Walking to Mackinac

Walking
to
Mackinac

David E. Bonior

Ann Arbor
THE UNIVERSITY OF MICHIGAN PRESS

A CIP catalog record for this book is available from the British Library.

Library of Congress Cataloging-in-Publication Data

Bonior, David E.
    Walking to Mackinac / David E. Bonior.
      p. cm.
    Includes bibliographical references.
    ISBN 0-472-11200-7 (cloth) — ISBN 0-472-08797-5 (paper)
    1. Bonior, David E.—Journeys—Michigan.   2. Hiking—Michigan.
    I. Title.
    GV199.42.M5 B66 2001
    917.7404'44—dc21   00-012730

At the request of the author, all royalties due to the author from the sale of
this book will be donated by the publisher to Rails-to-Trails Conservancy
of Michigan.

This book is for our children—
Andy, Julie, and Stephen—
and for Mary Strong.

Contents

Acknowledgments

To all the teachers and writers and friends who have opened my mind and eyes and heart to our world, I am deeply grateful. In my appreciation of what we saw on the walk and in writing this book, I called upon all of their lessons.

During our days walking, Stan Kemp, Chris Koch, and Ruth Gallop cheerfully helped us out. Thank you to each of them.

Tom Butts, then with the University of Michigan, made the initial contact with the University of Michigan Press. I thank him for his faith in me. The former director of the press, Colin Day, took a chance on this book—I hope he is not disappointed. In addition, he offered constructive criticism and thoughtful suggestions in delightful letters. The lengthy, thorough comments from the readers at the press were also extremely helpful.

From the outset my mother-in-law, Mary Strong, was an integral part of our walk. She followed the details of each stage with great interest and enthusiasm. During the intermittent months of writing, she offered unwavering support and invaluable advice. I appreciate the guidance and counsel she gave me during many conversations we had about the manuscript.

Without my wife there would have been no book. I wrote and rewrote each chapter on yellow legal pads. Judy prepared the manuscript. Her insights, criticisms, and editing skills pushed the book to completion.

Grateful acknowledgment is made to the following for permission to reprint lyrics.

"Iowa Fight Song" by Meredith Willson
Reprinted by permission of Frank Music Corp. and
Meredith Willson Music
© 1951 Frank Music Corp. and Meredith Willson Music

Lyric excerpt from "The Sound of Music"
by Richard Rodgers and Oscar Hammerstein II
Copyright © 1959 by Richard Rodgers and Oscar Hammerstein II

Prologue

Judy Bonior

I always look forward to what follows after he says, "I've got this great idea. . . ." As is the way with couples, my husband and I have established rituals to accommodate certain of our behaviors. They are neither original nor clever. Actually, they are simple and transparent. What is really important about them is that they work.

So, when David comes to me with another good idea, I try to be upbeat and positive in response. This is not my nature. Unfortunately, I am a pessimist. One friend said accurately of me, "Judy, you always see the hole in the doughnut." Truth be told, there is a hole in a doughnut. But, of course, there is also all that yummy dough. This is also true of David's ideas. A few are hollow; most are fabulous.

It is part of our ritual that I agree with any harebrained scheme that David proposes for the two of us. At least at first I agree. Occasionally they evaporate, others collapse, some mutate. Now and then I say flatly, "No!" But mainly we humor each other. As details emerge, I point out some problem I foresee. He rebuts. I reconsider. He presses forward. I equivocate. This is fun. Thrust and parry. The question slowly becomes: Where is the weight of the idea moving? Is it slipping into oblivion or heading toward reality? Is it just talk? Or have we each heard the same distant call to action?

We both share an intense interest in journeys. As a child, I daydreamed of being a pioneer. I was fascinated by Admiral Perry's North Pole expedition and Sir Edmund Hillary's conquest of Everest. David, in turn, enjoys reading about unusual challenges—hiking the length of the Appalachian Trail, biking across the United States, walking anywhere off the beaten track. He introduced me to two captivating books by Peter Jenkins, *A Walk Across America* and *The Walk West.*

For as long as I have known David, he has planned trips. He loves maps and is forever calculating the distance from here to there. This mileage is never to be covered conventionally. No, we are to walk, bike, or even boat. Over the years we narrowed the possibilities.

We decided our trip would be in Michigan. We would not walk the entire shoreline of the state or go the full diagonal from Lake Erie on the Ohio border to Ironwood at the westernmost tip of the Upper Peninsula. We would not do the more commonly hiked area of the Leelanau or the North Country Trail and would not follow any of the established cross-state routes. We would walk out of our front door in Mount Clemens and go north to Mackinaw City, creating our own way.

As the concept crystallized, so also did the circumstances. At the end of 1996 I would retire, so suddenly I would have lots of spare hours. Years are in shorter supply. Now in our early fifties, we were running out of time to undertake a great physical challenge. The congressional recess in August provided the opportunity, and with great excitement we began to plan. After discarding numerous wild logistical scenarios, we settled on the heretofore unthinkable, carrying all our gear on our backs and camping. But we innocently resolved to limit ourselves to ten pounds each and fifteen miles a day.

In February 1997 we visited David's father in Pompano Beach, Florida. David, his sister Nancy, and I walked seven miles along the ocean beach road. In March David purchased a *Michigan Atlas and Gazetteer*. Every night when he got home, no matter how late or how tired, he plotted our trip. It was astonishing to watch him. No general in history has more meticulously charted the course of his advance. In the end it was perfect. Not only did he find a suitable destination for each night and create an interesting walk combining trails, rails-to-trails, and back roads, but it was so firmly fixed in his head that during the three weeks of our 335-mile walk we made only one wrong turn.

The illusion of manageable fifteen-mile days gave way to the practical reality of finding shelter for the evening. Our days had to be stretched far beyond our original expectations, but in our exhilaration we were unfazed by mere numbers. In April we traced by car the first five days of the trip, making sure our chosen way would not unexpectedly dead-end and that campgrounds and motels were still in operation.

While David was engrossed in the big picture, I was sweating the small stuff. What will we wear? What will we carry? How will we even learn about any of this? I wanted a how-to manual that I could read from cover to cover and follow explicitly. I wanted my preparations to be as thorough as David's. After some searching, I found my bible, *Backpacking in the '90s* by Victoria Logue. It became something of a joke between us. During many a discussion David would finally ask in mock exasperation, "And what does *Backpacking in the '90s* have to say about this?"

Starting to share our idea with friends and family, we were met with responses ranging widely from enthusiastic support to disinterest to critical incredulity. We vowed to proceed with our grand notion, undaunted by doubters.

In May we made a substantial commitment by plunking down six hundred dollars at the REI sporting goods store. Here we took our second great leap of faith. The experienced salesperson disabused us of our ten pounds per person goal. In fact, he said we would be lucky to keep it to fifteen pounds. Counting on the expert design of the gear to absorb the weight difference effortlessly, we went ahead and purchased our backpacks, boots, and professional socks. On a sunny May 30 we made a trial run carrying twelve pounds on our backs. We hiked seven miles. Days later we were back at REI for tent, sleeping bags, air mattresses, and rain suits. I assembled the necessary minutia. Fortuitous business travel in June and July provided additional opportunities to hike longer distances in wilderness areas.

Ultimately, of course, the walk was to be undertaken by two people. Why we were doing this and whether we would succeed depended upon us, not our gear. Our roles from start to finish would be predictable and complementary. David is a natural leader—a quarterback, shortstop, and play-making guard, not to mention second-ranking Democrat in the U.S. House of Representatives; he is competitive to his core. If there is no challenge, he creates one. At the same time he is deeply contemplative— once a seminarian; widely read in fiction, history, the out-of-doors, and poetry; often lost in his own thoughts; he seeks texture and meaning in the process as well as the goal. I am a very good follower.

We were ready, determined, and eager to meet the challenge: to convene with nature; to inhale the beauty of Michigan; to learn our history; to test our flexibility, resourcefulness, and stamina; to expand our vision; to see our world differently; to walk every single step of the way—one million steps to Mackinaw City.

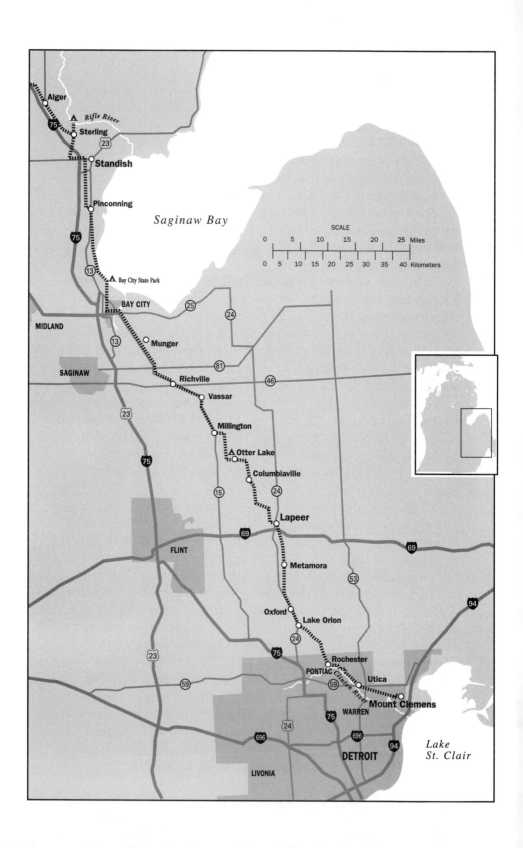

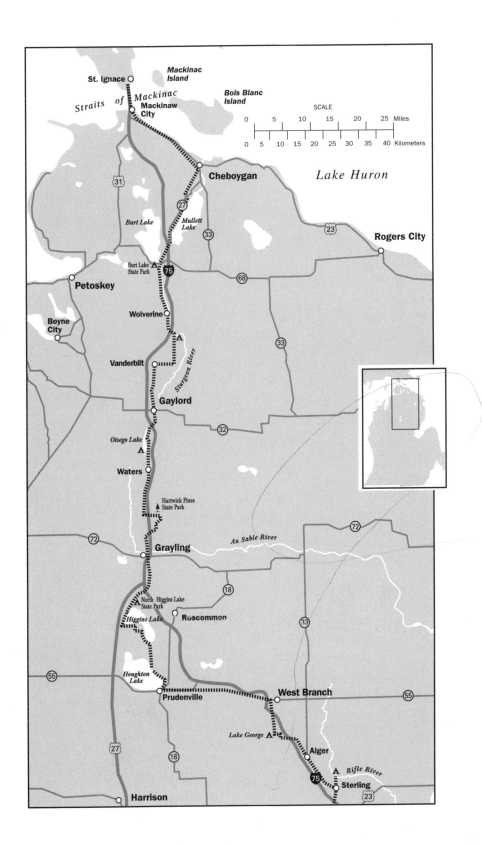

Chapter 1
Mount Clemens to Rochester

Anticipation. It does not let you sleep easily. The prospect of walking up the state of Michigan roils in our heads as we struggle nearly in vain for any rest at all. We twist and turn silently beside each other, our thoughts churning with excitement, trepidation, memories. Once again I fight "butterflies" as I ride the rosary-filled school bus taking my Notre Dame High School football team to its season opener. Countless election nights flicker by. Final exams, marathons, our wedding day, all jumble together. Lists of gear, hiking dos and don'ts, and the contents of our backpacks careen through my dreams. Our route up Michigan is like a crazy web spinning in my imagination. Finally, we face the first day, as "Monitor News" clicks on at 5:30 A.M.

Today, August 11, is the feast day of Saint Blane, a sixth-century Scottish bishop who is said to have gone on a pilgrimage to Rome, returning on foot through England. So this walking thing is not new. After toast and coffee we lace up our boots, strap on our packs, and step out into the gray and foggy morning with spirits high but plenty of unspoken questions and doubts nagging at us. Will our loads be too heavy? Will our boots serve us well? How will we do walking in a steady rain? The last question, at least, will be answered before day's end. The good Scottish bishop reportedly performed several miracles. We are hoping such intervention will not be necessary. Our friends at the Weather Channel, whom we are to rely on for a good portion of our trip, are predicting temperatures in the mid-fifties this morning—good walking weather—but rain as well.

With our disposable pocket camera we each take a photo of the other on our front stoop. Judy is dressed in green nylon walking shorts and a T-shirt with "St. Joan of Arc Grade School" on the front. Judy will prove to be as tough and resolute as the French heroine. I am wearing tan nylon walking shorts; my office softball team T-shirt, "Cool Whips," in reference to my leadership position as the Democratic Whip in the U.S. House of Representatives; and a United Steelworkers of America (USWA) baseball cap.

We step off! After crossing the Market Street Bridge over the Clinton River we pass St. Peter Roman Catholic Church and parish school whose history dates to 1843. My sister Nancy was married here in 1980. The traffic in front of the church is now bumper to bumper extending to the traffic light. Sitting in their cars several people recognize us and wave or beep their horns, wondering, we are sure, what their congressman and his wife are doing with back-packs at 7:00 A.M. in downtown Mount Clemens. Normally, if you are backpacking, you do it up north, not in Michigan's third most populated county.

As we pick up our pace through the city streets, Judy casually asks, "How does your pack feel?"

"Okay," I answer cautiously.

There it is—the fear that has been nagging at both of us. We are carrying almost three times the weight we originally planned for, nearly twice as much as we conceded to in the REI store. Both of us have had back trouble. My serious problems led to three operations to my lower back, including two laminectomies, which forced an end to running at age forty-seven. Some thirty years ago Judy discovered she had a curvature of the spine, which can be very painful if she does not stay in good condition.

We know the city concrete is unforgiving, so we look forward to our first trail outside the village of Utica, in River Bends Park. But for now it's close to thirty pounds each and cement under foot as we wind our way through the pleasant oak-lined streets of the older neighborhoods of Mount Clemens.

Founded on the banks of the Clinton River by Christian Clement in 1818, Mount Clemens was incorporated in 1837, when Michigan became the twenty-sixth state of the Union. The oil fever of 1865 was responsible for the discovery of the waters that made Mount Clemens famous. Prospectors drilling 1,300 feet downward hit not oil but water that was strongly impregnated with salts and minerals. Attempts to extract the salt failed when the presence of other minerals was deemed objectionable. For several years the healing waters from Mother Earth were wasted, unused until local sufferers discovered by mere chance the natural medicinal value. Then followed adoption of the water as a curative agent by local physicians and finally recognition by the broader medical world. Mount Clemens became known as Bath City or the Spa City. Construction of elaborate and ornate hotels and bathhouses put the city on the map. Tourists came from around the country to take the cure, and the city's bottled water found an international market. Spa City enjoyed a glamorous and prosperous era, which faded with the Depression. I remember my parents taking my sister and me on Sunday afternoon drives northward through Mount Clemens. We would hold our noses because of the sulfur smell of the waters.

The city fell on hard times. The springs were capped. It has only been in the last twenty years that the city of eighteen thousand has seen a renaissance. Most of the magnificent old hotels and bathhouses sadly are gone, but new civic leaders such as Dean Petitpren and Gabe Anton have put life back into our town.

At the west end of the city we pass the Grand Trunk railroad station built in 1859. Thomas Edison worked here as a railway newsboy and made friends with station agent J. U. MacKenzie. It is said that young Tom saved the agent's little boy from death by a train in 1862. By way of appreciation MacKenzie taught Tom railroad telegraphy. That skill became the basis of Edison's earliest inventions.

Beyond the station we enter Clinton Township and pass the Clinton Grove cemetery, where soldiers are buried from every U.S. war. An older couple holding hands is walking briskly on the cemetery roads getting their morning exercise.

"Not everyone would choose to walk there among the ghosts," I observe admiringly.

"Yeah, well not everyone would choose our walk either," snaps Judy.

I look quickly to see if she's lodging a none-too-subtle complaint, but, no, she is smiling. We share a laugh that relaxes us both.

A quarter-mile beyond the cemetery we cross a heavily trafficked Cass Avenue onto Clinton River Road. We walk beside the large white, ghostly hothouses, which are the distinctive sign of our local rose industry. This is also the site of the former village of Frederick, which was established to serve as a freight terminal for the Clinton-Kalamazoo Canal. It was once thought that Frederick would become an important port and metropolitan center until the ambitious project fell apart. Clinton Township has now established a park on this venerable site to recognize its rich history.

The canal, conceived at the peak of the era of canal building, just before the rise of railroads, was part of a Michigan internal improvement program that was announced by Governor Stevens T. Mason in 1837. The Clinton-Kalamazoo Canal would make it possible to cross southern Michigan by boat from Lake St. Clair to Lake Michigan. In July 1838, amid much fanfare, construction began at what is now the corner of Clinton River Drive and Canal Road. Hard times made it difficult to sell bonds to finance the project, and the money ran out in 1843, with only twelve miles completed. Excavation stopped, work ceased, and an angry group of workers who had been denied their rightful pay vandalized the locks and other parts of the canal. Our walk this first day will follow the old canal into the city of Rochester.

Now we face a seven-mile stretch along Canal Road bounded on both sides by subdivisions. We walk on sidewalks through the township of Clinton (pop. 100,000) and the city of Sterling Heights (130,000), both essentially bedroom communities cut by industrial corridors serving the auto industry. We are on the north side of the road where on occasion the remains of the canal are visible depending on how new development has altered the terrain. The canal often reappears as a wetland and therefore by law is protected from further destruction. And it is obvious why these small parcels are treasures. The wetland vegetation reveals red-wing blackbirds, scarlet epaulets proudly on display, gracefully bending the reed grasses on which they perch. The ditches proffer a colorful bouquet of fireweed, violet loosestrife, black-eyed Susans, and the delicate ivory doilies of Queen Anne's lace, softening the brick and mortar housing tracts we pass.

Our first inquiry occurs about one mile into our Canal Road walk. Two young women meet us on the sidewalk.

"Are you training for a hike?" one asks.

"No. Actually, we're on our hike," Judy answers.

"Where are you going?" the other asks.

"Mackinac," I answer, casually.

"Really? Wow! That's terrific. Good luck!"

We are actually feeling just a bit giddy—perhaps there are even signs of creeping overconfidence. The weight is riding lightly on our backs. Our identical pairs of boots cost an astonishingly high $189 each, but they are giving us the stability we need for the load and the distance. Judy is having one small problem with her pack, which is riding too low, below her hips, defeating the design purpose of resting on the hips and taking the weight off the back. We try to adjust her shoulder straps but realize the problem may require reassembling the pin placements. That will have to wait until we stop for the night. The rain has generously held off, but there is already mist in the air. We are anxious to get as far as we can before the rain begins in earnest.

As we approach the village of Utica, just beyond Sterling Heights an elderly woman working in her front garden calls out to us in a heavy colloquial accent, "Wherz ya goin'?" Again we answer Mackinac. She exclaims that she's never heard of such a thing and can hardly wait to tell her husband at dinner. It's obvious that we have added a little spice to her day. We wonder if her husband will believe her story.

By 10:30 A.M. we've reached Utica and the ten-mile point. Our goal is to average about three miles per hour, and we are right on target. Three cheers. We cross the expansion of M-59, the new suburban super-road that is being enlarged to relieve congestion in fast-growing northern Macomb County. This project has dramatically altered the city of Utica. The old village is located on a steep slope above the Clinton River. A German community settled in 1817, Utica was originally known as Hogs Hollow. For many years the town was primarily the home of retired farmers. Fifty years ago it was famous for all the rhubarb grown in its neighborhoods. Walking through the old section of Utica, we look for a way to enter River Bends Park, where we expect to find our first trail.

The ball field behind the Utica High School athletic field offers us a way into the park. We follow a path one-quarter mile over the railroad tracks into what was formerly known as the Rochester Utica State Recreation Area. Finally, we are off concrete and asphalt. The tranquil beauty of the little worn trail is a wonderful surprise. Judy is terribly allergic to poison ivy and poison oak, so we tread carefully. There are reeds nodding above our heads as we proceed northward between the Clinton River on our left and the canal and railroad tracks somewhere on our right. Foolishly, I have no compass, so maps, the sun, and landmarks will have to guide us. All around us are colorful wildflowers and beautiful butterflies. A host of swallowtails and monarchs reminds us of scenes in Gabriel

García Márquez's *One Hundred Years of Solitude.* This too feels like a magical place, awakening our hibernating senses—rich, musty smells; soft, springy ground; nature's designs and textures.

As we follow the trail northward we are accompanied by the quirky, soulful sounds of croaking frogs. Wading through a sea of seven-foot-high grasses, we spot our first deer thirty yards ahead. Despite frequent encounters with these beautiful animals, we are still struck by their grace. Motionless, we watch respectfully before gently alerting the doe to our presence.

A mile and a half up the trail we break into a baffling 300-yard clearing vaguely resembling a par four golf hole. Then Judy notices a contraption with a science fiction design, perhaps six feet high and bell shaped at the top with ribbed metal chains attached top and bottom to form a basket. This oddity is situated at a point where a golf green normally might be. To our amazement we find ourselves ambling through a frisbee golf course—a strange and unexpected discovery.

We walk the length of two holes before coming upon the park's picnic area nestled among a grove of hickory trees. The hickory is a rough, rugged hardwood tree. Hickory is far stronger than steel, weight for weight, more elastic, less brittle, and less heat conductive. The wood was used by early pioneers to construct covered wagons, which rolled west on hickory hubs.

In the park across the river from the picnic area and frisbee golf course lies the remains of historic Spring Hill Farm. In the 1840s Peter Lerrich, owner of the farm, assisted in building the Utica Methodist Church. Being a deeply religious man, he once salted a corn crop so that it would ferment too slowly to be used in the Utica distilleries. But it was the Lerrich family's abhorrence of slavery that reserved a place for them in history. They provided shelter, food, and clothing for runaway slaves before and during the Civil War. For many slaves their farm became a revered stop on the famed Underground Railroad to Canada and freedom. The Spring Hill Farm became the safest alternative route because many slave owners and their agents patrolled the closer and more obvious passage from Detroit across the Detroit River and into Canada. The Lerrich farm provided a respite for slaves traveling northeast to cross the St. Clair River at Algonac, Marysville, St. Clair, or Port Huron. They were guided to the farm by a "Beacon Tree," a virginal cedar standing over one hundred feet tall and visible from great distances. The Lerrichs would hang a quilt, one side green, the other red, to further signal the slaves when it was safe to enter the cave near the spring. To protect the escapees, Peter and Sarah Lerrich tried to keep their noble efforts secret even from their children, as their daughter Libereta describes.

> In the year of our Lord eighteen hundred and fifty, I was five years old, not old enough to go to school but just old enough to want to know the whys and wherefores about everything and must have stumped my mother for answers not too untruthful, for truthful answers she did not dare. . . . [My father] in turn would be asked by me, "Why was our house built way off here, forty rods away from the road . . . ?" And his answer would be, "Mother and I thought that it would be better to build here to be near the Spring-in-the-Hill, we must have water, you know." . . . [This] was much more truthful than poetical and silenced my tongue, but not my thoughts, as to why the bricks around said spring, that held the water back, were so wide, wide enough for a man to walk on, and why it looked like the inside of a log house in back of the water with the logs so nicely fitted and [grooved], and why the little ramshackled door at the bottom of the hill that always shut itself, was kept covered with a grapevine, running on nails; and why the vine never stuck fast to the door by tendrils as other wild vines did; and why we were told to always hang up the vines just as we found them "to keep the water cool." And why did the fried cake crock get empty so quickly? It did not seem reasonable that a six gallon crock could empty itself so often, but I was told if Mother did not complain about it, I needn't.

In the late 1930s the great heavyweight boxer from Detroit, Joe Louis, purchased the 250-acre Spring Hill Farm for $100,000. Louis turned the farm into a popular showplace for his passion, horses, building a track and restaurant. Rather improbably, in the 1950s and 1960s the property became a Nike missile site before being turned over to the National Guard and finally to the State Department of Natural Resources. The buildings of the Lerrich farm have long since disappeared, leaving only a few foundation stones, sidewalks, and the remains of several flower gardens. The Beacon Tree is now gone, cut by a former owner for fence posts after perhaps two hundred years of growing and giving life and hope. The land seems empty without it—a void in a distant glorious past.

To celebrate that past and preserve it for future generations, Congressman Louis Stokes of Ohio led an effort in Congress, which I joined, to pass the National Underground Railroad Network to Freedom Bill. The Underground Railroad stands as one of the most significant stories of American history. Prior to 1865 its complex network of individuals, sites, and routes represented the primary means for slaves to escape to freedom. The railroad spanned twenty-nine states; had branches in Canada, Mexico, and the Caribbean; and reached as far away as Africa, eventually helping hundreds of thousands of African Americans flee slavery. That brave struggle for freedom hallowed this very ground.

As we leave the park at Twenty-two Mile Road, the rain begins to fall. A large oak at the side of the road shelters us as we put on our rain gear. Proper rain gear is probably one of the most essential items on our clothing list. Wet clothes can lower your body temperature to the danger point. It doesn't have to be freezing or even near it for a hiker to become hypothermic when wearing wet clothes. The greatest risk of hypothermia comes when you least expect it. So the question for us was, what kind of gear? We rejected ponchos as the least effective option because in wind they are practically useless. We decided on rain suits (jacket and pants) but declined the most expensive brand with its supposed feature of breathability. The argument over whether or not this truly works centers on whether it is simultaneously breathable and waterproof. We have read that the fabric seems incapable of keeping up with the water vapor escaping the body while backpacking. The $300 high-end rain suits yielded to the $95 nylon suits that we purchased at the REI store.

We pull out our pack covers even though our backpacks are made of water-resistant material. Moisture has a way of finding seams and zippers and saturating your gear if the pack is left unprotected. The covers fit nicely over the full packs, allowing us to continue unhindered.

Judy is now dressed all in blue, and I am a vision in green as we move west toward Yates Cider Mill, with the old canal on our right behind a string of light industrial shops. The rain is now steady and strong. Two miles up the road, looking like two nuclear decontamination workers with our hoods drawn tightly around our faces, we coincidentally pass by a large scar on the park's surface. This actually was the location of an original Superfund toxic waste site, now controlled, all two hundred acres, by the State of Michigan.

Weariness sets in as we plod our way to Yates Cider Mill. We attempt a shortcut from the road to a trail by the river but soon find ourselves sinking in a field of mud. With our boots heavy we finally find the trail and walk three-quarters of a mile to the shelter of the mill and large red barn located at the convergence of the river and the old canal. The mill has been powered by water since 1803 and is now a popular gathering place for families who hike the nearby trails and for fishermen and canoeists. The Clinton River is wildly natural in this far northwestern part of the county.

The mill is also a very popular weekend destination in the fall for those seeking cider, apples, doughnuts, and a touch of the out-of-doors. We take refuge from the driving rain under an overhang at the mill and find it closed and deserted. We are alone, wet, and increasingly chilly. A fifteen-minute break allows us to try again to adjust Judy's pack and to quench our thirst. We have come fourteen miles, with three left to finish our day. Across the road from us lies Yates Roadside Park, a scenic but small facility on the banks of the river. And across the river is Bloomer Park, which hosts the terminus of the canal. Our goal is to cross into Bloomer Park and take the three-mile trail into Rochester. But Bloomer turns into a bummer.

To our surprise and disappointment a fence has been erected along the edge of the park across from the cider mill. We cross the road bridge to see if we can find an opening, but the fence is too high and new to overcome in the rain. Our other option is to ford the river, so we backtrack across the bridge and into Yates Roadside Park. But the water is now running too deep to wade across the river, and we resign ourselves to walking the park's perimeter into Rochester. Cars and trucks roar by, spraying us with more water. Not only are we denied our hope of being on a trail, but the course ahead seems endlessly miserable.

William S. Knudsen, then president of General Motors, once remarked that "the American is a person who insists on going from Point A to Point B *sitting.*" He could have added, "and dry." This is certainly true in Macomb County. The county was named in honor of Brigadier General Alexander Macomb, who during the War of 1812 defeated a British squadron on Lake Champlain. Heavily wooded like most of Michigan, its grand forests gave way to the ax and peavey and became rich in agricultural production. Its flat and fertile fields yielded bountiful harvests for neighboring Detroit and environs. The descendants of the early German and Belgian settlers and farmers witnessed a dramatic change after World War II, when auto plants began to mushroom throughout the county, and returning veterans moved to Macomb County to begin their family life in this newly created suburbia. Spilling out from the urban centers of Detroit and Hamtramck, this migration of Germans, Poles, Italians, Ukrainians, and others flavored Macomb County with their rich cultures. From this polyglot sprang churches, schools, cultural centers, and festivals (which were often held along the banks of the Clinton River)—traditions that still today create the mosaic of social and religious life in Macomb. From a population of 100,000 in 1940 to its present 750,000, the majority of its families are now connected in some way or another to the auto industry.

So, here, where the history, economy, and lifestyle are based on the automobile, we decide to walk! Not just any walk, but a twenty-one-day, 335-mile walk—17 miles the first day. When we share the idea of our adventure with hometown folks, they typically respond, "You're doing this on purpose?"

Today the northern half of the county is yielding swiftly to subdivisions and commercial development while still struggling to retain its farmlands. The expanding auto industry has altered the landscape. The presence of a record thirty-five golf courses (riding mainly) has for now helped stem the complete elimination of open land while providing green spaces and recreational outlets. In the lower eastern half of the county, bordering Lake St. Clair, which divides Michigan from Ontario, is the largest recreational boating fleet in the United States. Despite a short boating season of only six months, my congressional district has sixty-five thousand registered boats, the most in the nation.

So contrary to all conventional modes of travel here—minivan, electric golf cart, or cabin cruiser—we are walking in the pouring rain. We turn a corner and to our pleasant surprise find ourselves in the midst of a broad swath of colorful wildflowers. Buttercups, yarrow, mullein, and aster are radiant against the gray rain. Our spirits are lifted. Goldfinches and doves accompany us on our soaking-wet walk to town. The goldfinch will turn out to be a faithful companion all the way to Mackinac.

Rochester lies between the high banks of the Clinton River on the south and the wandering Paint Creek on the north. A New York family, the Grahams, settled the city in 1817. They named the town after Rochester, New York. Earlier in the century the steep hills and the broad, stream-laced valley attracted workers from the auto plants in Pontiac just a few miles to the west. Fifty years ago Rochester's industrial profile included a foundry, a knitting works, a paper company, and the Parke-Davis Biological Farm. Only Parke-Davis remains, but the area is also home to three other distinctive institutions, Meadowbrook Theater, Oakland University, and the Leader Dogs for the Blind. Today Rochester is an upper-middle-class suburb of 7,100 people located twenty-four miles north of Detroit. A true, old-fashioned main street is anchored by a variety of shops, restaurants, and parks.

Upon reaching the heart of town, we proceed three blocks north to the Spartan Inn, "Your home away from home." The lady at the front desk remembers us from our earlier visit in the summer to make reservations. We told her then of our plan, and it amused her that we would be walking into her motel. Either we did not impress her enough to be given a convenient room, or she sweetly sought a quiet corner for us. In any case we find ourselves in the farthest room possible from the office, in room 41 on the second floor. This pattern will become familiar over the course of our trip. After the relief of reaching our destination and checking in, hoisting our packs again and staggering to our room often seem the hardest steps of the day.

Our room is a simple sanctuary—small but very dry. We hang our damp clothing and dripping gear everywhere. Our legs ache. Yes we are used to running and biking, but walking seventeen miles with nearly thirty pounds on your back awakens a whole new set of muscles, which are now screaming their displeasure. The pain vividly reminds me of the first week of double-session football practice. It is a necessary passage for future success. After stretching our aching limbs, we take a ninety-minute fitful nap. When we rise, the rain has stopped.

The lady at the desk recommends the Rochester Cafe, three blocks south, for dinner. We choose a restaurant across the street. We should have followed her advice. After dinner we pick up a copy of the *Oakland Press* and retreat to our room for some planning, repairing, reading, and writing. The room is dimly lit for reading, but I pore over maps for tomorrow's short fourteen-mile walk and then write in my journal. Judy works on her pack. Out our window the August sky is streaked in yellow, orange, and reds. The gorgeous sunset bids a stunning farewell to our first day.

Judy is very sore and worries about the future, when our days will be longer and our loads heavier. She is excited to have completed day 1, but her natural caution focuses on potential problems. Mainly, she is concerned that this may be too great a risk for my back. I promise to admit any signs of trouble rather than keeping quiet, as is my habit.

The Tigers and Blue Jays game on TV is quiet comfort as we prepare for tomorrow. The forecast is for cloudy skies, a high of sixty-two, and rain late in the afternoon. At 9:30, just as we are about to drift off to sleep, there is a knock at the door. Our friend Stan Kemp has come to hear the story of the first day. He missed us earlier when we were out to dinner. We want to share our adventures with him, but exhaustion rules.

"I'm sorry to say, Stan, it's lights out for us in one hour," I tell him. "It's been a long day, and we hardly slept last night. You know, anticipation—."

Total Distance	335 miles
Walked Today	17 miles
Walking to Do	318 miles

Chapter 2

Rochester to Oxford

Tuesday, August 12

We awaken to the feast day of Saint Clare, a familiar name in this part of the state. On August 12, 1679, the French explorer Robert de la Salle and Father Louis Hennepen sailed northward onto the lake, which they christened St. Clair. Clare, a devoted follower of Saint Francis of Assisi—himself a lover of nature and a progenitor of environmentalism—renounced her nobility and material life to found the order of "Poor Clares," practicing austerity, sleeping on the ground, abstaining from meat, and adhering to silence. (In the Catholic Church hierarchy of sainthood, and there is one, Francis and Clare rank near the top, so admired are they for their strength of character.) Today the name St. Clair not only names the lake but also denotes the cities of St. Clair and St. Clair Shores and the St. Clair River, whose thirty-three miles drain Lake Huron into Lake St. Clair. Lake St. Clair is also the receptor of the Clinton River, from which we will diverge today. Confusing the history of the origin of all these Clairs is the naming of the county for Arthur St. Clair, a Revolutionary War general and first governor of the Northwest Territory.

In bed I stretch my back with a gentle series of exercises—leg pulls, pelvic tilts, and sit-ups. This early daily routine is as important to me as a good cup of coffee. Judy is up checking our clothes and gear, which all dried well. The Weather Channel confirms yesterday's forecast for today—cloudy, high 62, and a pretty certain prediction of afternoon showers. We again face the possibility of walking in the rain, but the short walk, just fourteen miles, may get us there ahead of it. Our legs are a bit stiff, and Judy's shoulders ache from the weight of the pack. She spent a part of last evening adjusting the pins on the lower part of her backpack to shorten the frame. We both hope she'll be more comfortable.

Next to our boots nothing is more critical to a successful journey than a properly fitted and well-designed pack. At the sporting goods store we purchased identical Kelty external frame packs weighing four pounds each. Our history of back problems steered us to a pack that rides on our hips and takes the strain off the shoulders and back. The selection process for a pack is as tough as finding a perfect pair of boots, since there are so many manufacturers offering hundreds of choices.

The pack options fall into three broad categories: external frame, internal frame, and the frameless rucksacks. We settle on the external design that distributes the weight equally and has a high center of gravity. It is made for gentle to moderate terrain (our route) and also has the advantage of a web backing that keeps the pack away from your back, allowing air to circulate between you and your pack. Our packs also have lightweight aluminum tubes with a nylon packcloth and thick, padded shoulder straps. We also appreciate having an outside water bottle holster and many outside pockets for easy and quick access to rain gear, pack covers, writing and reading materials, and binoculars. I especially like the thick foam hip belt with the easy-release buckle.

The key term here is *easy-release,* as I have an obsessive fear of bears. In July we spent five glorious days in the Land of the Midnight Sun, camping and hiking in Alaska's Arctic National Wildlife Refuge on the north slope of the Brooks Range, where the arctic plain meets the foothills on the Aichilik River—grizzly bear country. If pursued by a bear, we have been advised, we should drop our packs in order to divert the bear's attention. So an easy-release buckle takes on a life-or-death significance. In Michigan the black bear will be our concern and only in the northern half of our trip. But our recent Arctic experience with grizzly paw scratches and scat droppings near our campsite makes me sensitive to all precautions. My fear in the Arctic was of stumbling upon a grizzly while hiking through low-lying willows near the river. Though there were no actual bear sightings during our short stay, we were told by Jim Kurth, the refuge manager, that, while we didn't see them, they most assuredly saw us. His firm and scary declaration was followed two days later by a front-page story in the *Anchorage Daily News* describing an attack by a juvenile bear on a bush pilot who was jogging along a wilderness airstrip. While there are no grizzlies in Michigan, I want to be prepared for what I am certain will be our encounter with a black bear. Bears and disagreeable dogs are to occupy my thoughts for a good portion of our trip.

A final word on packs. We tested our packs in the sporting goods store by putting fifteen-pound weights in them and walking around the store. We agreed that the packs felt comfortable and fit properly. That positive feeling was confirmed in a series of practice walks. The difference now, of course, is that we are each carrying fifteen more pounds than we anticipated, which caused Judy's pack to sag too low on her hips yesterday. The hip belt should fit snugly around the top part of your hips and not catch your legs when walking or allow the pack to hang from your shoulders.

Today we will walk along the banks of the winding Paint Creek, which parts from the Clinton River and runs to the north of Rochester up to Lake Orion. After dressing and packing, we walk down to the motel lobby and enjoy coffee, juice, and doughnuts, part of the forty dollar room rate. Today's relatively short hike does not justify a country farm breakfast. While we both love to eat, through steely willpower, Judy has been able to maintain her 130-pound weight consistently on her 5'7" frame by regular running and one end-of-the-day meal. I, on the other hand, at 5'11", fluctuate between my 180-pound playing weight on the University of Iowa football team thirty years ago and 195 pounds. I begin this trip at 190 pounds, 10 heavier than I need to be, and I shall pay a price for my excess. On a previous bike tour in northern Michigan in which I did about fifty miles per day, I actually gained weight because I thought it was possible to indulge in a huge breakfast every morning. It always comes back to calories taken in versus calories expended. You gotta do the math.

Over coffee we strike up a conversation with the new motel clerk and a guest who is either a businessman or professor visiting nearby Oakland University. Curious about our packs and hiking boots, they pepper us with questions about the logistics of our trip. While they both find the idea of the journey interesting, the clerk, a student at St. Mary's College at Orchard Lake, thinks it totally crazy to walk 335 miles. Yet she is intrigued enough to leave her post and enthusiastically take a picture of us in front of the motel. In deference to our example the gentleman, who is from South Carolina but speaks with a South Asian accent, Indian or Pakistani, decides to walk the four miles to his appointment rather than taking a cab. Our first convert!

We in turn walk four blocks south on Main Street to the creek and trail head. The trail lives up to its billing as one of America's top rail-trails, a recipient of the 1992 U.S. "Enjoy Outdoors America" award, as well as other commendations for planning. It is built on the gentle grade of a former railroad with a smooth, firm, 10-foot-wide surface, making it comfortable for walking, running, biking, cross-country skiing, and even horseback riding. The trail crosses Paint Creek thirteen times as it meanders through fields, woodlands, hills, and marshes and away from busy roads and aggressive dogs.

We enter the trail next to the Rochester municipal park, one of six local and regional parks that are linked by the 10.4-mile trail to Lake Orion. Soon we approach the Dinosaur Hill Nature Preserve, a charming 17-acre preserve with a nature center and several short paths. Staying our course, we are rewarded with a glorious profusion of wildflowers crowding each side of the trail. This is only our second day, but we know already that these flowers—as stars or slippers or snowflakes, in gentle pastel blush or startling primary hue, standing as lonely sentinel or banked in madcap variety, scratching hold of some roadside gravel or thriving lushly in rich loam—will be one of the true gratifications of our walk. Tall dew-covered grasses bend and glisten in the early-morning calm. Our new friends the goldfinches dart and dive through the chicory, asters, mulleins, and thistle. These small yellow birds with black wings and undulating flight sing a simple ti-tee-di-di. They particularly thrive on thistle seeds.

Further up the trail we begin to pass walkers, runners, and cyclists. They all greet us in a friendly fashion, and several of the women inquire where we are going. We answer Mackinaw City, which is received with variations of surprise, admiration, and approval. The beauty and serenity seem to bring out the best in folks. Crossing a bridge over the creek, I notice below a small flat-bottom research boat and four state Department of Natural Resource workers getting ready to launch their skiff. "What's going on?" I ask. "Fish survey," is the laconic response. But a second fellow supplies further details. "Yesterday we counted fifty brown trout in a thousand-foot stretch near this location. Some are as long as eighteen inches. Stream's lookin' healthy." Wow! How fortunate to have this natural abundance in such easy proximity to a basically urban region. It is actually not unusual to see fly fishermen on the Clinton River even near the Yates Cider Mill. Here a nearby sign also tells of Trout Unlimited's efforts to help propagate fish in the creek. There are so many groups that participate in preserving the trail and its environment as a resource.

I want to photograph every wildflower. Like a kid in a toy store, I am excited by the glorious bounty that awaits us around each turn. While the right-of-way is only one hundred feet wide, this green space encompasses some of the loveliest scenery in southeast Michigan. From my reading I know that deer, turtles laying their eggs, great blue herons, and even coyotes are frequently spotted here. Even if we don't actually see these species, we are happy to know we are among them. A choir of frogs and birds serenades us as they busy themselves in the bordering wetlands.

About three miles up the trail we stop at the Paint Creek Cider Mill and Restaurant, which was converted from an old logging mill that dates back to 1835. This wood and flagstone structure blends naturally with its surroundings. Inside there is room for one hundred seated guests in the dining area and seventy more on the rustic deck overlooking the trail and creek. We enter the cider mill side of the building and order coffee and a doughnut. Here there are several small tables, and the area resembles an old-fashioned general store. I sip my coffee and write in my journal, while Judy paces about and, in her own journal words, "tries not to bug him." We think this might be a nice place to bring our hosts for this evening to dinner.

Before we return to the trail, I coax Judy to the front of the mill for a picture before a large water wheel. She strikes a confident pose. Something about this image of my wife—her determination, her still-great-looking legs—reminds me of my first sight of her almost thirty-four years ago.

"Eight ball in the side pocket." It's the fall of 1963, my freshman year, and I have found my sanctuary in the pool room at the University of Iowa student union. When I straightened from gently striking my cue, I saw her through the glass partition, tall with long wavy dark brown hair falling into the hood of her gold-colored car coat. She was wearing black flats and her long, shapely legs were striding purposefully to the river room, the haven for social and political activists.

Throughout our years on campus I would pass Judy in the union. At some point she started to return my shy nods or my bashful hellos as we made our way to our respective hangouts. She would eventually marry a talented football teammate of mine, and they would find their way to the nation's capital by way of the Washington Redskins. I married my college sweetheart and was elected to Congress in 1976.

The trail is almost all ours the rest of the way. Walkers and runners have finished and gone off to work. The dog walkers have done their early-morning duty. We pass two impressive-looking Oakland County sheriffs mounted on their huge horses, and we greet them respectfully. Only an occasional young runner or cyclist passes us the rest of the way. We approach a two-acre wetland on our right and watch a large sixteen-inch turtle basking in shallow water. Soon we are in an area abutting some distinctive, comfortable homes with backyards that take creative advantage of their unique location. One resident has steps leading up from the trail to a rest area with a bench and a cooler of water with a hospitable sign inviting travelers to help themselves. Another property owner displays an old horse watering fountain next to a hitching post along the trail. I remember in my youth that such water troughs were still used by the mounted police to refresh their steeds in downtown Detroit.

Curiously, having some knowledge of horses played a key role in my congressional career. When I arrived in Washington in 1976–77, Tip O'Neill had just become speaker of the House of Representatives. I was advised that a good way to learn how the House worked was to attend the weekly Whip meetings. So on Thursday mornings I would wander over to the Capitol and sit in the corner reading a newspaper. Tip would sit up front, and he would also read the newspaper, big stogie clamped in his teeth. At some point he realized we were both reading the sports pages about the football games coming up on Saturday.

So we got to talking about whether Boston College was favored— or Iowa or Michigan or "who do you like in this game?" We developed a relationship based on something very ordinary but satisfying to both of us.

A year later I got up enough nerve to ask Tip to come to my district. He agreed to do it, but I did not know how to meet him when he flew in because I did not have a big enough car. Nor did my father.

Mounted police on Paint Creek Trail

We debated about how to pick up the speaker at the airport, then my father said, "Why don't you just get Stan Shultz to drive him?"

Stan Shultz was a friend and the undertaker in town. Sure enough, Stan shows up with the hearse, a long Cadillac. Tip actually got a kick out of being picked up in a hearse. Tip sat in the front with Stan, and my father and I sat in the back seat. My dad and Tip naturally got into a conversation about politics and sports. The subject narrowed to horse racing.

Tip was trying to remember the name of the great horse that won the Kentucky Derby in 1960-something, 1964. He said it was a Canadian horse. I do not know horses from beans. But for some reason the name immediately popped into my head.

"It was Northern Dancer, Mr. Speaker."

He turned around in the front seat of the car, and he looked at me as if to say, You're on the right track, young man. I believe that moment led the speaker to appoint me to the Rules Committee, which established me on the leadership track.

Time passes easily as we pace ourselves without the worry of traffic or the fear of animals. Our packs fit comfortably. Judy is better, though not completely free of shoulder strain. My feet feel good on the smooth limestone surface. We talk about the concept of "greenways" and the linked recreational trail system. The idea is to encourage hiking, cycling, skiing, and even riding a horse to those special places in your community without the conflict, danger, and distraction of competing auto traffic. How appealing to be able to explore natural areas, recreational lands, and historic places on a day bike trip or a weekend excursion from your front door without driving hours to a tourist area. Letting children roam free and find their own adventure in a nonmotorized environment has great appeal. It is an idea that is sweeping the country. Linked recreation trail systems are being developed using abandoned railroads, safety paths along parkways, utility easements, and waterways. These networks provide an opportunity for neighbors to enjoy face-to-face encounters, make new friends, and foster and enhance a sense of community. Peggy Johnson, an old friend and a premiere environmental and community leader in the Clinton River Watershed, was one of the heroes in making the Paint Creek Trail a reality. She seized the opportunity to create connections across local jurisdictional boundaries.

Actually, in the spring of 1990 I had a similar idea and approached Tom Welsh, a friend and veteran community leader, road commissioner in Macomb County, and member of the Huron Clinton Metro Park Authority, the regional park authority in southeast Michigan. I proposed to Tom that we link the Metropolitan Beach Park on Lake St. Clair with Stony Creek Metro Park by way of a hike/bike trail that when completed would encompass a forty-four-mile loop. Tom was a doer and liked the idea right away. So, together with Bill Sherman, Bill Westrick, Chris Koch, and a few other very dedicated people, we went about selling this idea to the many communities it would pass through. In auto-sensitive Metro Detroit at first we did not encounter a lot of enthusiasm. But we went ahead anyway. Adjacent homeowners were worried about crime and property values, while many others thought the idea just folly. Today, like the Paint Creek Trail, which we will eventually reach via Stony Creek Park, our greenway idea has been a resounding success. Local officials have joined the effort. Realtors report that home buyers are now requesting property with easy access to the trail. Neighbors are visiting with one another on the trail, and parents feel more secure knowing their children have a traffic-free zone to ride their bikes, rollerblade, and skateboard. Soon the last few miles of the twenty-mile path linking the Metro Parks will be completed.

The Paint Creek Trail also links two major regional parks, Riverbends-Bloomer Park at the south end and Bald Mountain State Recreation Area, which we now pass at the north end of our trail walk. Then abruptly we find ourselves in a shopping center parking lot in the village of Lake Orion, one block from the lake itself. A small park near the creek in town is a pleasant rest stop. For fifteen minutes we enjoy the sense of near weightlessness without our packs on, loosening our boots and swigging water from our bottles while watching some youngsters on the swings and slides. Several little ones are scurrying about having great fun feeding the ducks near the water's edge. The park clears as a slight mist begins to fall, and we decide to walk up the main street in search of food. We find a health food store and pick up a few snacks. Eating on the go, we head through town on our four-mile walk to Frank and Gail's home on Indian Lake.

Lake Orion, population twenty-nine hundred, is located north of Pontiac, sitting at an elevation of 991 feet. M-24, or Lapeer Road, skirts the village and is a trunk line highway running into Michigan's thumb region. Originally named Canandiagua City, it was renamed in 1859 for the well-known constellation. The village was settled in 1819, and nine years later a dam was built there to join several small lakes, creating a single mile-wide lake. Around 1872 Lake Orion village became a popular railroad excursion and picnic point, and twenty-five years later, with the interurban electric railway built between Detroit and Flint, Lake Orion developed into a leading summer resort in southeastern Michigan. Today homes and cottages surround the lake. As we walk along the uneven sidewalks heaved up by old tree roots, Judy is reminded of parts of Northfield, Minnesota, where she spent her childhood. The homes are neat, modest wooden structures befitting the working/middle-class character of the town. Barking dogs announce our presence as we stroll west from the village center.

At Conklin Road we turn north, bisecting Long Lake, one of the dozen Long Lakes in Michigan. Straddling the road is another community of cottages. Several old fishermen in sun hats are out on the lake in small boats trying their luck at bass, crappie, and sunfish. A car with a young family, several small children in the back seat, pulls to a stop beside us, and the father asks for directions to any nearby campground. Our hiking attire and gear give them hope that we can help. We know there is nothing nearby, but I dig my maps out from the pocket of my shorts to show them where we are and how far they might have to go to find a resting spot for the night. Judy worries they are homeless, and it does seem unusual to be on the road with little ones and no idea of where you are or where to go. There are approximately 600,000 homeless in the United States and roughly 40 percent, or 240,000, are families with children. Often campgrounds provide shelter for families with no other options available. After a brief conversation we wish them well, feeling uncomfortable about their circumstances in contrast to ours.

Leaving development behind, we drop off the pavement's edge and find ourselves negotiating a deeply rutted stone and clay surface. The atmosphere of the walk changes with the type of road we travel. Now we find ourselves in a more natural setting with less traffic. That's generally good. Ironically, in this instance we cannot fully enjoy the views but must keep our heads down, mindful of each step so we don't fall or twist an ankle. Each combination of factors affects our moods, our very appreciation of where we are. At Indian Lake Road we turn east and walk beside several small wooded lakes. Lined with oaks and maples, the road rises and falls, beckoning us toward each next crest. Moraines, the residue of glacial halts and retreats, are strikingly apparent in Oakland County, the area where the Huron and Erie glacial lobes collided, leaving a jumble of hills and lakes. Here there are 1,600 bodies of water including marshes, swamps, 450 navigable lakes, and 3 rivers—all together creating hundreds of miles of shoreline.

It now begins to rain, but, being so close to our destination, we are reluctant to put on our rain gear. We walk by Indian Lake, which we later learn resembles a V with a peninsula in the middle. It is puzzling that we have not come to the street we are looking for. Though it has been a short and comfortable day, we are still ready to stop and feel slightly uneasy that we may have misunderstood the directions to our friends' home. We have little choice but to continue, but we quicken our pace. Farther up the road on our right is another lake, the other half of the V of Indian Lake. And soon, to our great relief, we spy the sign ahead for Ridgemont Road. Around a bend is a beautiful, spacious house ideally situated off the road and surrounded by a lush expanse of lawn sloping down to the lake. Upon seeing this Shangri-La, we share a spontaneous laugh. This is not what we had expected.

Earlier in the year, during our planning stage of the trip, we were faced with the problem of lodging in the Oxford area. There was no motel or campground that would not take us miles out of our way. One day last spring in a conversation with our friends, Frank and Gail, I mentioned this predicament. To my total surprise, they volunteered that they lived near Oxford, whereupon I boldly and unabashedly asked if we could pitch our tent in their backyard. They graciously responded with an offer of shelter—but inside their home. While I had been forthright and direct in making the request, I did not feel that I had placed them in an awkward position. Their offer seemed genuine.

Of course, little did we realize what a magnificent home and "yard" we were walking into. Our tiny tent would have been quite a silly sight in that location. The mere thought makes us giggle.

Their renovated split-level home is patterned after a Frank Lloyd Wright design, with low horizontal lines and protruding eaves. Consistent with his philosophy, the house echoes the rhythms and forms of the surrounding landscape. We look forward to a relaxing afternoon in this little slice of paradise.

At the end of the long winding driveway, on the front door we find a note from Gail welcoming us and giving us directions to the swimming beach, which is a half-mile away. The rain is falling harder now and, with the cool weather, cancels the appeal of swimming, but the comforts of our environment more than make up for any disappointment. We enter and find Gail downstairs in the gym running on a treadmill, in training for the Chicago marathon this fall. Before heading back to work, she gives us a tour of their home and invites us to make full use of all the amenities. The house is elegantly appointed with a clean open look and an expansive view of the lake. There is an inviting deck and fabulous rock garden with a path leading down to their dock. A nearby island disguises the size of Indian Lake and creates a sense of total privacy.

The outdoor hot tub is a splendid indulgence, even though our aches and pains are minimal. After a thorough soaking, we sit and read in the open solarium amid beautiful houseplants overlooking the lake. We feel very relaxed and restored. How much better this is than our tent pitched on the lawn! A groundhog plays peek-a-boo with us from beneath the deck.

The choice for dinner is easy—Frank and Gail read our minds and suggest the Paint Creek Cider Mill. In our boots, shorts, and sweatshirts we head out into the now hard-driving rain, this time on wheels. It is six miles back to the mill but seems longer as we wind through country roads, the rain obscuring the sights we missed by taking the trail. The restaurant deck would have been our preference, but the weather keeps us inside. The food is excellent. The wine even better. Inevitably, I turn to Frank and Gail with my favorite question, "How did you two meet?" They both laugh, and Frank says, "You tell the story, Gail. You tell it better than I do."

"It was 1986, I think," Gail begins. "Frank and I were both in the same health care field, but as far as we know had never met. I had attended a professional seminar during the day and went directly to the cocktail reception in the Amway Grand Plaza in Grand Rapids. Of course, everyone was in business attire, suit and tie. Except one guy. He walks in with just a shirt and casual slacks. Not even a belt. I noticed him right away. I liked his attitude. He was comfortable with himself."

"The truth is," Frank interjects, "I had left my clothes back in Oxford. Far from being laid-back and cool, I was just absent-minded. But we were immediately attracted to each other. In fact, our first date was to the theater in Detroit. We saw *A Streetcar Named Desire*." Their eyes catch each other's for a moment. That fleeting look of love between couples is often the reward for asking the question.

"So, did you two just walk into each other?" Gail asks teasingly.

"Actually, our story shares some of the elements of yours," I answer. "We met at the University of Iowa, but what matters is that we remet."

Judy at Paint Creek Cider Mill Restaurant

Judy interrupts. "I had already been working in Washington, DC, for Congressman John Brademas from Indiana for a year when David was elected to Congress in 1976. Our office, the Majority Whip's Office, was responsible for one of the orientation programs in December for the newly elected members. But I never made the connection then with our college days. It was only when David walked into our office several months later wearing blue jeans that it clicked. I remember thinking 'Oh, *that* David Bonior.'"

"David, you tell the rest," Judy instructs me.

"Well, the years passed. Brademas lost in the Democratic election debacle of 1980. Judy moved on to other offices on the Hill, Congressman now Senator Byron Dorgan of North Dakota, the Clerk's Office, and the Chaplain's Office. I struggled my first few terms trying to find my niche. We would occasionally pass each other in the halls or on the grounds of our new campus, Capitol Hill, acknowledging each other but not beyond our simple greetings. Both of our marriages crumbled. Yet it would be another decade before our paths would meet, not just cross.

"In 1987, with the retirement of Tip O'Neill, Jim Wright of Texas was elected Speaker of the House. Speaker Wright surprised everyone by making me his top appointment. I was honored to be his chief deputy majority whip."

Anxious to get involved in the tale, Judy asks, "Can't you hear the music building? Fate is intervening. We're about to be tossed together for good."

"It's true," I continue. "My new position on the leadership ladder provided me with an office in the Capitol and a small staff. I needed someone smart and politically savvy to put the office together. Judy applied. She had just the experience I was looking for."

"It was funny," says Judy. "I wasn't even looking for a job. But a friend asked me to interview as a favor to him. And it turned out to be a perfect spot for me. There were two other staff people, too. Four of us in a small space, and we got along really well and cared about the same issues and worked very hard. I loved that."

Judy always sounds wistful when she talks about giving up her job, so I am anxious to get back to the happy stuff. "Soon we were exchanging books in the office," I quickly add. "I would give Judy my Wallace Stegner, and she'd give me her Anita Brookner. We teased about baseball, her Orioles and my Tigers. Both of us were runners. Two and a half years later, in the summer of 1989, I worked up enough courage to ask Judy out."

"And finally, after all those years of sort of knowing each other, we were married in May of 1991," Judy finishes triumphantly.

"It's lucky you found each other," says Frank. "Otherwise, you each might have been walking alone."

"Not me," Judy says. "Maybe David would have done this alone, but I never would have even thought of it."

The wine is gone. Time to head home from the restaurant. By

10:30 we say good night. Lying together in bed, I whisper to Judy, "You're not sorry we're doing this, are you?"

She answers immediately, "Oh, no. I love our walk."

Good, I think to myself.

"I love you," she quietly adds.

"And I love you, too."

Total Walked	31 miles
Walked Today	14 miles
Walking to Do	304 miles

Chapter 3
Oxford to Lapeer

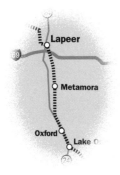

After a good night's rest, we ready ourselves for a twenty-two-mile walk to Lapeer. Gail is already off to work, so we breakfast only with Frank and thank him for their generosity. We know this will have been the highlight of comfort and luxury on our trip. In their garage we slip into our mud-caked boots and begin our four-mile journey to the village of Oxford in the early-morning mist. No sooner do we wind back up to the top of the driveway than the rain begins to fall. It's between a mist and a drizzle, which prompts me to call it "mizzle." It is 7:30 A.M., and the temperature is only in the mid-fifties. We decide to return to the house, under the overhanging eaves, to put on our rain gear. Starting out wet and cold is not a bright idea.

On Indian Lake Road we retrace for a half-mile our approach walk and then turn north up Marwood, a rolling unpaved road with stately homes barely visible beyond the trees on each side. At the corner of Marwood and Drahner Roads we approach a small marsh. We are both excited to see what appears to be a green heron, the most generally distributed small heron in the north. Quietly, we steal closer to get a better view of this fifteen-inch bird with a purple-black neck, yellow feet, and a long bill. Judy thinks it may be a rail, but then it flies off before we can firmly make an identification. For those few moments we enter a communion with this bird. It is an inspiring sight in the early morning.

We continue west on Drahner walking through an area called Grampian Hills, elevation twelve hundred feet. Drahner is flanked by hovering broad oaks, which with the added full spread of maples provide a canopy that almost protects us from the mizzle. Soon we march by Grampian, Handsome, and Tullamore Lakes. The last offers us a view of a large deer feeding in some marsh grasses near the far shore about a quarter of a mile away. We are taken by its size, thinking perhaps it could be a moose but knowing that there are no known Bullwinkles in Oakland County. Our road passes an Oakland County Youth Camp perched high on a hill, a children's nature center, and the Oxford Hill Golf and Country Club. We avoid walking farther to the heavily traveled M-24 and instead head north into Oxford along a back road that skirts an industrial park. This unpleasant bypass ends in Oxford village, population twenty-seven hundred, at an elevation of 1,059 feet. Founded in 1836 and named for the many oxen teams owned by the settlers, Oxford closely resembles the village of Lake Orion, both small midwestern, middle-class towns off the main transportation trunk line. Drenched, we walk through an older neighborhood to main street, where we get out of the rain in the Wildcat Cafe.

The cafe is a throwback to another time when we were adolescents and sought refuge in that special place for meeting after school or hanging out after ball games or just escaping an adult world that didn't seem to understand us. Yellow and blue cat paw prints border the walls, and old Oxford High School yearbooks going back forty years are stacked in the back. "Chef Doug" is at the grill flipping pancakes and listening to his young worker at the counter talking nonstop about his girlfriend's parents. On the bulletin board is an article entitled "Julia Child at 85 and Still Cooking." Placed throughout the diner are old racquets, helmets, and skateboards all evoking memories of cherished youthful endeavors. On the main wall of the cafe above the booths is a framed football jersey with the number 25. Circling the jersey are pictures of fresh-faced, young people. Presumably, this is a tribute to local high school stars—students and athletes. This authenticity cannot be duplicated by formulaic chain restaurants. There is nothing contrived here.

We are both surprised at how soaked we have gotten underneath our rain gear. Two wet travelers with packs squeezing into a cafe can be an unwelcome annoyance, so we quickly seek out a vacant corner to stash our gear. I dig out a dry T-shirt from my pack and go to change in the restroom. We intend only to get coffee but break down and order our second breakfast. Judy treats herself to pancakes, while I have oatmeal with brown sugar and a bagel. We spend a good deal of time drying out the insides of our rain gear and then writing in our journals. We each have a 3 x 5 inch, spiral flip waterproof notebook. The covers are made of "100 percent post-consumer recycled material," and the sheets are "all-weather writing paper," which was created to shed water and enhance the written image. We doubt if our scribbles need all this, but already being waterproof is critical.

Judy casually inquires about the wall of fame. We are unprepared for the response. Our young waitress tells us that the pictures on the wall are of students who died tragically young, including the owner's daughter. It is his tribute to them. If this is to be a place of remembrance, then all the Wildcats are to share in its past. Our waitress goes on to tell us that channel 50, a local Detroit TV station, heard about the wall of honor and remembrance and sent a crew out to do a human interest story. They got the story horribly wrong, broadcasting that all the students on the wall had been suicide victims, when in fact only one had been. This naturally devastated the town. Our waitress sent the station a long letter complaining about the inaccuracy of the report and telling of the pain it had caused the families of these deceased young people. She asked for a retraction and clarification on the air but received only a letter of apology.

At this point in her story, she pauses, takes a considered breath, and continues. "When I was ten years old and my brother seven, we were crossing the main street in town, right outside here. My little brother was hit by a car and killed as we crossed the street together. It took me so many years to deal with my own sadness and guilt. I am so angry at those TV people. They have no right to hurt these families again."

Her story stuns us. We can find no appropriate words but nod gravely in agreement and simply whisper, "Thank you." The rain and the cold delivered us to the Wildcat Cafe. We leave there warmed spiritually as well as physically.

We head up Washington Street for three blocks, passing many small businesses but no people, the rain having chased everyone indoors. We have Oxford to ourselves. Washington then becomes the dreaded major trunk line that we must travel for two miles before reaching the Metamora Road. Facing oncoming traffic, we are buffeted by the stinging wind bursts of double-wide trucks and speeding cars. The wet air that refills the vacuums left by these passing vehicles literally slaps us as we walk. Pushing forward, we pass a series of lakes, and one, Stony Lake, appears to have a shoreline on which we might have pitched a tent had we needed to. Mercifully, our highway experience ends, and we turn up the Metamora Road. It is a disappointment to find ourselves on a paved surface in a light industrial area. This is not the beautiful rolling horse country we were expecting. But two and a half miles later, as we approach the Lapeer County line, magnificent oak trees shade the road, and again the scene changes.

Oakland County is the tree's namesake. Tradition has it that oak is the king of trees. Donald Culross Peattie, in his poetic book *A Natural History of Trees*, called the white oak, throughout its range, the king of kings.

> The Tuliptree can grow taller, and the Sycamore in the days of the virgin forest had gigantic boles (trunks), but no other tree in our sylva has so great a spread. The mighty branches, themselves often fifty feet long or more, leave the trunk nearly at right angles and extend their arms benignantly above the generation of men who pass beneath them. Indeed the fortunate possessor of an old White Oak owns a sort of second home, an outdoor mansion of shade and greenery and leafy music. So deep is the tap root of such a tree, so wide the thrust of the innumerable horizontal roots, that if one could see its whole underground system this would look like a reflection, somewhat foreshortened, of the giant above the ground. (195–96)

Soon the foliage will turn to the color of wine, and then the weathered leaves will either cling in clumps to rustle in the wind or drop to cover the pastoral road on which we walk.

As we move up the road into Lapeer County, our way is lined with small farms, dried cornfields, and meadows dotted with horses. Lapeer is the southernmost county in what has become known as Michigan's Thumb. The shape of the Lower Peninsula of the state is so like a mitten that natives hold up their hand to point to a particular location. We are actually just at the inside of the joint of the thumb and palm. A century ago the Thumb was new crop land, much of it burned over from the great fire of 1881. Farmers of German and Yankee descent raised crops that can thrive in a short growing season such as potatoes, sugar beets, and navy beans (used in the bean soup served in the U.S. Capitol in Washington, DC). Today the Thumb is still mostly farmland tilled by the descendants of those pioneers.

The rain has stopped, and the sky struggles to reveal the first rays of sun we've seen. Monarchs, dramatic in their orange and black, and a variety of swallowtails share with us the many wildflowers along the fence rows. Just beyond Wolf Lake, two adolescent deer in their summer reddish-brown coats lazily feed in a meadow. They take a measure of us and with their juvenile assurance decide we are no threat and continue to browse. A half-mile farther several chestnut horses lift their heads from their grazing to eye these two strangely burdened folks. Their inquisitive stares call to mind Robert Frost's sweet lines, "My little horse must think it queer / To stop without a farmhouse near."

We stop and watch the horses, wishing we had sugar or sweets to offer. The moment is unexpectedly satisfying. The world around us is hushed and harmonious.

And the sun is actually shining. This means we are suffocating in our rain gear, and Judy suggests we stop for a break. We take off our rain jackets and pants and thread them through the straps on the outside of our packs so they will dry as we walk. Now it is time to turn our attention to our feet. The top of the second toe on Judy's left foot is building a bruise. I am developing a blister on my left heel. The gravel from the road also kicks up into our boots. I'm growing increasingly apprehensive that my boots do not fit properly. This is a surprise, since they felt great on our ten- to twelve-mile daily hikes in Alaska and Montana this summer. Now I feel they might be a quarter- to a half-size too big even taking into account the heavy trekking socks and the additional thin liner socks I'm wearing. The extra space may be causing friction on my feet. When we empty our boots, there is more gravel in mine than I care to think about—I imagine the rocks rubbing, rubbing, rubbing. We each bandage our tender spots, hoping this will suffice until we get to Lapeer.

The sun plays hide-and-seek among the clouds as we walk into the village of Metamora. This small town, population 552, is named after the Indian word for "hills." The clerk in the convenience store tells me the name means "among the hills." The first white settler came in 1843 and built a hotel. When the Detroit and Bay City Railroad was laid through these parts, a depot was built in town. The

With Katie Shaw outside Genoa Pizza Company in Metamora

village center has two blocks of business establishments, including the Genoa Pizza Parlor. As we walk by the pizza place, a laborer carrying a pizza swings into his pick-up truck and volunteers that the "best pizza in these here parts is right in there." We must look hungry. Taking the bait, we stop there, happy to rest after coming thirteen miles. Before entering the store, we take off our packs and lean them outside against the wall between two wiggly old benches. Across the street a crew of shirtless young men, still bronzed from the July sun, is laying asphalt in front of the party store. In Michigan we refer to convenience stores as "party stores," which must say something about us. Soda we call "pop," an onomatopoetic treat.

Inside we try to order two slices of pizza but are told that they just sold the last pizza (to guess who?). Katie Shaw, the young daughter of the owner, suggests pizza dough sticks, which we order and dip into pizza sauce. Very good and just right for me. Judy misses the cheese. I take my drink and food outside to sit in the 1:00 P.M. sun on the rickety old bench. Before me unfolds an interesting scene. While the asphalt is being laid and tamped, a thirteen- or fourteen-year-old girl watches from behind a clump of trees in a vacant lot next to the party store. My first thought is that she is peeking at the muscular, tanned workers but soon realize that her young girlfriend is emerging from the store carrying some juvenile contraband. My guess is cigarettes. The two girls disappear, having played their stealthy roles with the right degree of guilt and deception.

Katie is curious about our gear and where we are going. Like many young women we will meet over the course of our walk, she finds our story fascinating and liberating. Judy is already firmly convinced that this pattern of response is differentiated by gender. Grudgingly, I acknowledge some agreement. Our one nasty encounter so far was with a man we met early yesterday morning on the lovely Paint Creek Trail. He was walking a bulldog and asked if we were training for a hike. Evidently disbelieving our story, he essentially called us liars. Judy was so mad it almost ruined her day, until passing women all offered us encouragement and support. And so it is to be. Men rarely engage us and, when they do, usually feel challenged and have to either put us down or brag of some greater exploit of their own. This hostility is always unsettling. We are the first to acknowledge that others have undertaken far greater challenges. Ours is a pilgrimage, not a competition.

Katie is intrigued. She tells us that the longest walk of her life was four and a half miles after an argument with her father. Judy seizes any opportunity with all the young women we meet to deliver her message. She tells them that they can make their dreams come true, just as we are by taking this walk. They may sometimes feel trapped in these jobs or places, but if there is something else they want to do, even if people laugh at them or say it's impossible, they should persevere. After all, most people laugh at us, and here we are, on the road following our dream. It sounds obvious, but many young girls in particular still do not know what opportunities are available to them. They respond to Judy's words, agreeing that it would be exciting to do something challenging, interesting, educational, and healthy. Katie tells us she will always remember meeting us. That, too, will be a common response. Before we say goodbye we take a picture with her in front of the store.

On our way again, the road stays paved north of town, and the traffic thickens as we travel precariously along the narrow shoulder of the road. The houses we pass display innovative and curious yard objects. An old green bicycle serves as a mount for a mailbox. This is matched earlier in the day by an old plow converted for the mail. We've seen flowers blooming in a wringer washer and even in the bowl and tank of an old commode. One yard has a full-sized statue of a cow tied to a tree. Most popular of all is a wood carving of a small boy peeing in the garden. Judy doesn't care for those, but I think they're kind of innocent. In any case these sights tickle our imaginations as we push up Metamora Road. After two miles of cars we are weary of walking on the lip of a ditch. Searching for relief, we turn west onto Sutton Road for a half-mile and then up Clark.

Clark is heavenly, just the sort of road we dream of walking. Unpaved and deserted, it is lined with oak, maple, and pine. We pause to read a sign beyond a low iron gate overlooking a well-tended cemetery. "Clarks cemetery founded in 1862 by Mrs. Clark" I muse about the year 1862. The Civil War and a country in despair. Lincoln at the brink, the Union torn apart. Austin Blair, Michigan's abolitionist governor, who earlier had proposed granting African Americans the right to vote, sends ninety thousand Michigan soldiers to Washington, the first western regiment to reach the capital. President Lincoln declares, "Thank God for Michigan." That year was also a time of hope. Not forty miles east of here, in Port Huron, Michigan, Thomas Alva Edison builds his first electrical battery and begins his many experiments, which will eventually change the history of mankind dramatically.

On up Clark Road we collapse next to a bean field. Dropping our packs to the ground, we pillow our heads on them and find ourselves eye level with the endless rows of beans. We are bushed and hurting. Our feet are crying, "No mas," as bruises, blisters, and hot spots multiply. Judy's hip is beginning to ache, a problem she has experienced with her running, too. We lie in the warm sun, drinking from our water bottles and gathering our strength. I drift back again to 1862 and the hot, long march of thousands of troops through the Shenandoah Valley. We will soon be sheltered in comfort, whereas those poor souls for the most part knew only misery. It is time for us to find that comfortable shelter. We stagger forth.

The traffic increases at Hunter Creek Road as the late afternoon hour ushers workers to their homes. We pass under Interstate 69 and angle over to M-24, where we hope to spot the Best Western Motel located in a shopping and fast-food strip near the entrance to the city of Lapeer. I suggest we cut through a ballfield and find the motel north of our present location. Judy seems sure that it is due west a few blocks. She rarely questions my lead, but at this point each extra step matters, and I sense a rising tension in her voice. We follow her intuition, wisely, as we finally glimpse our destination ahead. My thoughts now wander to the motel swimming pool and how refreshing it's going to be after twenty-two miles of hoofing it. I dream of floating in cool water, no pressure at all on my feet, legs, and hips. And then crawling into the whirlpool, where hot-water jets massage my shoulders and balls of my battered feet. These visions carry me across the highway and into the motel lobby.

It is now 4:45 in the afternoon, and the lobby is empty. Confident that our timely reservations for a Wednesday night will guarantee us a convenient room, we pick up our key and a letter from Judy's mother. The desk clerk tells us, "Room 231, upstairs, down the hall, in the back of the motel."

Judy mutters, "What is going on here?" We are feeling quite put upon. Do we smell? Are they ashamed of us? Are they political enemies? Are we reading too much into this? Of course. But don't they realize how absolutely exhausted we are? We struggle back into our packs, walk up the stairs and down seemingly endless corridors. Our room is the very farthest from the front desk. Fortunately, it is agreeable, with a king-sized bed about three times the area of our tent space, a table, and two comfortable chairs. Out our window is a string of fast-food restaurants, all the better to make a dinner selection. The end of each day's walk is the same. Drop our packs. Kick off our boots. Rest.

Before we go down to the pool I check in by phone with the office and make what turns out to be a foolish request. In preparing for our expedition, we had overlooked any study of butterflies. We are frustrated by our ignorance. So I blithely ask a fellow nature lover in the office to fax us some information. Then we head off to the soothing waters. In the swimming pool we experiment with every aquatic suspension position, permitting our tired bodies to float aimlessly. The contrast of the 102 degree whirlpool almost lulls us to sleep. This pampering is a welcome relief for our languid bodies. We are the only people in the pool.

The fax is awaiting us after our soak. There are eighteen pages of black-and-white butterfly images. Useless, of course, and for the tidy sum of eighteen dollars. We won't do that again. Our hunger pangs call, so we limp over to the Burger King in our extra footwear. We have identical thick blue flip-flops, which we purchased for seven dollars a pair at KMart. We look dippy, but they are a relief from our boots, and we are glad to have them.

Bringing our hamburgers and fries back to our room, we eat in comfort and share observations about the day. Two treats remain. Judy heads out once more and brings back hot fudge and hot butterscotch Dairy Queen sundaes for herself and me, respectively. I have certain diet restrictions, and Judy abides by them even if I don't. One item I'm to steer clear of is caffeine. Our second indulgence is the letter from Mary Strong.

Judy's parents were both academics, and she was raised among books, conversation, and letters. One of her fondest memories of her father, who died when she was just fourteen, is sitting in the living room with him while they each quietly read their own book. When he took his sabbatical from Carleton College in Northfield, Minnesota, when she was but nine, her father sent Judy postcards nearly every day. Hers was and is a writing family. Judy's mother has kept her daughter's correspondence detailing in weekly missives her life at the University of Iowa and afterward as a young mother. And to this day Mary Strong writes to us weekly, although Judy has succumbed to the ease of the phone. One of the most amusing of the family writing stories occurred when Judy went on a congressional delegation trip with her first Capitol Hill boss, John Brademas. Among the participants on this trip to Spain and Portugal in January 1980 was the late congressman from Queens, New York, Benjamin Rosenthal. This was Judy's first trip overseas, and her enthusiasm delighted this experienced congressional traveler. In addition, her mother sent her letters on the trip. Congressman Rosenthal was so taken with this concept that he would rush to the hotel desk at each new destination to claim Judy's letters. Then he would read them aloud to the assembled delegation at the briefings in the control room. You might wonder if a bunch of strangers could be interested in a simple mother-to-daughter correspondence, but it is a sign of the quality of Mary's letters that they were.

So, when we sent a copy of our itinerary to Mary Strong as we did to other family members and a few close friends, we rather expected that she might be in touch with us along the way. As a frequent and serious writer, Mary always takes advantage of the stationery provided in hotel rooms. My guess is that in these days of primarily electronic communication those sheets of paper often go untouched by months' worth of guests. But our letterhead and envelope sent to Lapeer, Michigan, from Somerset, New Jersey, had been supplied by Hotel Accademia in Verona, Italy, where Mary had visited in June.

Her first paragraph speaks most personally to us: "If you are reading this, it means that I have had better luck reaching you in Lapeer than you did me in Venezia [Judy's letter to her mother in Venice in June had been returned] but also that you've completed the third day of your walk through Michigan. The third day, as you found in the book on hiking in the 90s, was the one on which the strains showed up. I just hope you've been the exception to the rule and that you're enjoying the experience you're having good or bad."

We fall into a deep sleep. We are surviving the bad and enjoying the good, which seems a satisfactory record after three days.

Total Walked	53 miles
Walked Today	22 miles
Walking to Do	282 miles

Chapter 4
Lapeer to Otter Lake

Thursday, August 14

Better give your path to a dog, than be bitten by him in contesting for the right. Even killing the dog would not cure the bite.

—Abraham Lincoln

We are up at 6:00 A.M. Ready to go, we traipse back down the long hallways to the lobby, where I pay the bill and we help ourselves to doughnuts and coffee. Nursing our coffee, we roam into the entrance of a bar/restaurant called Firehouse Willie's. Peeking through the windows, we can see a festive sports motif. The hallway is lined with famous pictures of well-known sports teams and celebrities. A sketch of "Firehouse Willie" is added to each photograph, revealing a large, bearded man wearing thick red suspenders. Below the photo is a caption. For instance, beneath Willie in the team picture of the 1984 World Champion Detroit Tigers, is written, "Willie pitches Tigers to a pennant—goes 22–3 and wins the Cy Young Award." Amused by Willie's flights of fancy, we head out into the crisp sunny morning to pursue our own.

Lapeer is the seat of county government for Lapeer County. With a current population of six thousand, it is a handsome town that evolved from a French trading village. Its name is an anglicized version of the French word *la pierre,* meaning "stone" or "flint." In 1831 the Pontiac Mill Company established a sawmill here at Farmers Creek. The town was originally platted and recorded as Whiteville in 1833 and changed to its present name a year later. From a lumbering village it developed into a manufacturing center for bookcases, cabinets, and cedar chests. Today, in addition to its government role, it has become a community of suburbanites from nearby Metro Detroit and Flint and retired farmers who have left their mark on the rich agricultural lands of the Thumb.

Walking through town on Lapeer Road, we are treated to large, old, charming houses with broad porches and high cupolas. A few blocks to our east rises the old courthouse constructed in 1837 in Greek Revival style.

A mile and a half up Lapeer Road we turn west on Oregon Avenue and walk with the sun low to our backs. Our shadows cast out from our feet to well above our heads before us. We stalk our own resemblances. I pull out our camera and tell Judy to wave while I shoot our ground reflection, which is thrown long and wide on the grassy easement between the sidewalk and road. We are enjoying this serendipitous moment. An older man in excellent shape and wearing a sleeveless "grandpa undershirt" walks by us at a rigorous pace. In answer to his query we announce our Mackinac destination. He smartly responds, "When I finish my five miles, that is it!" Today we need to make eighteen miles to reach our campsite at Otter Lake, where our friend Stan will meet us. Passing the high school on our left, I get the feeling we have overshot our mark. Sure enough, on checking the map I see we have missed our turn north by about a mile. Instead of retracing our steps, we mistakenly decide to take Millville Road north.

The road has virtually no shoulder, just a narrow gravel strip next to a drainage ditch, which opens up on the other side to an expansive soybean field. I walk in the lead. My body tenses as we encounter heavy morning commuter traffic. Folks are on their way to work, school, or errands, and we receive many inquisitive looks. Judy says I'm down in the dumps today. I confess that the traffic and my feet have me bummed out. Blisters continue to broaden on both heels. The pain in my feet erodes my determination and focuses my thoughts on the end of the day. This is not a healthy formula for a 335-mile walk. I know I can get through this day. But what about the rest of the journey? We will still have 264 miles to go when tomorrow dawns.

When we left Mount Clemens on Monday, I had just recovered from something the doctors call keratolysis exfoliation, which is the breaking of the outer layer of skin. My hands and feet were peeling at an excessive rate, and I needed a steroid to stop my shedding. Doctors believe this condition is related to a strep infection. But *stress* may also play a role in it. Was it Alfred E. Newman who once

Stalking our own shadows in Lapeer

said, "What, me worry?" Well the upshot here is that my new skin is tender and, I guess, susceptible to blisters. I am worried. I can't bear to imagine aborting our adventure after all the preparation we have invested. My mind fast-forwards to meeting Stan at the lake campground. Catching sight of the waving soybean rows to my left, I wish we could wade through those soft green fields. Judy, on the other hand (or is it foot), is in high spirits on this sunny day and is in love with her boots and the walk.

We finally abandon the busy thoroughfare after forty minutes and strike out west on Bolton Road toward Bronson Lake. In an excited voice Judy suddenly exclaims, "Did you see that?"

"See what?"

A red fox has just dashed across the road in front of us. This carnivorous mammal from the dog family is most active at night, so this appearance is one of nature's unexpected treats. Judy describes the fox as about two feet in length, with reddish fur, a pointed face, and a long tail. The fox was prized for trapping in earlier Michigan history, when the fur trade was king. I miss this sighting because I often walk with my head down, a bad habit from my youth.

Yet my downcast demeanor is soon rewarded. On the shoulder of the road there appears a curious, coincidental collection. Set not twelve inches apart from one another lie a discarded audiotape, a stilled monarch butterfly, and a dead eastern bluebird. The monarch and bluebird are perfect specimens still in full color. Judy picks up the tape and reads, "Jimi Hendrix, Kiss the Sky." The monarch, orange with prominent black veins, travels great distances to Mexico and California to winter. Like Hendrix, this one ran out of energy and kissed the sky good-bye. The bluebird we think just recently fell from the sky, as its bright blue plumage and red breast make it appear to be only napping. Couple this scene with the title of the book Judy is reading, *A Happy Death,* and we nervously laugh about what the future portends.

The paved portion of Bolton Road ends near a large entrance sign to a boy scout camp, Camp Homoloka, Tall Pines Council. We examine our map and conclude that the camp trail is what is designated. We are reluctant to go into the camp for fear of being turned away but are loath to retrace our steps. Deciding to chance it, we proceed up the dirt road, lined with Burma Shave–type signs extolling the virtues of scouting. "A scout is brave." "A scout is loyal." "A scout is trustworthy."

With prompting from Judy, I take the trustworthy sign to heart and decide to announce ourselves to the camp custodian who resides one-quarter of a mile into the campground. The camp is empty, which raises our hopes that we will be granted permission to use its trail. We approach the back door of the house and begin to make our case. I'm prepared, if our request is faring poorly, to recite the scout pledge, which I remember, amazingly, after forty years. Judy explains that we are hiking to Mackinac and our atlas has led us to this trail, pointing out to our host the exact spot on the map. After initially balking, he eventually lets us pass, and we are escorted down the trail by a tiny furry black dog with no bark who is determined to guide us with all the spunk and loyalty of Dorothy's Toto.

It is easy to imagine scores of boys thrilling to the wonders of this sylvan back country. We spy through an opening in the woods Horton Lake, where swimming lessons are taught and canoeing takes on a sense of pioneering adventure. Indian lore richly infuses scouting traditions, and we picture troops encircling a campfire in an open meadow as they share in a powwow. I recall those memorable events years ago as a scout, in the summer of 1957, camping at the D Bar A, a boy scout camp near our walk along the Metamora Road.

Several peacocks appear ahead of us. This ornamental bird, which once lived in the wilds of the Orient but is now raised in captivity, has historically been a symbol of pride and seems too regal for our simple, rustic surroundings. Before losing ourselves in the woods, we stop at a picnic table to change the moleskin on my heels. Our little furry friend patiently waits for us to finish and then leads us up and down on a winding trail through a woods of oak, pine, and beach with ground ferns carpeting the forest floor. The quiet walk on a dirt surface smoothed over time by the pounding feet of energized twelve-year-olds is a pleasant respite after gravel roads and shoulders. A mile and a half later the trail ends at a fence, which we must scale. Fortunately, the gate seems to be sturdy and should provide solid footing for our leap over. We remove our packs. I go over first, and Judy hands over the packs before joining me. We are actually reluctant to bid our puppy companion farewell. Dogs will be a serious problem for us along the way, but this one was adorable. On the other side we are not sure of our location, but across the road a friendly neighbor points us in the direction of Bronson Lake. I get our bearings, and we make our way along the northeast part of the lake. Small boats tied to docks bounce merrily on the wind-rippled lake, and the three-quarters of a mile passes pleasantly.

Next, unpaved Klan Road takes us north through prosperous farm country. The sun still shines brightly, drying up puddles from the past week's worth of rain. We hope for some tan so that we will look convincingly weather-beaten by the end of our walk. For the first time on our trip we actually feel hot. Sheep, cows, pigs, horses, chickens, roosters, and ducks are our companions. We break into appropriate song. "Old MacDonald Had a Farm" and "Oats, Peas, Beans, and Barley Grow" head our list of farm favorites. We sing all the verses with full sound effects. As we cross a railroad grade, I conclude with a rousing "I've Been Workin' on the Railroad." Life seems grand. Then we enter a stretch of particularly vicious canines.

I wonder if it was our off-key voices raised in song that set off a chain reaction of barks and growls that dominoes up the road for three miles. The tension heightens as German shepherds and other large snarleyyows set their sights on us. We are both dreadfully afraid of dogs. But Judy has read about how to handle this predicament and is determined to maintain her poise. She instructs me to cross to the other side of the road from the dogs, to avoid eye contact with them, to walk at a normal pace, and to keep my arms at my sides. I want to ready myself for battle but yield to her advice. Anticipating these encounters, we tried to purchase mace but had to settle for pepper spray. Mace is only legal in Michigan for letter carriers and law enforcement officials. Many times on our walk, when faced with an especially threatening dog, we think of our friends Pat Carroll and Mike Sheridan of the South Macomb Letter Carriers. But I guess friends don't ask friends to lend them unauthorized substances. We carry pepper spray and a billy club, which is threaded through the top flap of my pack. The pepper spray is also designed for surly black bears and hostile Homo sapiens. The spray is intended to cause an animal temporary visual and breathing problems, but we easily imagine distempering our foe or finding the spray blown back into our own faces. All in all, this little canister is a very questionable weapon to rely on for protection. I'd feel better now with the club in my hand, but Judy says it will just incite the dogs to attack.

Lest we appear a bit paranoid about "man's best friend," consider these 1998 research findings from the Center of Injury Research and Control at the University of Pittsburgh. Nearly 4.5 million dog bites occur annually in the United States, sending 334,000 victims to hospital emergency rooms. That is more ER visits than injury from skateboards, baby walkers, and in-line skates combined. Dog bites kill about twenty people a year, and dogs apparently seem to prefer biting males. I do have reason to fear.

I walk the length of Klan Road with my finger on the pepper spray button. Every homestead we pass is guarded by a dog, sometimes two or more, that rushes to its property line ready for our unwelcome entry. This happens at least a dozen times. We are saved on several other occasions by owners who call off their "pets." As we approach each new property line, we tense, searching for sight or sound of danger, prepared to cross the road or defend ourselves. The adrenaline surges. We are actually nearly consumed with terror. A huge, barking, snarling dog races toward us. What will we do if we are attacked? These bounding beasts appear to be ready to have us for their next meal. But at the last moment they always pull up short. Judy's advice is right on target. Still, the fear is exhausting. My courage spent, I convince Judy to take a break at the intersection of Klan and Peters Road. As we rest, I look back to the road we've just traveled. Now safely at the other end, I can admire the ordered horse pastures, ranch home estates, and grand sweep of the fields.

A mile up Peters Road we enter Columbiaville. This village of 957 is located on the Holloway Reservoir, which is a product of the dammed Flint River. Founded in 1847, it was originally named Niverville after George and Henry Nivers, who built a sawmill on the river. The name was changed to Columbiaville to honor Columbia County, New York, from which a number of early prominent settlers had migrated. We stop at the local market for fruit, chips, and drinks then drift a couple of blocks to a small park set just above the bank of the reservoir. Dumping our packs, we collapse upon them and remove our boots and socks to let our feet dry and breathe.

An adolescent boy emerges over the lip of the bank. His behavior is strange, and his body language signals that we have invaded his space. While we snack gazing out over the water, he circles behind us, pacing and throwing stones at a gravel pile only a few feet away. He makes us feel so ill at ease that Judy imagines he might turn and start casting the stones at us. I feel like closing my eyes and drifting off for fifteen minutes, letting the warmth of the sun work its restorative powers, but his presence makes me edgy. After twenty-five minutes of building tension we gather our gear and begin our final six-mile leg to Otter Lake, which we hope to reach before 3:00 P.M. Our break has not been restful, and in retrospect Judy thinks maybe the kid was just trying to get our attention. It's true that I normally would have talked to anybody throwing something. In fact, I might have joined him pitching stones into the water. After all, playing catch with any kind of ball is one of my all-time favorite pastimes. We were both just too tired to engage him, and we feel sort of guilty for not trying.

A bridge dedication sign at the entrance to the road across the narrowed part of the reservoir announces that construction occurred in 1978 with federal and local dollars. That was the year we passed the Accelerated Public Works Bill, providing four billion dollars of 80 to 90 percent federal dollars for roads, bridges, firehouses, and municipal buildings. At that time I was a member of the House Public Works and Transportation Committee and its Subcommittee on Surface Transportation. I was able to get thirty-three such projects for my congressional district. It honestly gives me great pleasure to visit the results of our legislative labors, especially after a generation of use. I like seeing the firehalls in Marine City and Berlin Township, the civic center in Clinton Township, the track at Port Huron Northern High School, and all the other projects that would bore anyone else to death. And those are twenty-year-old efforts. Catching a glimpse of more recent accomplishments such as our bike path or the second span of the Blue Water Bridge makes me positively ebullient. Such are the joys of a legislator.

As we cross the narrows, we enjoy the colorful canvasback ducks, scoots, and a blue heron stalking near the water's edge. For the next three miles we walk north through a rural landscape, passing Hemmingway Lake as we tack west into Otter Lake. The sign greeting us at the village limit reads, "Laws regulating peddlers and solicitors strictly enforced." It seems unduly harsh, but we assume that we will be welcome.

Otter Lake village is one-half in Genesee County and the other in Lapeer County. With only five hundred souls, the village is named after the lake, which once held an abundant otter population. Like other communities in the area, Otter Lake is a product of the lumbering era. It was platted in 1874, the same year that the Pere Marquette Railroad came through town. Today the small outpost hosts a campground on the lake, a bar, Joyce's Cafe, several other modest stores, and a gas station/convenience store.

We arrive right on time, at 3:00 P.M. Dave Marginet is the tall, thin, sixtyish resident campground manager with a fine weathered face. He's got a good "listening-to" voice. "It's quite something to see you two just walk in here this way. I don't remember we've ever had a hiker here. A cyclist now and then. But no hikers." We believe that, for we've passed no other hikers ourselves.

"Have you seen a friend of ours who is meeting us here?"

"Oh, he's been here," answers Dave. "We've been talking. He'll be back." Dave has a stable of regulars who park their trailers and return on weekends as well as the drive-in types with pop-ups and tents.

Dave sends us to site 9 ½, which is on the lake's edge and is supplied with the usual picnic table and fire ring. Next to us a grandpa and his six-year-old grandson are fishing, duplicating a ritual we shared with our children when they were little ones long, long ago. Stephen is now thirty-one, Julie twenty-seven, and Andy twenty-four.

Stan returns from the local store with BBQ potato chips and beer, just what we need at the end of a long day. We sit around the picnic table relating tales of our days and occasionally picking up bits of conversation nearby about the fish in Otter Lake. Stan fills us with stories about the whole camping and recreational vehicle business. A car aficionado, he entertainingly holds forth on the makes and models of various vehicles in our camp. Suddenly we hear, "Look Grandpa!" The little guy is holding up a wiggling four-inch sunfish, proud as he can be. Grandpa takes it off the hook for him. The lake beyond us is round, dotted with lilypads in bloom and calm in its wooded glen. Toward evening we hear the haunting call of a loon from the far shore. It is good to be here.

Stan unloads our tent and sleeping gear from the trunk of his car. The untold secret of our walk so far is that we haven't even been carrying a full load. When we discovered how much overweight we were last weekend in Mount Clemens, we decided to take Stan up on his offer of assistance. Since our first three nights on the road did not involve camping, we sorted out that equipment and left it for him to bring to us at Otter Lake.

We have a Walrus Archrival tunnel tent that weighs a mere four pounds and eight ounces. Tunnel tents are gaining in popularity because of their light weight and compact "covered wagon" two-hoop design. For us the problems are a very tight fit and virtually no headroom. Of course, the trick is to strike just the right balance between weight and space. Judy is worried about her tendency to be claustrophobic. On the other hand, carrying more tent than the trip calls for can be almost as much of a mistake as not having an adequate tent. The rule of thumb is not to carry more than four pounds of tent per person (three pounds each is better). We plan to split the weight between us, with one carrying the stakes, poles, and footprint and the other the heavier tent and flysheet. The literature claimed that our tent would hold two people, and it meant that exactly. No room for gear. Space for us to turn only if we roll as one. The tent has wonderful ventilation with no-see-um netting to keep out the smallest of bugs while allowing us to view the moon and the stars. Regretfully, the dewpoint and rainy weather require us to use the waterproof flysheet, obscuring the night sky and impeding fresh air.

The tent is quick to erect, taking no more than ten minutes. The aluminum stakes and shock cord poles, which snap together for threading at the foot and head of the tent, make it easy to complete the job. As advised, we practiced pitching the tent in our yard before we left. Judy also waterproofed the seams again, even though they claimed to be factory sealed. For added protection from dampness we first lay a ground cloth known as a footprint because it is the precise shape of the tent floor and same material as the flysheet. This first effort at setting up the tent is a success, except that I bend two of the aluminum stakes by stepping on them. The better way to accomplish this task is to use the heel of your boot as a hammer, exerting just enough percussion to sink the stake without bending it. Do I sense a slight annoyance in Judy at this carelessness on my part? She is ever so much more careful at her tasks than I am. We both admit that there are pros and cons to both approaches, so our tempers rarely flare. We've situated our tent on a slight incline, with the foot toward the water's edge. Next we inflate our air mattresses and pillows, put our sleeping bags in place, and generally ready our little home so that we will be prepared when darkness falls. Stan watches all of this with considerable amusement.

Pleased with our efforts, we drive with Stan into nearby Otisville to the drugstore for supplies. Judy is disappointed that it doesn't seem strange to ride in a car. Maybe we can't ever get to that point living in the United States, where the automobile generally rules all. Earlier in the day I lost my twelve-dollar runner's watch somewhere in the scout camp. We need a watch to time our travels and our pace as well as to wake us in the morning. Judy had bought a watch with a light for the trip so she could check on the time in the middle of the night. But I need my own. I find one for eighteen dollars. I also stock up on moleskin for my blistered feet and foot pads to try cushioning the balls of my feet, which also hurt. We also buy another recyclable camera.

Back in Otter Lake we take dinner in Joyce's Cafe. The food is not the point of our choice. Rather, we want to be part of the place where we find ourselves, and Joyce's is that. Next to us, Dave, the campground manager, is eating with friends, and the swirling conversation centers on rainy weather and poor fishing. We return the two blocks to the camp and check out the weather forecast on the TV in the small recreation room. Possible rain tonight and tomorrow. This has to be the wettest August on record, or else there is just a cloud following us. We bid Stan farewell and many thanks for his help. After brushing our teeth in the simple but clean and modern bathroom facilities, we prepare our site for the night.

Following some discussion, we decide to put our pack covers on our backpacks and then put each in a large plastic trash bag. We leave them on top of the picnic table for the night, where they may get rained on, rather than under the table, where they might be invaded by animals. There is always the risk of theft too, so we take our valuables into the tent with us. Our boots, which are irreplaceable, are in the "vestibule" of our tent, created by the flysheet. Now we enter our tent.

Welcome to the most cramped quarters of your life. We hardly know whether to laugh or cry. Yet I proceed to react in ways that will guarantee both responses before long. With memories of freezing in my tent while camping as a boy, I wildly overdress in my insulated winter long underwear, top and bottoms, and heavy wool socks. So pillow conscious am I that I stuff my empty pillowcase with nearly everything in my pack, including, unbelievably, my toiletry items, only sans razor. Judy meanwhile has neatly folded a mere two or three clothing items into her pillowcase. Dressed in her usual night attire of T-shirt and panties, she is lying comfortably in her sleeping bag eyeing me with sheer bewilderment and mild amusement. Knowing better than to say anything, she waits. Before long I am drenched in perspiration. It is very hard to remove sticky long underwear in a tiny tent. For the next ninety minutes I am tussling with my clothes, my sleeping bag, which of course becomes twisted, and my stupid pillow, which is hard as a rock with sharp protrusions. All of this activity is taking place in a tunnel! Length, only at our toes, nine feet; width, only at our shoulders, five feet; height, only above our heads, thirty-eight inches. This scene will be one of the comedic low-lights of our trip. In fact, Judy still laughs aloud when we reminisce about the first night in our tent.

Finally, we are settled. Under my head is my soft expanded camp pillow. It appealed to me in the REI store because in its compact form it looks like a football. Under my legs for back support is my pillowcase now properly filled by Judy. We turn to reading with our flashlights, hoping that we will become sleepy enough to drift off in our not-altogether-comfortable conditions. Unfortunately, our ill-considered choice of books doesn't help. I had picked up an Elmore Leonard, whom I often find entertaining, particularly because the stories are frequently set in Detroit. But I can tell at once that this one is not going to be my favorite. And Judy brought Camus's *A Happy Death* solely because it was slim. We are definitely not having an existential experience. And two fifty-two-year-olds zipped into mummy bags in a toy tent is a quintessentially American reality—not French or Algerian at all.

Haunting me as we try to sleep is the certainty that we have made a major miscalculation in placing our tent on a slight slope. It seemed at the time that having our heads a bit higher than our feet would be the natural position. But I can already feel all my upper body weight bearing down on my hips. One inch of padding beneath me might not be enough.

"Sweet dreams," Judy whispers in the darkness.

Total Walked	71 Miles
Walked Today	18 Miles
Walking to Do	264 Miles

Chapter 5
Otter Lake to Vassar

A dog in the distance barks all night. The pitch of the tent suggests we may slowly slide into the lake—a sensation that only intensifies through the long, dark hours. My inflatable three-quarters-length sleeping pad is a quarter-length too short and a half-inch too thin. My pelvic bones feel as if they have been scratching for arrowheads. Our sleep is so restless and disturbed that we are up before the alarm on my new watch goes off. The tent itself, aside from being too cramped, holds up well in the light rain, keeping us warm and essentially dry. Judy is delighted with our self-sufficiency; I am already less enamored of this camping business.

After some easy back stretches, I gather my clothes strewn around us in the tent, and we fold and pack our gear. Working from the inside, we stuff our sleeping bags and pillows into their sacks and deflate and roll up our skinny sleeping pads. Like turtles living in their shells, we next unzip the flap and poke our heads outside to feel the dampness and see the cold, steely gray skies. The campground is as silent as a graveyard. We quietly slip into our flip-flops and shuffle to the community restrooms and showers. When we return, I take a sweet picture of Judy next to our tent with the lake in the background.

Today's challenge is to walk seventeen miles via back country roads and M-15 into Vassar with an extra six pounds on each of our backs. My feet, the rainy weather, and the additional weight present significant hurdles.

Breaking camp goes well. We dry the tent, fly cover, and footprint as best we can before stuffing them into their nylon sacks. It's important that they are dry in case we decide to camp tonight in the

At Otter Lake—could a tent for two be any smaller?

Vassar village campsite beside the Cass River. The weather report for today and tonight is grim, with heavy thunderstorms expected.

After packing, I spend forty-five minutes working on taping my feet, a ritual that will occupy part of each morning for the rest of our journey. Sitting on the picnic table, I cut moleskin patches with my Swiss army knife scissors. Never go camping or hiking without a Swiss army knife ensemble. Everything from knives, scissors, bottle and can openers, tweezers, and screwdriver to toothpick is available. I use them all. My heels require a half-dollar-size patch with a hole cut in the middle to match the blister. The opening allows the air to dry the blister and protects it from friction from the boot. I cover with moleskin four other "hot spots." It is now 7:30 A.M., and still there are no other signs of life in the campground. Quietly, we lift our heavier loads onto our backs and steal away a third of a mile to the gas station and party store.

Dave, the campground manager, is sipping coffee in one of the two booths, watching as the village slowly awakens. Two young women are behind the counter waiting on customers rushing off to work. The aroma of freshly brewing coffee permeates the store. After buying our coffee, juice, and energy bars, we slide into the remaining booth next to Dave and casually inquire, "What's the deal with the barking dog?"

"That damn dog has been barking all summer," he responds.

Incredulous, I pursue with the obvious next question, "You mean this town of five hundred folks lets one household disturb their sleep all summer with this barking dog?"

"Yup."

Judy remembers the sign at the village entrance announcing, "Laws regulating peddlers and solicitors strictly enforced," and concludes that dogs have more rights than people. After our light breakfast we bid Dave and Otter Lake farewell. Outside we put on our pack covers as angry skies threaten once again. We leave by Lake Road and after one mile turn north on Sheridan Road and head into Tuscola County.

Tuscola County was established in 1840 and named by settlers with a word Henry B. Schoolcraft was believed to have invented. Schoolcraft is a significant figure in Michigan history. Known as one of the nation's leading experts in Indian culture, in 1823 he married a European-educated granddaughter of an Ojibway (also known as Chippewa) chief. Lamentably, neither his knowledge nor his experience apparently enlightened him. The objectionable Indian Treaty of 1836, which Schoolcraft secured, stole from the tribes 16,000,000 acres of land, nearly half the state. He should have stuck to linguistics. His word, *Tuscola,* was thought to mean "level land," and indeed it is almost billiard table flat. Once an important logging region, this area is now largely agricultural. Sugar beet farms are especially prominent here.

Sheridan Road is lined with vast fields of beets, beans, and corn on either side of us. Traffic is almost nonexistent as we walk the paved road. Cattails standing like sentries in the ditches remind

Judy of her youth in Minnesota. Queen Anne's lace lavishes the roadsides with its delicate white canopies. These so-called weeds, easily dismissed when we whiz by in cars, are truly beautiful. A couple of miles up the road we pass Harvey Lake, where Judy spots what we think may be a whistling swan, though they are rare in these parts. Years of protection have made swans very tame. We are able to approach closely and watch this haughty bird watch us. Horses in a nearby pasture approach and gaze almost lovingly at us. Cows follow us with mournful, bewildered expressions.

Sheridan Road proves a pleasant experience. Then suddenly our rural reverie is interrupted by a loud crack from the heavens. The sky is now dark and ominous. We scramble into our rain suits. The rain is pummeling us, and we are miles from a town. Two farmers, fixing some broken equipment along the road and hurrying to finish before the storm hits, pay us no heed. What will we do if lightning strikes, as it surely will?

In *Backpacking in the '90s* we are startled to learn that lightning claims more victims in the United States in an average year than any other natural disaster, including floods, earthquakes, and tornadoes. Each year between one hundred to three hundred people are killed by lightning, particularly between May and September. Amazingly, lightning strikes a hundred times a second worldwide. Cloud-to-ground lightning can injure in four different ways: by direct strike; by the splash or side flash, when it hits something else but flashes through the air to hit you as well; by ground current (the most common method of injuring people), when the lightning strikes a tree, for instance, and the current runs through the ground or water and into you; and by the blast effect, when you are thrown by the sudden expansion of air caused by a strike. We are prime targets on this August day.

Nervous and exposed in the flat Tuscola countryside with nothing around us except our metal tubular packs and fields of vegetables, we ponder our peril as we see lightning in the clouds. We quicken our pace, looking for a barn or farmhouse. The wind picks up, and we peer through our hoods into sheets of rain, hoping to get a better sense of the cloud-to-cloud lightning we hear in the distance. Having learned that lightning can strike from a mile away, we begin to count once we see the flash. If we hear thunder after seeing a bolt of lightning before we finish counting to five, then we know we are within range of being hit. We count, "One one-thousand, two one-thousand," and hear the rumbling thunder. As a kid, I was told that the sound of thunder was Saint Peter bowling in heaven. I wonder if there is a patron saint for bowling. But kidding is not appropriate now. Judy is as skittish as the horses we see racing for cover. Our vulnerability is real. Our options for shelter are few. The ditch next to the road is rapidly collecting water. There are no stands of trees in sight, although a group of small trees in a wooded area would be preferable to our exposure on the open road. About a quarter-mile from the intersection of Sheridan and Millington Roads we spot several homes. The corner house displays a sign advertising homegrown fruits and vegetables. They must be used to strangers stopping by. We dash for their open garage door, hoping they will understand our plight.

As we plunge through the puddles in the driveway, a tall, still able-bodied, elderly man with a seasoned face, genial expression, and large, strong hands descends steps from the attached house into the garage. He greets us in a friendly but cautious manner, perhaps thinking to himself, "I want to help, but first let's see what I've got here." He looks us over quizzically.

Two cars nearly fill this two and a half–car garage, with the remainder occupied by gardening paraphernalia. We have decided that Judy will make the first contact. While I stand back and hold my breath, she approaches and pleadingly asks if we can take refuge in his garage to escape the rain and lightning. He readily obliges. We are saved. Not only may we stay, but he immediately drags out three white plastic-stamped deck chairs, the kind you see in nearly every American yard, and sets them along the back bumpers of the cars, facing the storm and the vegetable stand, where corn, beans, and tomatoes are sold to folks traveling Millington Road into town. We pull off our rain hoods. He introduces himself as Charlie Simpson and asks us to sit a spell. We are as curious about him as he is about us. Charlie takes the center chair.

The rain is now falling so hard that the garage gutter is overflowing, occasionally splashing us. With our packs stored in a dry part of the garage we sit back and watch the storm sweep over the great expanse of bean fields across the road. It is a wondrous sight that for me evokes memories of Iowa. Simple yet refined in its natural design—the waving green fields, the sheets of angled rain, the brilliant quick bolts of lightning followed by the reverberating booms of thunder. It is a setting ripe for reminiscence. Between us sits Charlie, preparing to share with us the breadth of his life.

Charlie is seventy-nine years old. He is one of ten children raised in southeast Missouri, where his parents ran a boarding house for lumberjacks. There were eighteen woodsmen who slept in a bunkhouse and took their meals in shifts in the family house. Charlie recalls the stove at home being hot from 4:00 A.M. until ten at night. "You learn to get along that way; you learn to share," he says. He goes on to tell us about his favorite schoolteacher. She was named Marietta Georgia by her father after the city he had passed through during his service in the Civil War. Marietta had a profound influence on our host. Here Charlie pauses. And then as if transported back to that English literature class some seventy years ago, he recites for us Henry Wadsworth Longfellow's poem "The Village Blacksmith." Recalling stanza after stanza from memory, feeling each word and taking the pleasure of each meter and rhyme, he mesmerizes us.

> Under a spreading chestnut tree
> The village smithy stands;
> The smith, a mighty man is he,
> With large and sinewy hands;
> And the muscles of his brawny arms
> Are strong as iron bands.

He continues for all eight verses. Charlie may be dreaming of himself as a young man. We marvel at his memory, but even more touching is his willingness to share his passion with two strangers. We talk a little poetry, and then, in a melancholy voice and with the gleam of mist in his eyes, Charlie slips into a haunting ballad of a child's death.

I ask how it was that he came to Michigan. He tells a familiar story. He came in 1936, one of thousands who left their roots in Tennessee, Kentucky, and Missouri in search of jobs in the auto plants up north. He became a die maker in a General Motors plant. A member of the United Automobile Workers Union, he must have arrived at the time of the difficult struggles for union representation that took place in 1936–37. Charlie eventually taught welding at various General Motors schools. Like so many workers in the auto industry,

Charlie also acquired land that he farmed. With some sadness he tells us he recently sold his farm. Pointing to fields "over yonder," where we had just passed the two farmers working on their equipment, he says proudly, "That's our farm." I guess it will always be "their" farm.

Behind us we hear the door from the house open. A cheerful voice calls out, "What's taking you so long, Charlie?" Spying company, she joins us, pulling up a chair beside Judy. So we meet Norma, Charlie's second wife. She is a lovely, open-faced woman with a smile that brightens even this stormy day.

Charlie continues his story, telling us that he has fourteen children, three with Norma. The conversation flows easily about family, neighbors, and friends—the good old days and the familiar rituals. Charlie excuses himself and disappears into the house. In a few minutes he's back with his guitar and entertains us with a few ballads, sung with the same sentimentality as his poetry. We are enjoying ourselves but, being ever mindful of the miles ahead, know that we have to leave the comfort of the Simpsons. They ask us to send them a postcard when we reach our destination. Judy takes their address. In heartfelt response to our thank-yous for taking us in from the storm, Norma gives Judy, wet and all, a big hug and says, "I'm so glad you picked our house." So are we! This is what we hoped for on our journey.

With our hood straps cinched securely under our chins we resume our walk into Millington. The electrical storm has passed, but the rain is still torrential. The road is fairly busy with cars and an occasional truck blowing by us at fifty or sixty miles per hour. We walk the stone-covered shoulder with nothing but sheets of water in front of us and fields of corn, beets, and beans to our sides. On a dry day it might be a pleasant walk even with the intermittent traffic, but today we are only thinking about lunch under a dry roof. Just before entering town, we pass a farm with two elaborately decorated barns. On the side of the first barn are larger-than-life-sized cut-outs in black wood, like giant puzzle pieces of cows, horses, bluebirds, cardinals, a farmer and his wife, farm equipment, and more; on the second are similar silhouettes of rabbit, bear, deer, other animals, and hunters. Even viewed in the falling rain, the scale of this undertaking is noteworthy. Beyond the farm the sign welcoming us to Millington reads, "A Friendly and Progressive Community." Now there is a proper and optimistic greeting. The village is obviously readying for an event this evening. Lawn chairs are set at the edges of front yards and along the curbs, and floats are parked on side streets and in driveways. As Millington prepares for its evening parade, the town waits and worries about the weather. We empathize.

In 1859 the first sawmill was built at this site on Millington Creek. The creek had in all likelihood been named after Dr. Abel Millington, who came from Vermont to Michigan in the early 1820s and was involved in numerous land deals. It is just as well that an unrecorded name, Podunk, did not stick. The first church and post office were built in 1857 and the village incorporated in 1877. An important personage in the area was a Native American known as Indian Dave, who was here to greet the first white settlers. He died in 1909 at the age of 106. Those early settlers were originally lumbermen and farmers, and the town grew around those occupations, with businesses such as shingle making and blacksmithing.

In the heart of town we turn up M-15, the road to Vassar and Bay City. One block up we take cover in the Millington Cafe. It is now 12:30, and at least thirty people are having lunch. All eyes are on us as we struggle with our wet packs through the narrow door. Fortunately, there is a table in an empty corner, and we settle there, leaning our packs against the edge of our table. After removing our rain suits, we fish out dry T-shirts and head for the restrooms. Everything is a bit of a production, and Judy is always self-conscious about causing a scene. It is true that we are the only ones changing our clothes in the restaurant.

Our waitress asks about our circumstances and seems positively stunned by our ambition. She also probably anticipates that we will order a large meal. I don't disappoint her and go for carbohydrates and protein—a hot roast beef sandwich and a bowl of clam chowder, the latter a Friday favorite. Judy has hot tea and the salad bar while jealously eyeing my heartier fare. An avid people watcher, Judy has focused on a table of elderly women who are dressed in their best and brightly made-up for this lunch together. She warns me that one of the ladies is approaching us, probably as a curious emissary. Sweetly introducing herself as Norma (the second Norma we've encountered today), our visitor gets right to the point. "My sisters and I are lunching today, and we couldn't help but notice when you came in. Do you mind if I ask?" she asks. We assure her that we don't mind. Then I briefly fill her in on our itinerary. In response, without missing a beat, Norma graciously offers us a flattened bag of "nutty doughnuts." We can hardly control ourselves. Is this a joke on us or them? Norma spends quite a bit of time on a mysterious explanation of how it is she has nutty doughnuts to spare. Then, satisfied that she has good gossip to share about us, she returns to her table. We are not sure now if the stares we are receiving are in admiration, pity, or bewilderment. What we are sure of is that we have a bag of smashed nutty doughnuts—perhaps the most fitting food of our trip. And we have a really good laugh, which is nutrition for our somewhat bedraggled souls.

After lunch we linger a while and write in our journals until most of the patrons have left. Our waitress, who wears her lustrous auburn hair in a thick braid long enough to sit on, doesn't seem to mind that we are slow to leave. She advises us that bad storms are expected late tonight. She also confirms that Vassar is seven miles up M-15. We in turn wish her a clear evening for the annual parade.

Outside the cafe we sit on a street curb as I change the moleskin on my heels and put on dry socks. The rain has stopped. We cheer for the sun when it pops out between the scuttling clouds. Acting optimistically, we pack up our rain suits and pack covers and thread our wet T-shirts and socks outside our packs, hoping the seven miles to Vassar will be sunny enough for them to dry. On this fifth day of our walk we are beginning to look like scruffy pros rather than the spiffy play actors of just this past Monday.

Across the street from us, in an empty used car lot, motor enthusiasts tune up about fifty small engines attached to a variety of odd contraptions. Going nowhere, these little machines make a terrific racket, pounding and burping and coughing all the while throwing out puffs of black smoke into the damp air. The men are having the time of their lives in the midst of this noise and pollution. Judy and I are struck again by the anomaly of our walk within this motor-crazed world.

There is a choice to be made about our route to Vassar. The obvious course is along M-15, a moderately traveled two-lane road with wide shoulders. It is direct but not very interesting. The other, more intriguing option is the abandoned Huron and Eastern Railroad bed that runs parallel with the road and avoids traffic. A disadvantage is the possibility of tripping over the railroad ties, especially since we will be tired at the end of the day's walk and are slightly unbalanced by our heavier packs. Also, we reason that the proximity of the tracks to the back property of homes and businesses might invite a junkyard dog attack. Any dog argument always seems to carry the day. So up M-15 we go.

We're not far out of town, but my blisters are still bothering me badly. It is deeply frustrating to be fighting this constant pain. Every stop involves the burden of taking our packs off and then heaving all that weight back on and readjusting the load, not to mention the time that ticks off our walking clock. But I have to endeavor again to get some relief. We find a sign for a concrete company with a perfect ledge for sitting, and I try a new adjustment. Setting off anew, I can tell right away that I've actually made things worse! So back again we go to the sign ledge and through the whole rigmarole once more. As I'm studying my sad feet, a young woman from the company approaches us across their lawn. Fearing that we are in trouble, Judy quickly apologizes for stopping on their property. The woman laughs and responds, "Oh that's no problem. We've all been watching you through the windows, and I was just the one with the courage to come out and ask, 'Where are you going? Where did you come from? And how many times is he going to change his socks?'" Her good humor is just what we need. She also graciously offers the use of their toilet facilities and water, but we're anxious to move on. Her three questions will be a mantra we repeat when times are tough and we need a funny distraction.

This afternoon is rather tedious. The miles seem longer, the weight on our backs and on my feet heavier. We catch sight of a home or business on the horizon and mark the passage of distance as it grows closer. We look forward to our next stop.

To pass the time as we walk, we reminisce about our conversation with Charlie. He came from humble means, worked hard all his life, and is now able to enjoy his retirement in dignity and comfort. It is the American miracle of the twentieth century—the emergence of a huge and prosperous middle class. And for working people the engine of that success was and still is labor unions. Yet the history of labor is largely forgotten and unions often unfairly reviled. In Michigan the sit-down strike on December 30, 1936, at the two Fisher Body plants in Flint led to the signing of the first collective bargaining agreement between the United Automobile Workers of America and General Motors. Those strikers literally did not leave the plants until February 11, 1937. But their courage won the union that protected Charlie for a lifetime of work. Next workers took possession of six Chrysler plants and stayed in. My dad still talks about going to one of the factories in Detroit as a teenager and throwing sandwiches over the fence to the strikers. After Chrysler, Reo and Hudson signed agreements with the auto workers' union, the slogan became "GM—Chrysler—Ford Next." Because Henry Ford refused to recognize unions, the UAW hired a small plane to fly over the River Rouge Plant pulling the one-word message: "Organize." When union men tried to distribute literature near the plant on May 26, 1937, they were attacked by Ford's private security force; the confrontation became known as the Battle of the Overpass. The bravery of the early brothers and sisters in organized labor has always been an inspiration to me. I'm excited about the labor movement resurgence in this country. Just talking about the possibilities energizes me now.

About four miles beyond Millington we treat ourselves to a ten-minute rest at a convenience store and gas station. As always, we take advantage of the bathrooms first. Then we indulge in a refreshing, old-fashioned treat—orange sherbet push-ups. We are encouraged by two young women's interest in our adventure. They once had a long-distance cyclist stop there but never hikers. Like many people we meet, they have no idea of mileage, even over distances they travel every day. With complete confidence they give us wildly different and inaccurate estimates of how far we have yet to go today.

We have three choices for our night's stay in Vassar. For style there is a bed and breakfast in a grand 1880 lumberman's house, described as a Victorian respite, on the cliff overlooking the Cass River. For atmosphere there is the city campground in the park along the river in the center of town. For convenience there is the Vassar Inn, a mile and a half on the far side of town, that much closer to Bay City, our next night's destination. The B&B sounds great, but cats are allowed, which might well trigger our allergies and especially my asthma. The campground is preferable, but, with possible severe thunderstorms tonight and the long walk tomorrow in mind, we choose shelter and one and a half miles extra today. Still, we regret that we will not have an evening befitting two wayfarers, camping alone on the grassy bank along the cool, clear river in town.

Vassar is easy on the eyes. There is a quiet dignity to the small town center of handsome old red-brick buildings. With a current population of twenty-six hundred, the city sits at an elevation of six hundred feet. When it was first settled, along the Cass River in 1849, the pioneers quickly exploited the cork pine forest in the vicinity and with that wealth built fine homes on the crest of the hill. The village was named for Matthew Vassar, an uncle of one of the first settlers and founder of Vassar College in Poughkeepsie, New York. The *Vassar Pioneer Times,* first appearing in 1857, is the oldest continuously operating weekly newspaper in Michigan. In the summer the main road through town is lined with petunia beds.

I gaze longingly toward the campground as we trudge through town. My body begs to stop, but my head knows the motel is the right decision. To forestall any chance of backtracking, we've already called ahead from the gas station to make sure we will have a room.

Across the river rises a long steep hill that will take us to the other side of town. Judy walks in the lead, her stride steady and confident. I'm pushing myself to keep up with her. We finally resort to boisterous singing to carry me up the hill. "Climb ev'ry mountain," "The hills are alive with the sound of music," "I found my thrill on Blueberry Hill," and other ascendancy favorites propel me over the top. But, alas, over the crest there is still no sign of the motel. Now I require serious motivation. We launch into a medley of every Big Ten fight song we can recall from our student days. Of course, we start with the Iowa fight song. "You gotta fight, fight, fight for Iowa, let every loyal Iowan sing; You gotta cheer, cheer, cheer for Iowa, until the bells and rafters ring." Then on to "Minnesota Hats Off to Thee," "On Wisconsin," the Michigan State fight song, and finally, at the sight of the motel sign, with our caps off, the University of Michigan's fight song, "Hail to the Victors." We care not who is listening or watching. I need to dig deep to finish the day, and this does the trick. It is 5:00 P.M. as we stagger into the motel lobby, our voices as tired as our bodies.

The Vassar Inn is not an especially pleasant experience. Exhausted, we reel back in terror as we are met by two huge, barking, black and white German shepherd/huskies lunging toward us from behind the counter. Here for obvious security reasons, they scare the hell out of us. I guess we appear threatening to them, setting off all their alarms. After a tense few minutes registering, we are given room number 1, right next door to the office. We break our cycle of being farthest from the office, but being next to these dogs is not necessarily a bonus.

The room is small and dreary. We take off our packs and boots and collapse on the bed. "What is it," we wonder, "about motels?" They always advertise cable TV, never good beds and adequate light. Maybe we're the only ones actually looking for a sound night's sleep and a good read before drifting off. After a short rest we clean our boots and hang up our damp stuff. While I shower, Judy walks back to the grocery store we spotted two blocks from the motel to find dinner and breakfast.

After dinner we turn on the TV to get the news and weather. It's funny for now the news that interests us most is what the weather will be. The weather is the same. Heavy rain and storms are expected tonight—after the Millington parade, we hope, which should be under way about now. The prediction for tomorrow is for good weather in the morning, turning to showers later in the day. The rain seems unrelenting.

We switch to the soft drone of the Tigers and Royals baseball game. The easy rhythm of baseball with the intermittent slap of ball into catcher's mitt or the crack of bat on ball provides a relaxing backdrop while we recapture the day in our journals. Our eyelids are heavy when we put down our pencils.

Total Walked	88 miles
Walked Today	17 miles
Walking to Do	247 miles

Chapter 6

Vassar to Bay City

Suffering produces perseverance; perseverance, character; and character, hope. And hope does not disappoint us.

—Romans 5:3–4

Our most challenging day lies ahead—twenty-four miles to Bay City with thirty-seven pounds on each of our backs. After my blister patching we are on the road by 7:30. We share a nectarine as we walk along M-15 on this humid Saturday morning. Traffic seems inordinately light. Folks must be catching up on their sleep. It's still too early for chores and errands. A mile into our day we find ourselves in farm country. Handsome stone farmhouses framed by freshly painted red barns are a frequent sight. Several farms boast green historical markers that designate them as centennial farms. Vast fields of corn, soybeans, green beans, white beans, and sugar beets dominate the fertile landscape as far as the eye can see.

Four miles up the road we enter the tiny village of Richville, a German-American community formerly known as Frankenhiet, founded in 1850. Across the road from the Richville Lutheran Church we discover a small park that features wood signs engraved with mottoes and proverbs that are fun to read. These eighteen-by-twenty-four-inch signs stand like centurions in front of young trees, which are evenly spaced in the park. Judy is delighted with the humorous bits of wisdom dispensed here. One she thinks particularly suits her. I take her picture hugging a small oak tree by a sign that reads: "Great oak trees start out as little nuts that hold their ground."

We continue through the pristine farm country down the quiet but endless road. By 9:15 A.M. we've covered five miles. Judy's stride

Centennial farm outside of Vassar

is consistent and strong. The distance between us is growing as I lag behind her. The idea of nineteen more miles starts to wear on me. Our boots have steel plates in the soles to absorb the roll of our feet on the egg-sized stones along the wide shoulder of the road. But the stones still win out and grind away under my feet. My trotters feel abused and seem to be screaming, "Why are you doing this to me?"

The heavier load is already beginning to take a mental toll and to strain my upper back. I am feeling desperate. Panic suddenly starts to overcome me. Nearly overwhelmed by pain and fatigue, I begin to doubt that I can finish today. How could I have let myself start in such poor shape? I'm so mad at myself even though the condition of my feet ("at bottom" the cause of my problems) is just bad luck, not an issue of fault. What keeps me moving now is my concern about disappointing Judy. After all, I had convinced her that we could finish this together, getting through the tough days. Now that tough day is here, and I am crumbling, while she is exhibiting all the confidence and strength of a Perry or Hillary.

"Great oak trees start out as little nuts that hold their ground." Richville

I catch up with her and suggest a water break. We unload our packs, and I take deep swigs of now-warm water. Judy knows I'm hurting and discouraged. Finally, I confess that I might need to hitchhike into Bay City. Silence. Disappointment fills the air. We are each thinking the unthinkable—failure. Judy offers to support me in whatever decision I make, leaving open for me the option to continue. A break in the walk would tarnish our goal. She suggests that she take some of my weight. I agree, knowing that a lighter load might make some difference, although I am not entirely hopeful. Judy takes my sleeping pad, the first aid kit, and a few other items totaling about six or seven pounds. She now is carrying close to forty-three pounds. With my lighter load I struggle forward trying to match her strides.

I now know I will have to draw upon every imaginable technique and all my reserves to get us through this day together. I begin with song—chants I make up in order to put one foot in front of the

The endless road from Vassar to Bay City with full pack

other. The "fight songs" will be saved for the finish, if it is to be. I remember what it was like to run marathons—the Detroit, the Marine Corps in Washington, DC, and the New York City marathons. Hitting the "wall" at twenty miles is the ultimate test. Your body says no more, but your mind, if it's strong, can push you beyond that limit. Perhaps if I can conquer my mental anguish I can finish. I owe it to Judy to break through the wall. I decide that if my back cooperates, I will battle onward. I am talking myself into continuing. My determination is mounting. Memories flood over me of all the times in my life when people told me I "couldn't" because I was "not able to." I rekindle the fires of outrage at those who would try to thwart me. I've fortified my mind, my will. I have toughened my spirit!

Suddenly a black and white pick-up truck driving toward us slows down and pulls off on the shoulder. I pick up my pace to catch up with Judy. Two men are visible in the front seat, and they slowly pull up to us. The driver rolls down his window and asks, "Are you Senator Bonjour?" Surprised, I identify us but wonder if they are admirers, detractors, or carrying a message from work or, God forbid, a family emergency. Bracing ourselves for the worst, it is easy to relax as we hear the story. They've been looking for us for more than twenty-four hours. It seems that Stan, worried about us hiking and camping with the threat of severe thunderstorms, called the Vassar Department of Public Works to alert them. The DPW called the Police Department. The job fell to Officer Jim Smith. By the time word reached him, Smith believed he was on the lookout for a single, elderly congressman who might have been caught in the storm camping in town along the Cass River. This was a mighty unusual request, but Officer Smith took the assignment very seriously. There was no trace of a hiker in town. Because the chief was out of town, Officer Smith requested permission of the city manager to patrol beyond city limits. That range is not covered by Vassar jurisdiction, however, so Officer Smith has been combing the roads in Tuscola County overnight on his own time, in his own truck, also checking back at the campground seven times. That's why he's not in uniform. He's rather surprised that there are two of us and visibly relieved to have found us, not at all annoyed at being unnecessarily inconvenienced.

It is such a sweet story really. Our dear friend Stan in his concern raises the alarm; a total stranger rigorously pursues this odd mission, and all the while we are oblivious to the whole thing. Later, in response to a call requesting information on Vassar, the city manager sends us a promotional video. The opening and closing shots are titled "Vassar—We're Looking for You." We can vouch for that.

We thank Officer Smith and his companion profusely for their concern, time, and courtesy and snap a photo of them. Before leaving us, Smith asks if we need a lift. Without a thought of the irony, I decline and say we are fine. As he drives off, Judy looks at me in amazement. For the first time in hours we both laugh. Had he come along thirty minutes earlier, before I had worked on my mind, I would have been in the bed of his pickup, riding into Bay City. Pride and stubbornness put us back on the road, our battered feet again tackling the rocky shoulder, our walk still intact.

Up the road we see a large sign, "Big Chief Sugar–Monitor Sugar Company and Sugarbeet Growers." It feels like a personal greeting. The northern part of my congressional district and on up into the

Vassar police officer Jim Smith, the Good Samaritan

thumb of Michigan is sugar beet farm country. We wade into the field, and Judy takes a picture of me, soaked in perspiration, next to the sign with the research buildings in the background. We think it will be fun to share it with our sugar beet friends.

Fortified with another dose of friendship, my spirits are lifted as we continue on our journey north. I savor all those encounters: Stan's thoughtfulness, Jim Smith's kindness, friends remembered by a silly picture. This tug of war in my mind for control of my body will occupy me throughout the long day. And the gestures of friendship, many from strangers, will be the mental medicine I need to continue. Also, I use my hands behind me, under the backpack to lift the weight off my back while walking, giving myself momentary relief. My mid- and upper back are feeling the strain. Increasingly, my worry shifts from my feet to my back. I know that once those muscles start to tighten I'm in for a domino effect down to my lower back, and then I'm done for. I take two Tylenol to ease the pain.

We enter Blumfield Corners in the northeast corner of Saginaw County. Populated by German immigrants who had fled their home- land to escape persecution, they named their settlement for Robert Blum, who was shot in 1848 by the king's soldiers. *Saginaw* is an Ojibway Indian word meaning "place of the Saux Indians." Now a farming region dominated by sugar beet production, this county of 230,000 in its early days witnessed the historic harvest of white pine, which changed the face of the land.

We have come a mere seven miles, with seventeen more to go. The merciless sun beats down upon us. The high humidity sucks all the oxygen from the air. We are listless and dripping wet. It seems as if everything is working against us today. For another hour we struggle up the endless road until we reach the intersection of M-15 and M-81. Stumbling into a gas station / convenience store, a blast of cold air nearly takes our breath away. Out of the sun, heat, and humidity the contrast is too much. It feels like we've mistakenly entered a walk-in freezer. I worry that my back muscles will freeze up on me. During a break in their stream of customers, the two women employees inquire where we are going. We try to answer with conviction, hiding our current doubts, summoning at least a moment of enthusiasm. It works. They are amazed that we plan to go all the way "to the top." So are we! We each buy a sandwich, cookie, and cold drink and hurry back into the heat, collapsing against the building in the shade. For five precious minutes we savor being off our feet.

I think to myself, what can I discard from my pack to lighten the load? Blue jeans—they are heavy, and I have not worn them yet. The same goes for my long johns. But can we afford to be without them as we go north and the days and nights become cooler? I certainly could do without 50 percent of the toiletries, saving perhaps two pounds. I long for our magic formula of fifteen pounds and fifteen miles per day. But the geography of our trip requires many longer days to locate nightly shelter. My mind skips to all the poor souls marching with full packs during war, any war. Imagine twenty-five miles a day over difficult terrain, under life-threatening conditions, in extreme heat and cold—crummy food, fear, and dirt your con- stant companions! Things could be worse for us. I try to hold that thought. Still, as I gaze ahead at the intersection and watch as cars pull up and stop at the light, another thought prevails. A perfect place to hitch a ride. Memories of hitchhiking in my teenage years flash before me. The temptation grows. But I dismiss it and suggest we find a tree to shade us while we eat our lunch.

We cross back to the other side of the road and resume our walk up M-15 looking for a shade tree. Two miles further we find a farmhouse with a large white oak just off the road. There are no signs of life about. Judy knocks on the side door but gets no response. We decide to take the liberty of availing ourselves of the soft, shaded grass and settle down with our backs against the magnificent trunk. After eating in silence, our talk turns to strategies for getting me into Bay City. We agree to take it two miles at a time, building on each success. It does not feel that we are ever making any progress on this long, flat road. This must be how people go mad in the desert. The horizon is forever hovering in the distance, unchanging, unyielding, out of reach. So we will mark each two miles with a brief rest.

Farm after farm, field after field, we trudge on. For one rest stop we pause in the shadows of a recreational vehicle that is for sale. Maybe we should buy it. Several miles up the road at the intersection of M-15 and M-138 we are overjoyed to see John's Bar. This is no roadside dive but instead resembles a ranch home of light yellow brick with a large attached side addition. It is your quintessential clean, friendly country tavern. My spirits rise as soon as we enter the premises. Inside, a large man with a wide smile says he saw us walking up the road earlier in the day and wondered where we were headed. He is tickled to hear our destination.

Judy leans her pack against the back of a booth under a large window and heads for the restroom. I slide gratefully into the booth and order a diet Coke for Judy and a nonalcoholic beer for me. The fellow at the bar tells me to check the temperature gauge outside my window. Ninety degrees! No wonder we're wilting. The cold drink and convivial atmosphere start to revive me almost immediately.

There are several families in the open, light-filled tavern. We feel as if we are in someone's home rather than a bar. A young father in his late twenties, the same age as our kids, plays with his precious infant at the next table, showing off the little boy to the other guys. Judy and I muse that we could easily be that child's grandparents. Than we look at our sweaty, exhausted selves and wonder if this is appropriate behavior for grandparents.

Before we leave Judy takes my picture behind the bar with the

Relief from the heat at John's Bar, Munger

waitress, who is the daughter of the owner, and Joe the bartender. On the wall is the exact picture of Tiger Stadium that Judy gave to me for winning the Whip race and which now hangs in my office in the U.S. Capitol. Like our walk, Tiger Stadium is the stuff of dreams to me. With Fenway it was the oldest of the major league baseball parks. Because these old ballfields hold so many memories and are natural links between generations, in addition to being architectural gems, we should preserve them as national treasures. I actually introduced a bill in Congress to prevent five of our greatest stadiums from being demolished, including Fenway in Boston and my beloved Tiger Stadium in Detroit. It's no surprise to me that these good people near the little village of Munger would also hold dear the great baseball park at the corner of Michigan and Trumbull.

Refreshed by the nice folks at John's Bar, we set out again into the heat, now taking care to drink regularly from our water bottles, which were refilled by Joe with cold bar water. A light breeze has picked up, slightly cooling our ruddy faces. We have been lucky not to encounter any nasty dogs. I believe that the combination of this tough day and mean dogs would have sent me over the edge. More farm country ahead. We pass potato farms as well as white, navy, and soybean fields. Our eyes are busy searching the landscape ahead for an indication that we are closing in on our destination. We have come to rely on an old-fashioned landmark to provide the promise of day's end. And, finally, there it is. The Bay City water tower. It is our Holy Grail. They come in all shapes, sizes, colors, and ornamentation, but every town has one, and the water towers have become our beacons. That the sight of this strictly utilitarian, often unsightly structure gives us such an emotional rush and mental lift is proof of how completely we have crossed into a new world along our walk.

Soon we will be at the Tuscola Motel, where we had originally inquired about a room. Our other choice was to walk two miles farther into Bay City and stay at the more comfortable Clements Inn, a bed and breakfast. We reserved a room at the inn but left ourselves the option of stopping at the motel. Pleased that I seem to have broken through the psychological barrier of the wall, I grow confident that I can surmount the final two miles into town after one last rest stop. Across the road from the Tuscola Motel we see a store with the sign "Country Market Meats—Home Made Sausage." This is German and Polish country, and I have the feeling that something good is inside.

We leave our bulky packs leaning against the outside wall of the little store. This time the rush of cool air feels good as we walk inside. We both make a beeline for a frosty cold pop. I take two more Tylenol for my aching back. With a cold drink in one hand and a bag of barbecue chips in the other, I can relax and absorb the ambience. Spotting an old chair in the corner, I ask the two young women behind the counters if I might sit. Of course I can. We are definitely objects of curiosity. An older woman behind the meat counter goes in the back and pulls out a stool for Judy. In opposite corners of the store we settle in for some conversation. They are as eager to hear our story as we are to hear theirs. After I tell our tale, they volunteer that a cyclist stopped in on his way down from Mackinaw City earlier in the summer. I guess it might be the same chap who stopped in the gas station near Vassar and perhaps the same fellow who Dave made reference to at Otter Lake.

One of the young women is particularly taken with our walk. She tells me she can imagine doing it. She runs two miles several times a week (a good idea for someone working in a sausage store). We tease each other about exercise and eating Polish sausage. She offers a sample of freshly made liverwurst, a favorite of mine but not a regular part of my low-fat diet. What a delicious treat at the end of a grueling day. I am now convinced that with my tasty little meal of chips, sausage, and Seven-Up that I've got just enough fuel to finish the remaining two miles. Knowing that we are off M-15, formerly and appropriately called Tuscola "Stone" Road, is a welcome relief. The surfaces now will be asphalt and grass—no more rollercoaster ride for the tenderized balls of my feet.

In her corner Judy hears an interesting story from the older woman who is the daughter of the store owner and keeper of its history. She has worked there forty-five years and now is semiretired, living next door and caring for her eighty-nine-year-old mother, who suffers from dementia. She recalls for Judy the glory days of the store, especially before holidays, Easter being the most celebrated. People would line up in their cars as early as 4:00 A.M. waiting for the store to open at 8:00. She would take pity on them and beckon them into the store early. So anxious were they to buy the meat of their choice before it was all sold out that some would even have forgotten to put their teeth in that morning. She chuckles recalling this memory of better days when the meat store was a community center, before the impersonal supermarkets destroyed their business. She is a cute little lady in curlers, happy to have visitors and making sure we are comfortable. If we were camping tonight, a nice ring of sausage would be great roasting over a slow fire. It's time to go, so with many thanks for their kind hospitality we say our good-byes and leave behind this little corner of another time, wondering how much longer it will last.

Another mile up the road we take a photo of the "Welcome to Bay City" sign. No one else can possibly understand how much this simple sign means to us. We have now walked 111 miles since our journey began.

Bay City is a beautiful place of forty thousand, named for its location on Saginaw Bay. Felled trees once were the principal source of the city's prosperity; standing trees along its residential streets are the main source of the city's beauty today. Past a quaint cemetery and up a few blocks we reach M-25, or Center Avenue, a wide street lined with mature hardwoods and stately old wood homes. These obviously were once the homes of prosperous mill owners, lumber inspectors, bankers, and others of wealth. The Lumbering Society dominated Bay City during the nineteenth century, when most of these fine homes were built.

After 1860 the lumbering industry developed rapidly, and communities on the Lower Saginaw River became the centers of milling activity. In 1872 there were thirty-six mills between the southern boundaries of Portsmouth (now incorporated into Bay City) and the mouth of the river, a distance of eight miles. Some of them were among the largest in the country. The settlements constituted a one-industry town; the whine of saws biting into logs was heard ten hours a day, and the smell of fresh lumber was said to be strong enough to flavor food.

We are a pitiful sight by now this particular day. The magnificent trees graciously offer us their shade, but we are not really fit for their company. The irony, of course, is that the lumber and sawmill barons preserved a wooded beauty for themselves while making their fortunes from clear-cutting the great white pine forest of the Saginaw Valley.

At 4:30 P.M., nine hours after we began this excruciating day, we approach the Clements Inn. This handsome Victorian home was built in the 1880s by lumber magnate William L. Clements, who was a former regent at the University of Michigan and owned a famous collection of manuscripts relating to the American Revolution. In addition, he was the donor of the Clements Library of Early American History at Ann Arbor as well as the present Bay City Public Library further up Center Avenue.

On the front lawn is a flower "bed" created within a border of a real brass bed frame that has been painted white. Literally on our last legs, we walk up the five creaking wooden stairs, across the veranda, and into the foyer. We wait patiently as the clerk politely helps a new arrival. Finally, Karen Hepp, who owns the inn along with her husband, Brian, walks into the foyer from the parlor, sees us, and says, "You must be the maniacs." That's us. Upstairs each room is named after a Victorian novelist, among them Emily Brontë, Louisa May Alcott, and Charles Dickens, which of course is ours. We open the door to Dickens Room, and on the bed piled high with pillows is a copy of *A Tale of Two Cities*. Never has that familiar first sentence seemed so appropriate.

It was the best of times, it was the worst of times, it was the age of wisdom, it was the age of foolishness, it was the epoch of belief, it was the epoch of incredulity, it was the season of Light, it was the season of Darkness, it was the spring of hope, it was the winter of despair, we had everything before us, we had nothing before us, we were all going direct to Heaven, we were all going direct the other way.

Our day precisely! Our sentiments exactly!

The room is charmingly decorated in period colors, style, and furnishings. Yet there are also modern conveniences such as a small TV and VCR unobtrusively integrated into the pleasant space. Waiting invitingly on a small table is a pitcher of ice water, an assortment of hard candies, some scrumptious cookies, and a little fruit. The spacious white bathroom has as its centerpiece a huge old claw-footed tub with an all-around shower curtain.

We each take a long, hot shower to wash away twenty-four miles of pain and agony along with the sweat and grime. As I feel the healing effects of the water on my body, I fervently hope that in this day we will have met the worst and survived. Clean clothes are a joy. I collapse on the bed. The owners kindly allow Judy to do two loads of laundry, and then she walks to a convenience store for provisions. After a simple supper in our room we stroll in the cooling night air to an ice cream parlor for dessert. Back at the inn we read a letter from Judy's mother, write in our journals, and fall quickly to sleep. No walking tomorrow. On the seventh day we shall rest.

Total Walked	112 miles
Walked Today	24 miles
Walking to Do	223 miles

Chapter 7
Bay City State Park

Sunday, August 17

Saginaw Bay

⑬ ▲ Bay City State Park

BAY CITY ㉕

While not precisely heaven, our day of rest on Sunday feels like a little slice of bliss. We planned our schedule to have a day off from walking every six days, and that turns out to be a very good idea. It was in part the anticipation of having a day off to recover our strength and heal our wounds that propelled me through yesterday. The only way we could complete those grueling twenty-four miles was knowing that we would have two nights and a full day to recuperate. Now we have the satisfaction of having completed one-third of our goal.

Awakened by the 8:00 A.M. light pouring through our lace-curtained windows, we gingerly test our bodies and find ourselves surprisingly refreshed. We have slept long, like adolescents—eleven hours. After our morning routine we repack our clean clothes and amble downstairs for the 9:30 breakfast shift. This time we are more observant and notice the organ pipes built into the curving staircase.

The dining room, like the rest of the house, has been lovingly and elegantly restored. Here there is lustrous, dark wood paneling providing a nice backdrop for the finely decorated china setting on the ample table. Before us is a great spread of food, including an assortment of freshly baked breads, cheeses, jams, fruit, and cereals of various kinds. A selection of cold meats, a choice of juices, and hot drinks complete the fare. It looks very inviting. Perhaps this was how we were meant to live!

Breakfast is presided over by the owners, Karen and Brian. Besides ourselves, seated at the table are three young couples, each of whom is sharing a romantic interlude. One couple was married just yesterday and is headed for Harrisonburg, Virginia, in the beautiful Shenandoah Valley, where our youngest son, Andy, went to college at James Madison University. Along with the newlyweds we are joined by a couple celebrating their second wedding anniversary. He is a medical intern, and his cheery wife is a teacher. The third young couple have a sadder story. They are from Bloomfield Township in Oakland County, Michigan, a very prosperous area. The young husband appears to have recently suffered a stroke or perhaps a head injury. His speech is halting and his thoughts labored. His wife watches him with love and compassion and pride in his courage, but also etched in her face is the pain of the long struggle ahead of them.

Our place of rest today is the nearby Bay City State Park, on the shores of Saginaw Bay. Michigan boasts an amazingly high number of state parks, ninety-six, which are no further than an hour's drive from one to the next. The first was established in 1919 in an effort to preserve the state's natural treasures. Now more than twenty-five million people visit these parks and recreation areas each year. Early Michigan pioneers found a vast mosaic of undisturbed forests, sand dunes, prairies, and wetlands supporting a rich diversity of native plant and animal life. For two centuries thereafter, however, the landscape was ravaged. Today it is only because of our park system that our remaining natural wonders are protected from the ax, the plow, and the bulldozer. Michigan is particularly rich in water resources. Four of the five Great Lakes touch Michigan shores, creating three thousand miles of shoreline. There are also more than eleven thousand inland lakes and thirty-six thousand miles of rivers and streams—much to be saved!

We are excited to test this unique and highly regarded park system. The state park system is a wonderful bargain especially for families. In addition to being accessible, it's relatively inexpensive. For twenty dollars in 1997 you get unlimited entry for a year to almost all of the ninety-six parks, which are spread over four coastlines and scattered throughout the interior of both peninsulas. We are two of the over five million campers who use the park campgrounds annually. We are disappointed to find out, however, that in the Lower Peninsula you can only make reservations for a minimum of two nights. We end up paying thirty-three dollars for our one-night visit—twelve dollars each for the mandatory minimum reservation, plus a five-dollar reservation fee and a four-dollar administrative fee. We learn along the way that we would not have needed reservations on Sunday or weeknights. The other annoyance is that the phone reservation service is contracted to a company in Illinois. So much for state loyalty.

Across State Park Drive from the picnic area and the beach is the park campground. A dense woods screens the area from the road and the rest of the park. Rain begins to fall as we walk in from the road to the registration guard house at the entrance to the campground. Inside the tiny building we are given the choice of a pet or a no-pet campsite. We look at each other. "No pets, please." Rather than put up our tent in the rain, we ask the young woman in the guard house if we can hang out with her for awhile. "Sure," she says, so we take off our packs, sit on the concrete floor, and watch the parade of departing campers. The cold weather scares some people off, and the beginning of a new week summons others home. Schools will also soon be opening for the new year, so attention is turning from summer fun.

After about thirty minutes the rain stops, and we dash through the empty campground for site number 59 in the far back. Fearing more rain, we quickly take advantage of the hiatus to put up our tent. We are alone among the trees, with only one other site occupied in our "no pet" section. Eager to escape the cold, windy, wet weather, we crawl inside our tent and read for a while. The gray light filtered through our tent actually seems brighter inside than out. We are happy to be resting.

Sooner than we expect, the inertia of just lying around starts to annoy us. We had planned these stops in the parks expecting warm, sunny days and hoping to swim. Despite the weather, we are anxious to see the beach, which stretches nearly a mile along the bay. We slip into our flip-flops, put on our sweatshirts under our rain jackets and walk out to the bay. Our feet feel liberated in the cool, breezy air. We find a quiet spot on the beach and snuggle up next to each other to keep warm. The bay is gray and wind-whipped. The sky and water are colored the same, merging seamlessly on the horizon, only the white of the capped waves breaking the grayness. The crashing surf may be Herman Melville speaking:

> There is, one knows not what sweet mystery about
> This sea, whose gently awful stirrings seems
> To speak of some hidden soul beneath.

Or Matthew Arnold:

> Listen! You hear the grating roar
> Of pebbles which the waves draw back, and fling,
> At their return, up the high strand.
> Begin, and cease, and then again begin,
> With tremulous cadence slow, and bring
> The eternal note of sadness in.

Our sadness is more disappointment at not being able to test the water and bask in the sun on this fine sandy beach. But by our age we have learned at last to take pleasure in what is at hand rather than just to lament what might be.

Chilled, we walk from the exposed beach to the nearby small lagoon that is today home to the annual Saginaw Bay Waterfowl Festival. Scores of families circle the lagoon with checklists in hand, identifying the waterfowl decoys that have been placed there or nearby on the shore. We sit on a wooden bench overlooking the lagoon and watch fathers and sons bonding in the ritual of this non-violent hunt. Canvasback, ring-necked, wood, mallard, and teal ducks as well as several types of herons appear in their natural habitat. After thirty minutes of watching people watch birds, we decide to wander over to the Visitor Center.

The center is jammed with people. Folks are looking at a wide variety of displays, exhibits, and interactive devices that tell the natural history, geology, ecology, and wildlife story of the Saginaw Bay. We even come upon a live alpaca. I fantasize about how wonderful it would be to have this animal carry our gear. Because of my back problems, Judy has insisted that she always carry our luggage. As a result, I have affectionately called her my Sherpa. Seeing the alpaca, I look at Judy and announce, "Your Sherpa relief."

We are now looking for a park ranger who might give us some advice about tomorrow's walk along the rails-to-trail path that hugs the shore of the bay between the water and the Tobico Marsh. We know from our previous scouting expedition that the trail merges with a road and dead-ends about three miles up the coast. Yet the trail shows up on our map as continuing. Our question to the ranger is, are we within our rights to continue along the shore on this public right of way? A mistake here could cost us six extra miles of walking if we have to turn at a "dead end" and retrace our steps.

Well, we have asked the right man. He's obviously excited by our query. He tells us it is our duty to continue up the trail. Indeed, it is public right of way. We can detect tension here between the cottage owners on the bay and the state Department of Natural Resources. On one side are the owners, who want their privacy; on the other side are those who want to protect access for the public. Our ranger appears to be almost using us as a pawn in this war. Always cautious, Judy asks the ranger directly, "What about all the signs that say Private Property and No Trespassing?"

"Ignore them," is his instant response. Then he adds, "Where you want to go is most certainly public right-of-way no matter how the owners try to pretend that it is not." Finally, he imparts this bit of commentary, "You two shouldn't have any trouble. Now, if you showed up in a leather jacket and a dirt bike, that might be another matter."

We are relieved that we can take our preferred route but only partially encouraged by his advice. The hike along the marsh and the shore of the bay is much more appealing than M-13 or other back roads. Bolstered by the ranger's assurances of our legal rights, we agree to "go for it."

With time on our hands (and not on our feet) we follow a crowd into a theater, where we expect to see a film on waterfowl. Instead, we are treated to a concert of popular and folk music—and it is quite a good one at that. Mike and Theresa Irish accompanied on guitar by Dave Ingersol remind us of Peter, Paul, and Mary, whose songs they sing, along with a few Simon and Garfunkel, Linda Ronstadt, and Christopher Cross. We enjoy tapping our feet and humming along to the familiar tunes. It's a warm way to spend a cold afternoon.

Growing hungry, we leave the nature center and walk a few hundred yards to the Muscle Beach Drive In, an ice cream, hot dog, and hamburger place. Normally, this spot would be "rockin'" on an August Sunday afternoon so near the beach. But the weather has chased people away; even our waterfowl friends are not interested. Inside three seventeen or eighteen-year-old girls work in the kitchen behind a counter separating them from the customers and a half-dozen small booths. Bored, the girls start bantering with us. Looking for something to warm us up, Judy orders a steak sandwich, and I have a hamburger and a hot dog. We share an order of onion rings. The only fair way to eat onion rings or garlic while living in a small tent is to do it together. For dessert we can't resist ice cream, even in the cold. The staff goes to the trouble of brewing a fresh pot of decaf coffee for me. I don't imagine anyone else will pass this way today for the rest of that pot of coffee.

But the young women are curious about us. Our unlikely story of adventure sparks their own imaginations. They pepper us with questions about specific details. How do we know where we're going? What about going to the bathroom? Are we ever afraid? Do we get sick of each other? And finally the key question. How did we think of the idea? After we talk a bit about taking a chance on your own dreams, one of the girls blurts out, "I've always wanted to be a stewardess, but everyone always laughs at me. I'm going home tonight and tell my parents that I can do it." Yes. Again we've made the connection. She figured out what our experience means to her. In this first week, at our lowest points, others have lent us inspiration from their own lives to help us overcome our tribulations. We are very happy to reciprocate.

It takes no more than five minutes to return to our tent. We are met, however, by a nightmarish sight. Our tent is alive with scurrying black ants. In our hurry to pitch our tent before the rain resumed, we set it up too close to an anthill. Fortunately, they haven't gotten inside, but Judy finds it disconcerting to watch them crawl over the tent just above us with only the netting separating us from the ant army. Occasionally, she punches the tent wall to send them all flying, but without fail the ants come marching back. In our tent we read and write for a couple of hours before venturing back out about 5:00 P.M.

Judy suggests a fire. She finds some still-smoldering embers at an abandoned campsite and carefully carries them to our fire ring. I gather leftover wood from other empty campsites and also find kindling in the wooded area nearby. An hour later, with twigs shaped in the form of a tepee over the hot embers, we feed scraps of paper scavenged from the trash bin into our creation. Slowly a fire takes hold and burns nicely. Sitting close to the fire, we bathe in its smoke, while the heat chases away our goosebumps. Proud of our first campfire, we sip warm beer left over from last night's makeshift dinner in the Charles Dickens room.

Our lone neighbors also have a fire going, but it's larger and more ferocious than our little flame. While gathering wood, the man asks me if I'm Congressman Bonior. I'm secretly pleased to be recognized in this remote location. It turns out that the man, Bill Davidson, and his friend Christina are also from Mount Clemens. They entertain us with an exciting camping moment earlier in the weekend when they set their picnic table on fire. The fire melted the plastic red and white checkerboard tablecloth to the top of the pine table.

We sit quietly dreaming around our own little fire. Judy is obviously content, happy with the simple natural things that life offers. Tonight it's a warm fire and the cadence of crickets, her thoughts perhaps drifting back to the beach and the pounding of waves on the shore. When I look at her like this, transfixed by a flame, I see a bright, resourceful, and generous woman. But, like the great oaks rising above us, dwarfing our little campsite, it is her integrity that shines above all else. A liberal, she is also passionate about personal responsibility and has little tolerance for those who don't accept their own. Her life operates within a structure of honesty with herself and others. At times that insistence on honesty collides with other realities. There is no guile here! And, because there isn't, you usually know just where you stand with her. If you stand at all, it can be the most rewarding of experiences—the opportunity to live, learn, and love within an honest relationship. So, yes, I can surely picture her on a wagon train passing through the Rockies or on a raft battling her way up the Missouri River, strong and a pioneer to her core. And, as I watch her mesmerized by the dancing low flames of our fading fire, I think how much I love her and what a lucky man I am.

Total Walked	112 miles
Walked Today	0 miles
Walking to Do	223 miles

Chapter 8

Bay City State Park to Pinconning

Monday, August 18

Saginaw Bay

Judy sleeps well; for her the little tent is fun. By her nature she is drawn to its economy of size. She has built a life around the wise and frugal use of resources, a saver of things in the best sense of the word. A passionate recycler, no empty ketchup bottle or corn can escapes its allotted bin. She dislikes shopping, except for food, and is uncomfortable spending money on herself. When I present her with a new sweater or blouse, she will squirrel it away and savor its newness only to appear in it for the first time a year later at some unexpected moment. In essence she is a woman of the thirties—the pioneering 1830s and the Depression-hardened 1930s—raised on the values of thrift, generosity, and need. This Spartan life is a perfect fit for her.

On this trip we are reversing roles. Judy, forever the pessimist, is now full of joy and hope. I, on the other hand, have put aside my optimism for mild bouts of despair. This ridiculously tiny tent does not get me off to a good start today. My sleep is tortured. Last night my hip bones pained me. My sleeping pad is just too thin to cushion my body's heavier weight. Given that I can't sleep, it is especially irritating that there is no room to toss and turn! And now, driven by bathroom needs, we have to climb out of our sleeping bags into the decidedly cold 6:00 A.M. air. Fog nestles in the trees, and I turn to Carl Sandburg for solace.

> The fog comes
> on little cat feet.
> It sits looking
> over harbor and city

on silent haunches
And then, moves on.

The forecast today is for sixty degrees and partly cloudy skies. We will probably get to see the sun. A short day of fifteen miles of trails and beach roads along the Saginaw Bay beckons us. Refreshed, at least by our day of leisure, we look forward to the wildlife in the Tobico Marsh and to challenging the obstructed right-of-way.

The Tobico Marsh sits just north of the park. Because of its "exceptional value in illustrating the nation's natural heritage," the marsh has been registered as a National Natural Landmark. The first mile of trail cuts through deep woods and marshes before edging the eastern side of the vast wetlands. There are two tall observation towers on the east side of the marsh. Tobico Marsh is nationally famous for its wetland bird life. More than two hundred different species of birds have been spotted in the marsh, and rare Michigan species such as the ruddy duck and yellow-headed blackbird nest there. Deer, beaver, mink, fox, rabbit, turkey, coyote, and muskrat also inhabit the area.

As we walk out of the campground toward the trailhead to the marsh, a ranger near the visitor center asks where we are going. When we respond Mackinac, she smiles widely and wishes us well. With that positive send-off, our backpacks feel less burdensome, and our steps are light on the paved trail into the marsh. We stop at several observation points displaying charts and drawings of the vegetation and animal life. Captivated by the sounds and sights, we stop to enjoy the birds feeding—titmouse, red-winged blackbirds, jays, capped chickadees, and our favorite friend, the goldfinch. The splashes of color darting amid the greens of the trees and grasses accompanied by the competing calls are a fine morning show.

Judy is taken with the sign in front of a stand of cattails. It describes the difference between the male and the female—who would have known? It seems the males are the ones with fluffy white fuzz—rather like my beard. Another exhibit explains the presence of a willful wildflower, the purple loosestrife. Introduced from Europe, this fuchsia beauty is slender and graceful, with the flower blooming in a loose spike along the four-sided stems. Unfortunately, this striking flower is choking the marshland with its many seeds and tough root system. It has no predator to keep it in balance.

It is cool this morning, and we find ourselves walking briskly, invigorated by our surroundings. The marshland is a wonder of opportunity. Regretfully, as Curtis Badger notes in his book *Salt Tide,* marshes have a negative connotation for many people and have been unfairly maligned for centuries. The bad guys in old Tarzan movies were forever sinking into swampy mud pits. And who can forget Humphrey Bogart covered with leeches in *The African Queen?* In our imaginations marshes are scary places with poisonous snakes, disease-carrying insects, foul smells, quicksand, and labyrinthine waterways, where one is doomed to be lost forever. Absolutely nothing good could come from a marsh. Only evil and death lurk there. Such are the misconceptions.

As the legal debate over protecting marshes raged throughout the 1970s, scientists produced evidence demonstrating the remarkable fecundity and usefulness of marshes. We now know that the biomass produced annually by a natural marsh rivals that of the country's most fertile and chemically manipulated farmlands. Marshes are responsible for millions of dollars worth of fish and shellfish, which support coastal economies and help feed the world. Marshes protect the mainland from storms. Marshes filter contaminants from surface water and return it to aquifers in a more pure state. But perhaps the highest value of a natural marshland lies in its wildness, its ability to offer an escape from the world humans have created, a place where nature reigns. The St. Johns Marsh in St. Clair County in my congressional district was saved by concerned citizens for all the purposes I've mentioned. It has been the lifeblood of Lake St. Clair and a habitat for magnificent white swans. We made a very wise choice in the 1970s to preserve our marsh. State and federal laws soon followed to extend protection to such special environments.

About forty minutes into our walk the trail unofficially ends. We find ourselves on Killarney Beach Road, a narrow beach road that parallels the abandoned railroad line. With marsh on our left and cozy cottages lining Saginaw Bay on our right, we continue toward our rendezvous with Dead End and No Trespassing signs. We have a mile to go before we face our inevitable confrontation with the property owners, who are assuming unauthorized control of public land for their private convenience. We are both apprehensive.

An older woman with arms pumping, out for her morning constitutional, pauses to greet us and in a curious tone asks where we are going. She is obviously surprised when we announce Mackinac. As she is clearly a resident, we hold our breath for her reaction. Confirming our concerns, she says that she doubts we will be able to get beyond the fence ahead of us. With unfelt bravura we say we will take our chances, hoping that she doesn't go home and call some security firm to chase us down. Now we are wondering aloud if we have walked three miles in vain and if we will be forced to retrace our way, making the day twenty-one miles instead of fifteen, not to mention forgoing the scenic route along the bay. Fortified by our conversation with the ranger, we proceed.

There ahead of us at the end of the road are the dreaded fence and threatening signs: Do Not Enter, Private Property, No Public Access. I search in vain for a hole to climb through as Judy watches for activity in the nearby house, and we both listen for dogs. It appears that our options are to climb over the high fence or see if we can skirt it by walking through an overgrown tennis court and then some ten yards to the beach. Scaling fences we can save for later. At our age we ought to explore other possibilities first. Luckily, it seems that there is no one at home in the cottage. But we are perplexed because on the other side of the fence there is no evidence of even an overgrown trail. I decide to leave my pack with Judy and go on a scouting mission to see if there is a way for us to proceed. Judy anxiously tells me to be careful and to hurry back. Cutting through the tennis court to the water, I find high waves pounding against the strand, making the beach impassable. My only choice is to tack back inland and follow the fence line north in the direction we want to go. Pushing through bushes and tangled weeds for about a hundred yards, I'm overjoyed when the fence abruptly ends. Victory, I think, and double back to find Judy. Although I've been gone a mere ten or fifteen minutes, she is immensely relieved to see me. It's the first time our little team has been separated on the trail, and she tells me she's happy to have her buddy back at her side. Judy follows me to the next leg of our exploration. We have overcome the first private obstacle to public passage and feel a bit daring.

Before we can bask in our boldness we come upon a bevy of threatening No Entry signs. A barking dog reinforces the warning. Yikes, as Judy says, now what do we do? Ahead of us appears to be another beach road with abutting cottages. But how do we get there? We stop to assess our position and decide that the right-of-way follows a gravel path next to the driveway of the sign monger. With pepper spray in hand and the billy club in accessible position, we move forward, certain that we are headed into trouble. Will it be a canine attack or, worse yet, a gun-toting homeowner waiting for us as we cross into enemy territory? As a teenager this might be great sport, but at our age it lacks allure. This is hardly fun but, rather, some small stab at survival. We have only the courage of our convictions, no surging adolescent hormones and certainly no peer pressure, to incite us. Public means public—or it should.

Despite a series of warning yaps from the dog, we pass with quickened step without incident. But what this mutt has done is alert every other dog up the way that aliens are about to approach. We are met with excited barking but no loose dogs. And it is a relief once again to be on an obviously public road, where we are less likely to be challenged. We enjoy glimpses of the bay between cottages and over decks and patios under a dazzling blue sky.

Past the northern boundary of Tobico Marsh we come upon a private wildlife preserve. There are perhaps ten acres of attractive red barns and sheds highlighted by a windmill tower and lighthouse. Within the fenced area are geese, ducks, goats, peacocks, and guinea hens, all dotted about an expansive fish pond. The grounds are picture-book perfect, with manicured lawns, little bridges, and a few graceful willow trees.

All of a sudden our idyllic road veers inland. Again we are puzzled about how to proceed. Just as we are giving up hope of finding access back to the beach road, a middle-aged man driving a van pulls up to answer our question. Calling out the open window on the passenger side, he volunteers, "You must be looking for the secret passage." He then shows us the well-hidden public path through a backyard that will take us to the beach road leading up through the community of Brissette Beach. We chat a bit about our walk. The seventeen-year-old girl in the passenger seat of the van is visiting from Crimea in Ukraine on a student exchange program. Her face brightens when I mention that my maternal grandparents were from Lviv in western Ukraine but falls when I admit I can't speak the language. As chance would have it, our very agreeable guide will be joining fifty other sponsoring families and their exchange students in walking across the Mackinac Bridge on Labor Day. In parting, we make plans to find them there.

At the six-mile point we stop for a break at the Linwood Beach Marina. This neat and prosperous-looking business is filled with fishing gear and boating equipment. A pleasant proprietor offers us complimentary coffee, including decaf, and we purchase a few snacks to take outside by the water's edge. The sun is now bright above, the clouds blown away across the bay. I snap a photo of Judy watching three young boys fishing off a nearby bridge. These excited ten-year-olds scampering about have yet to learn the patience required to actually catch a fish. On his way to his car the proprietor asks us our destination. We reply, and he responds with an enthusiastic "Excellent." It's nice to have this male reinforcement. I was beginning to get a complex about my gender.

After a fifteen-minute rest we hoist on our backpacks and walk into the village of Linwood. First known as Terry's Station when the Michigan Central Railroad came through here in 1872, the new name is descriptive of the wooded area that it once was. In the village we go north on Elevator Road, which is a disappointing departure from the earlier scenic route. Rural and isolated, it is alive with barking dogs. Thirty edgy minutes up the road we are happy to emerge along the shore at the Nayanquing Point State Wildlife Area. Once again puzzled, we stop to assess where the rails-to-trails path, which is indicated on our map, might be. In the distance is a farmhouse backed up to the woods, where we suspect the trail may begin. But between us and that point is a long dirt driveway that does not appear welcoming. Another tricky decision.

Just then we are rescued by an elderly couple in a van. In the back seat three young children drape themselves over the front seat, peering over their grandparents' shoulders at these two confused hikers. The grandfather, wearing a Notre Dame cap, asks where we are headed. To the amusement of the kids, I answer, "Big Mac." Immediately intrigued, he asks if we have ever read Peter Jenkins's books on walking across America. Yes, we exclaim with big smiles, they were an inspiration to us. Having noticed our confusion as he approached us, this second guardian of our day advises us to take the dirt road as it does indeed join the trail in the woods a hundred yards ahead. With a happy grin he promises, "You'll be closer to Momma Nature if you take the trail into Pinconning." As we finish our conversation, we think we see the sparkle of wanderlust flit across his eyes, and there is a longing in his "Good luck" as they drive off, as if to say, "I wish I could join you."

Our earlier apprehension over passing through the yard ahead of us now heightens as we are alone once more. Alone, that is, except for a man wielding a strange homemade tool, a two-by-two-foot board nailed at the end of a six-foot pole. He is bashing away with this weapon in the reeds not thirty yards from where we are standing. Judy has many theories about his behavior, none of them benign. We are extremely leery of this fellow but decide to give it a try. I greet him in what I hope is a calm and casual manner. He doesn't turn on us as Judy had feared, so I carefully ask him what he is doing. "Killing frogs," he laconically answers. Of course. How silly of us not to have known. So next I ask if the frogs are for fishing bait. This time he looks at us as if we are nuts. "No," he responds, "they're for eatin'." Wishing him good hunting, we proceed at a fast clip through his yard off into the wooded area, where we easily find the old railroad bed and trail. It runs straight and long.

No sooner do we comment upon the tranquillity of this secluded trail than we are attacked by swarms of mosquitoes. They are annoying enough that we take turns spraying each other with repellent. Out come our trusty bandannas to swat the mosquitoes and horseflies that are following us. We hike for three and one-half miles through woods, marshes, and the occasional bean field. The shore of the bay begins to slant east, and we skirt the marshy edge of the State Wildlife Area. The walk is flat and easy, except for the pesky insects, which are particularly fond of me. About two miles up the trail we spot the shadow of a large bird overhead. As it passes over us, it looks like a short-eared owl, streaked a tawny brown with an irregular flight pattern. This hunter likes to feed on rodents and insects. We wouldn't mind at all if the owl would dine on the hoards that are now feasting on me and driving us nuts with their buzzing attacks.

At Almeda Beach Road we decide to leave the trail and angle toward Pinconning, our destination for the evening. At Old State Road we stop for a rest on a shaded concrete bridge. A weathered green metal plate announces that the bridge was dedicated in 1948. We sip tepid water from our bottles and munch on Triscuits as we lean over and watch the cool stream below run its course to the bay. Across the road from where we rest is the Fraser Township Cemetery, an immaculately tended permanent resting place of our past. I'm drawn to the serenity and history of cemeteries, which have a way of humbling the living while at the same time reconnecting us to nature. Dust to dust. When I was a small boy I remember my father crossing himself when he passed a church or cemetery. I now do the same out of respect for him as much as for those interred in this peaceful patch of our earth.

We trudge the last two and a half miles up M-13, an unappealing and busy road connecting Bay City and Pinconning. As we approach our motel, we keep our eyes peeled for places that might sell any kind of padding or air mattress for our future camping endeavors. But there is nothing. By 2:00 P.M. we have finished our fifteen miles for the day and arrive at our destination.

Opinniconning is an Indian word meaning "place of the potato." On older maps the Pinconning is called the Potato River. The town is named after the river and today has a population of about fifteen hundred. Settled in 1866, the community was an important rail center in the logging days. It evolved into a trading center for the exchange of sugar beets, beans, and chicory. Eventually, dairy became increasingly important, and Pinconning gained the reputation as the "cheese capital" of Michigan. Billboards along I-75 boast of the cheese experience in Pinconning. And the all-important water tower is yellow-orange like a great ball of cheese.

We stay tonight at the Pinconning Trail House Motel, "Your first stop before the Gateway to the North." It is not clear to us what that means, but on a previous scouting trip we found the motel to be clean and serviceable, which is all that matters to us. We have lots of mail waiting for us. There is a letter from Judy's mother, a recharged battery for our cell phone, and three lightweight books on trees, butterflies, and wildflowers. We look forward to our reading.

Our room is number 8, across the driveway from the office and no stairs to climb. The room contains two double beds. While we prefer a single queen-sized bed, after our cramped night in our tent, we shall each luxuriate in our very own double bed. We take our boots off outside so as not to track the day's dirt into our room. Judy feels badly about my severely blistered and bandaged heels and takes a picture of them. This will not be a happy memory.

After a refreshing shower, washing away a gamey concoction of perspiration, repellent, and dirt, we slip into our flip-flops and walk next-door for an early dinner at Pertles. We've heard of early-bird specials, but this is ridiculous. Who cares. I have meat loaf with mashed potatoes, and Judy, with a Pinconning-inspired craving for melted cheese, has nachos. Our waitress, Devina, is chatty and inquisitive. She is particularly interested in my taped-up feet. It seems she too has injured her heels from being on her feet so much in the restaurant business. Of course, her nerve damage and pain have far greater implications for her livelihood than my temporary problems. She also laments that she is too tired to exercise after work and wishes she could resume her walking routine with her daughter in order to lose weight.

During dinner we pore over our books, excitedly identifying the trees and wildflowers we didn't know when we passed them. Aware as we are now of the toll of extra weight, we reluctantly realize that we cannot carry one single extra item. After catching up with today's entries in our journals, we walk to the post office to mail back the books. From there we search through town for foam padding. Stops at the hardware store, drug store, and used furniture store yield nothing, though everyone has tried to be helpful. I'm starting to get new blisters from my flip-flops, so we head back to the motel. My plan is to catch the last rays of the sun on the lawn and read the *Bay City Times.* Judy heads off to continue the hunt for foam.

As H. B. Kaltenback, the legendary newscaster, often said, "There is good news tonight!!" On the front page is a story announcing the end of the United Parcel Service strike. The result is a major victory for a resurgent labor movement. A key goal of the strike was to force UPS to reduce its growing reliance on low-paid, part-time workers. This issue captured the attention and sympathy of the public. Many American workers understand that their jobs are being threatened by temporary workers who earn low wages and receive no benefits. Temporary Manpower Services employs more workers than any other major corporation in America. Across the country people understood what UPS employees were up against. In the end the workers won ten thousand new full-time jobs with good benefits by combining existing low-wage part-time positions. They also won wage and pension increases for full-time workers. At the time the company was earning over one billion dollars per year but was not sharing its enormous profits with its productive work force. The Teamsters succeeded by putting together a community coalition of the union, clergy, sympathetic business people, and government leaders, who joined in rallies and marches around the country. The issues were easily understood, and the union communicated clearly and organized effectively. Because this was a domestic product, the company was unable to just move their operations to Mexico or overseas, nor could they even realistically threaten to do so.

Blisters, blisters, and more blisters. Pinconning

One hundred twelve years earlier in the very area we have just walked, the Knights of Labor concluded a similar, successful strike against the lumber barons who were deforesting the Lower Peninsula of Michigan. By the turn of the nineteenth century the great pine tracts along the Kennebec and Penobscot Rivers in Maine were nearly exhausted. The wood from those forests had built the East Coast of the United States. The opening of the Erie Canal brought thousands to the Western Reserve in Ohio and then on up to Michigan. The great gold fever of 1848 enticed easterners westward to California and Michigan. It was not, however, the yellow gold fever of California mining that lured them to Michigan but rather the promise of "green gold," which eventually outvalued the precious metal by more than a billion dollars. Michigan's green gold was the white pine.

For the rest of the century and into the next, Michigan white pine built the country: its houses, barns, sheds, wagons, fences, bridges, roads, boarding houses, saloons, churches, sidewalks, ships, steamboats, railroad ties and trestles. In 1800 the forests covered all but one-eighteenth of the state. By 1900 most of those forests were gone. During the second half of the century thousands of square miles of fine-grained white pine were ruthlessly cleared in the Saginaw River Basin as well as the rest of the peninsula. The Au Sable and Saginaw Rivers, each with dozens of tributaries, were the channels down which the logs flowed to Lake Huron. In 1849 there were 558 sawmills in Michigan. Saginaw and the city of Muskegon on the western side of the state led the world in lumber production for many years, and the state was number one in the country. Believing the resource was inexhaustible, an army of lumbermen cut its way northward, leaving in its wake a wealth of forest folklore and millions of acres of barren land.

Along the Saginaw River between Bay City and Saginaw, a stretch of twenty miles, there were by 1870 over one hundred mills running full blast day and night. The mill hands worked twelve-hour shifts six days a week under the most primitive and wretched conditions. There were 306 saloons in Saginaw. Water Street in Bay City was so notorious it was known as Hell's Half Mile.

It was under these circumstances that the Knights of Labor representing the Saginaw Valley lumbermen under the slogan "Ten hours or no sawdust" pulled off a spectacular victory for labor. The strike began in July 1885 and involved fifty-five hundred workers, 10 percent of whom were children. Like the teamsters in the UPS strike, they had a compelling story to tell of child labor, oppressive hours, no benefits, and no time for family. And, like their descendants, they organized and told it well.

The first strikers charted a steamboat and a barge and steamed upriver from Saginaw, stopping at every mill town to parade behind a brass band and an American flag, resuming their journey only after every lumber worker had stopped work and the mill fires had been banked. Thus, all the seventy-eight mills and fifty-eight salt blocks in the valley were shut down. Twenty companies of state militia and 250 Chicago Pinkertons were dispatched to the area, and the strike leader, Representative Thomas Barry of Saginaw, was arrested repeatedly until his bail finally amounted to twenty-five thousand dollars. After three months, however, the strikers won their demands.

Sitting on the lawn outside our motel room in the late afternoon sun, I feel lazy and contented, but the UPS story yanks me back to reality. Justice for workers did not and still does not come without a struggle in this country. Many men and women marched, rallied, went to jail, and were beaten and even killed for the benefits that are too often taken for granted today. The fight for a decent wage, fair working hours, overtime pay, health and pension benefits, vacation time, the minimum wage, health and safety laws, workers' compensation, unemployment compensation and employee stock options, sick leave, maternity leave, and the weekend were all advanced by organized labor on behalf of worker justice. And the irony, of course, is that the unions through their struggle for organized workers also raised the standards for nonunion workers as well, even for those who view labor unions with contempt.

There is also sad news in the paper today. I am stunned to see that State Senator Doug Carl of Macomb County has died of a heart attack at forty-six years of age. Senator Carl was my Republican opponent for Congress in 1988 and 1992. On the obituary page is the name of Allie Matuzak, who passed away at age ninety-two. I wonder if she might be related to Julie Matuzak, who works on my Mount Clemens staff and has relatives in the Harrison and Bay City area.

As I'm mulling over the meaning of all this, Judy returns from her hunt for a thicker sleeping pad for me. Under her arm is a rolled piece of ancient charcoal-gray foam secured with several equally old thick rubber bands. It's hard to imagine what that ugly foam had been intended for originally, but now it will serve to soften the ground for me. Judy tells me the story of finding this relic at Morgan's Bargain Barn, which seemed to her to house nothing less than a decade old, virtually nothing useful, almost nothing accessible, and everything under an inch of dust. It was only her fear that we might have to give up the walk that convinced her to venture into the deepest recesses of this peculiar place. There was one other piece of foam. It was hot pink.

We spend the rest of the evening quietly. Judy calls her mom. I refresh my acquaintance with the maps for tomorrow's walk to the Cedar Springs Campground just north of Sterling. When I call Stan, he kindly volunteers to drive up tomorrow to pick up our packs at the motel and transport them to our campground. He wants to show us the hot spots in Sterling and will camp with us tomorrow evening. At 10:00 we fall soundly asleep, only to be jarred awake at

11:30 by the phone, ringing loudly. It's Stephen. He's worked for a dozen years in bars and restaurants, so this seems like a reasonable time of the day to him to make a call. He wants to consult with his mother about a job interview. Judy is confident that she has been useless to him.

Total Walked	127 miles
Walked Today	15 miles
Walking to Do	208 miles

Chapter 9
Pinconning to the Rifle River

Tuesday, August 19

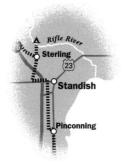

Never underestimate the pleasure of a good night's sleep. Our double beds last night sure beat our cramped tent and the hard ground. Today our destination is the Cedar Springs campground north of Sterling on the Rifle River. Rather than brood about the upcoming night, however, we approach the day with optimism. The forecast is for a cool, sunny morning. And the big bonus is—no packs to carry!

By 8:00 A.M. we are out of our room and crossing the parking lot to the office to arrange to leave our packs for Stan to pick up. To our disappointment we are greeted by a sign on the door that announces, "Back at 9:00 A.M." With an hour to wait, we cross M-13 to a restaurant for breakfast. The place is filled with the regulars—farmers, small business folks, friends—who share a large circular table in the center of the restaurant. Overlapping streams of stories, conversation, and laughter radiate from this happy spot and create a mood of energy and joviality.

I order pancakes, and Judy has eggs, toast, and coffee. In the booth next to ours, a State Farm insurance salesman shares his newest joke with his morning companions.

> A married couple are talking and the husband wonders aloud what would happen if he were to die. He asks his wife, if you remarry, would you let your new husband drive my car?
>
> Yes, answers his wife.
>
> Would you let him sleep in our bed?

Yes, she says.
How about sit in my easy chair?
Yes, she says again.
Would he use my golf clubs, too?
No, his wife responds.
Relieved, he asks her, why not?
Because, says his wife, he is left-handed.

The booth explodes in laughter with one exception. The salesman's wife sits in stony silence.

At 9:15 we are back at the motel, where the testy owner is not pleased with our request but reluctantly allows us to store our packs in the laundry room. Light of foot we set off buoyantly with only our water bottles, camera, pepper spray, and the billy club wrapped in a plastic bag so we don't look threatening. A mile up M-13 we turn west on Cody Estey Road and stop at the township hall to get advice on the best road to travel north. Inside, a cordial, helpful woman suggests we take Mackinaw Road, which she describes as scenic and paved but with little traffic. She often rides her bike there. Intrigued with our walk, she suggests putting our adventure into their monthly newsletter. We awkwardly decline, embarrassed at putting a damper on her enthusiasm after her kindness to us. Having sought no press, we are slightly uneasy about identifying ourselves. We are also vain enough to want any picture of us on this walk to be taken with our packs on.

Our old friend the goldfinch greets us as we turn north on Mackinaw Road. Ahead there is not a vehicle or a person in sight. But the sky is alive with swallows, purple martins, jays, and black-capped chickadees. Overhead the telephone line is a solid row of dozens of doves. It is as if we are within an invisible aviary.

I was hoping for a painless day without the extra weight of my pack, but that is not to be. Blisters are seriously aggravating my heels. By our measure we have walked 129 miles so far. Or, more precisely, in my case 227,040 painful steps. The building trouble in my boots robs me once again of a pleasant walk through this bucolic setting. Three miles up Mackinaw Road the surface changes to gravel when we enter Arenac County. After passing several handsome farms we approach the Saganing River. The bridge over the river looks like a good place to check out my feet.

Our arrival startles a green heron, which rises in flight, dropping a fish into the river. We have cost him a meal. At the bridge we peer over just in time to see a basketball-sized painted turtle retreat from sunning itself and dive deep into an eddy of cool, swirling water. Having scared away the natural inhabitants of this place, we turn to more prosaic matters, my feet.

I take off my boots and survey the damage. After examining the hot spots on my right foot, it appears that bandaging each of them with moleskin will suffice. They are not yet certifiable blisters. My left foot is another matter. This blister is a doozie, big as a quarter and bulging with liquid. Against all sensible medical advice, I decide to lance it. In the midst of this makeshift surgery the heron returns for another try at lunch. We are clearly no threat to him.

Bandaged and back into my boots, I'm ready to try again. A mile and a half farther up the road we find ourselves in a bit of a jam. We can continue straight on a "seasonal road" and then probably have to climb fences to cross US-23, a major four-lane divided highway. Or we can backtrack two miles to avoid that main road. Never anxious to add miles, we decide to take our chances and proceed north.

A seasonal road is nothing more than two parallel ruts, perfect for an off-road vehicle in summer or a snowmobile in winter. They are great for hiking because the way is cleared but there is no traffic. This road follows along the edge of a large bean field, which is "guarded" by two giant scarecrows. They are constructed of two eight-foot wooden crosses and dressed in colorful old clothes with milk cartons dangling from strings off their arms to scare away the birds. We somehow identify with them, all alone like we are at the edge of this field. Each of us takes the other's picture with our new comrades. As gestures of fellowship, I tie my bandanna around my scarecrow's neck and Judy offers hers a drink from her water bottle.

At the end of the field we are stopped by a fence. To our left are signs announcing a hunting club. We can hear the hum of the traffic on US-23 through the trees beyond us. We will have to climb this fence, which is topped by a strand of barbed wire. Fortunately we are not the first to scale this barrier. The barbed wire already sags from the weight of other crossings. But we take our time figuring how to overcome this obstacle. Our first aid kit has been sent ahead with our backpacks. I go first. Judy holds the wire down as I climb to the top and then vault over. I do the same for her as she more carefully navigates her safe passage. We next make our way through the underbrush of an overgrown trail another hundred yards, where we are again confronted by a fence. Presumably there to keep humans from crossing this busy and dangerous highway, this fence also serves to keep wildlife from becoming roadkill. We follow deer tracks along the fence line, and they lead us to a ravine that the animals use to duck under the fence. We lie down on the grass and shimmy under too. After carefully crossing the highway and scaling a bent fence on the other side, we are on our way again, thankful we didn't have our packs for these latest maneuvers.

Soon we find ourselves walking through Maple Acres Farm on Deep River Road. If it sounds like a storybook, it also looks like one. Surrounded by a white painted wooden fence, dairy cows and horses graze in a pasture. The road is lined on both sides with silver maples. The nature writer Donald Peattie characterized these grand trees as having "an air at once of dignity and lovely grace, a combination rare in a tree as in a human." He goes on to say, "It cannot grow without lending grace to any spot; it makes a railroad station look like a home and adds a century to the appearance of a village street." Under the sweeping bough of one maple I take a photo of Judy by the fence with a Holstein staring back at us. Curious horses follow us along the fence line, apparently happy for a little distraction on this quiet, lazy summer day.

The spell is broken as we turn onto Johnsfield Road, nine miles from the start of our day. Tension rapidly overtakes us. On our left growling dogs and empty dog houses on inhospitable properties stretch ahead. On our right posted on trees at the edge of a woods are signs in menacing red letters warning, "No Trespassing: Prison Property." Nowhere to run. Nowhere to hide here. My first reaction is to get ready for an attack by the dogs. Judy's first reaction is fear that we will be mistaken for just-released inmates or, even worse, escapees. We wish we had our packs to legitimize ourselves on this lonely, desolate road. The ferocious, barking dogs spot us and rush to the road. Our fear builds. We cross to the prison side of the road and pray they don't attack. One dog comes closer. I tighten my grip on the club and ready my finger on the pepper spray. We quicken our pace trying not to confront them directly but keeping an eye on our pursuers over our shoulders. They soon turn off but have given us a good scare and have alerted other dogs up the road.

Ahead of us we spot a mailbox with an "Elect Sabo" bumper sticker stuck to it. I quickly take a picture so we can give it to our friend from Minnesota, Congressman Martin Olav Sabo. Just beyond this point on our right is a gorgeous horse farm set back into the woods. The horses are feeding from a long trough deep in the shadows. The patterned trunks of the sycamore trees stand out as if dappled with sunshine and accent the black and chestnut steeds that feed nearby. We want to spend more time taking in this beautiful setting, but the dog problem is too near for comfort.

Ahead we see cleared land and a curious outpost that we recognize as we get closer as migrant quarters. There are two trailers and seven plain modular buildings. Latin popular music plays from a boombox. Hanging on the fence posts are shoes, muddied and wet from the nearby fields, drying in the noonday sun, laces dripping down the poles. The little encampment is surrounded by corn and bean fields. Across the road workers are picking melons and throwing them to others on trucks for transport. The rhythm of their labor is hypnotic. Stoop, pick, stand, throw, catch, place. Over and over in the hot sun. We feel sort of foolish just walking in the face of this backbreaking work.

Behind the buildings clothes hang out to dry. Precious little children are playing in the front along the road. One three-year-old waves both of his hands at the same time at us while alternating his gestures with a "Hi" and then a "Bye." We of course are coming but also leaving at the same time. He hits it perfectly and enjoys his little joke.

All of this reminds me of my third year in the State House in Lansing, when I authored a wage bill for migrant workers. For decades migrant workers have been moving their families to follow the harvests of fruits and vegetables. Michigan ranks high in agricultural production that needs picking, from the beans and beets of the Saginaw Valley to the fruit trees in the western part of the Lower Peninsula near Lake Michigan. The plight of these workers was chronicled poignantly in 1960 by Edward R. Murrow's acclaimed television documentary "Harvest of Shame." Judy still vividly remembers more than forty years ago reading a series of books for youngsters by Lois Lenski, who told the stories of these difficult lives through the eyes of the children. Unfortunately, the conditions described in these books—*Strawberry Girl, Blueberry Boy, Judy's Journey*—are still true today.

Workers still spend twelve-hour days at stoop labor in the fields for pitiful wages. There are often no sanitation facilities. Housing is deplorable or nonexistent, forcing many to live in their cars. The children face frequent interruptions in their schooling or leave the classroom permanently to take their places in the fields, which, because they are sprayed and poisoned with chemicals, cause serious health problems. Not surprisingly, life expectancy for migrant workers is far lower than for the average American worker.

The bill I wrote in 1973 would have corrected some of these outrages in Michigan and insured a fairer wage. Sadly, it was defeated in the House by a 49–47 vote. It still stands as one of the most devastating days of my legislative career. Eventually, some of these reforms were written into law, but how much more suffering had to occur before we began to pay the workers who pick the very food we eat the dignity and respect they deserve.

Still today these injustices exist. In April 1997 I traveled to California to march with Arturo Rodriguez and the United Farmworkers of America, the union founded by Cesar Chavez, to ask for justice for strawberry workers. Thirty thousand people gathered in the town of Watsonville to demonstrate support for virtually the same issues that compelled Murrow in the 1950s and me in the 1970s and which remain unresolved in the 1990s. The day prior to the march I visited a seven-member migrant family in their fourteen-by-twenty-foot, one-room home, where hanging sheets and blankets afford the only privacy. This is our own country. This is the hidden cost of the fabulous foods we take for granted. Judy and I fuel each other's rage over these injustices as we walk up to M-61 and then west under Interstate 75.

Ahead is a Shell gas station. We have come eleven miles, and this is the perfect spot for lunch. I grab a soda, chips, and a can of baked beans. Judy is trying to include more calcium in her diet, so she selects chocolate milk and a granola bar. We take our food outside to a grassy slope and eat in silence.

Slowly we begin to focus on the curious farm adjacent to the service station. Scrawled in big letters on the barn is the simple designation "Sam's Place." Sam must be a man of eclectic tastes. Advertised for sale are used books and engine repair. Corralled around the barn mingle an odd assortment of creatures—geese, goats, horses, and, yes, we are seeing this correctly, ostriches. Ah ha! Ostrich burgers. You see them listed on restaurant menus. These large flightless birds can reach eight feet tall and weigh two to three hundred pounds. But for some reason I can't get beyond the feathers, which isn't an appetizing thought. They are quite a sight, however, strutting about. We snap a photo before we are off to the village of Sterling.

There is little traffic, and we are escorted down this back road

by our usual companions, the goldfinches. We delight in their dipping flight patterns and the happy yellow of the male. Like us, they
travel as couples. I am envious, however. Oddly, I've always wanted
to fly. Now I know why. It's less painful than walking. My feet still
hurt, but the sky is blue, and I think I'll make it to the Rifle River.
Just to make sure I'm distracted, we launch into a loud medley of
service and patriotic songs, ending with a rousing version of "Stars
and Stripes Forever," which we dedicate to our friend Jerry Colbert.
Jerry produces the Memorial Day and July Fourth concerts at the
U.S. Capitol, which are seen by millions on Public Broadcasting
across the United States. To carry us into Sterling we even mimic
the exploding sounds of the fireworks.

Sterling was named after lumberman William Sterling and established here with a mill in 1871. Today this sleepy village of five hundred hosts a couple of bars and Iva's Chicken Restaurant. These establishments are frequented by the locals but also by travelers coming
off nearby I-75 and by tourists who vacation along the Rifle River.

After a restroom stop at another gas station and an ice cream
treat to keep me going, we trudge the last three miles of the day.
Even without our packs, I'm feeling whipped. The sun has shone all
day, and it has taken more than a bit out of me. I'm definitely thinking how lucky we are not to have the additional thirty-seven pounds
or so on our backs today. Perhaps the cloudy, cool, and rainy days
were more of a blessing than I realized.

As we approach the river valley, the road slopes down hill, and
on both sides before us are campgrounds with hundreds of canoes
stored on racks. And there is the river. A boyish energy now over-
comes my weariness as I imagine a tube ride on those cool waters.
But, alas, my body is no longer an eager instrument of my will. After
nineteen miles I need rest.

We register and are given site number 30, a beautiful grassy spot
on the river. We buy some beer and chips, head for our picnic bench,
take off our boots and socks, and collapse. Across from us a creek
flows over the three-foot-high bank into the river below. The sound
of this little waterfall is soothing and relaxing. It's very peaceful
here. We are happy to rest and wait for Stan.

I met Stan in 1972 at the Macomb County Probate Court, where
we were both employed. I had just returned home from serving four
years in the Air Force, and Stan had been teaching English in Japan.
He landed my former job as a probation officer for juvenile delin-
quents, and I became an adoption caseworker. In hindsight we may

have each needed doses of the services we were dispensing to others, but then we were young and eager. Stan was a couple of years older than I and stood five feet eleven inches. He is as trim today as he was twenty-six years ago. Sandy haired and mustached, his high energy and curiosity sparkle in his eyes. He is restless, a wanderer, and possesses a unique sense of humor. Our common interests were many—sports, travel, reading—but it was politics that cemented our friendship.

Stan is what some people might call a "character." He is bright, funny, offbeat, and inquisitive about almost all things in life. When we first met, we learned that our fathers had been acquaintances when they were our ages back in Hamtramck, a Polish enclave within the city of Detroit. Stan senior owned a pool hall during the Depression, and my father was a frequent visitor—thus my love of eight ball! We share a common Polish heritage and family history.

Stan can easily talk international politics or used cars, nature or technology, trees or cement. When he is around you can feel his energy. He looks for the spaces that others ignore or take for granted or discard. Whether it's a peanut farm in Georgia or an Indian reservation in New Mexico, he has a story, and it usually ends with a lesson in human nature.

Stan has worked off and on in politics. As an aide to me in Lansing when I chaired the House Marine Affairs Committee in the early 1970s, we wrote the first law in the country to ban the manufacturing, sale, and use of polychlorinated biphenyl (PCB). This chemical was killing the robust fishing industry in Michigan. High concentrations of PCBs were found in the fatty part of Great Lakes fish. Our bill, which became law, would serve as a model for other states and eventually would be adopted by Congress and signed into national law. When I went to Washington, Stan came along as a staff assistant for a year. He also ran for county commissioner in a very Republican area of Macomb County in 1974, losing by only one hundred votes, nearly pulling off an upset. He presently lives in Texas but still comes up often to the family home in Washington Township to help out his mother, Alfreda.

Within minutes of our sitting down Stan drives up with our gear, ready to show us the sights in Sterling. We prevail upon him to rest with us for a while. So, we sip our suds and occasionally wade into the shallow river to cool our dogs. After a debate focused on inches and where to pitch our tent—Stan will sleep in his car—

we settle on a spot and have it up in ten minutes. Here we commit a fundamental camping error. The weatherman is calling for bad weather tonight and the next couple of days. He calls it "a paper boy's nightmare—wet, windy, and cold." But we are seduced by the August sun, which has been in hiding this past week. We decide to roll up our rain cover so we can gaze at the stars from inside our tent when we return from dinner. And we are off.

Stan's tour of Sterling begins badly, as Iva's is closed on Tuesdays. The famous chicken restaurant is all Stan has talked about for two days. The old, large, white house sits in the center of the village on the main road, its ample parking lot deserted. Our memory of Iva's will be the sight of rows of white aprons drying in the breeze in the backyard. Stan is heartbroken. But there is other fun ahead.

Stan thrives on the ordinary as well as the extraordinary. He is a connoisseur of the offbeat. He has traveled the back roads of America selling clothing and hauling autos and searching for adventure. Every experience is a story; every person has a lesson to teach. To appreciate Stan and to learn from him, you have to enter his world, see through his eyes, and feel through his sensibilities. The next stop on our tour will be a Stan special. He is an expert on trucks, cars, and heavy equipment. We are about to see a combination machinery graveyard and cow pasture. Just outside Sterling along I-75, covering a multiacre site, is every imaginable type of semi-trailer, bulldozer, dump truck, end loader, and more, many with bushes growing through the windows, some on their sides. Grazing among all of this steel, rubber, and rust is a herd of cows. Strangest thing I ever saw. Stan wants to drive through it all, but Judy and I find it a rather sad sight. It seems to us a melancholy preview of the future, when our earth no longer has room for both our inventions and ourselves.

Thirsty and hungry, we stop in town at Mr. G's, the dankest and darkest bar I've ever been in. You know how it takes a few minutes for your eyes to adjust to a movie theater if you walk in from the light? Well, mine never adjust in Mr. G's. I am operating on smells and sounds, the loudest of which is a jukebox somewhere in the pitch blackness. We are "escorted" through the darkness to a table, where Judy fumbles about for a chair. With Iva's closed, this seems our only option for food and drink.

Stan is seduced by the jukebox, which is filled with old country favorites. The Texan in him surfaces. In the dark bar one ray of light beams like some UFO in the sky on a moonless night, pulsating with twangs and laments and mixed with a dash of country humor. Stan gets up from his chair and gropes in the darkness as he feels his way to the box in the far corner of Mr. G's. He studies the choices like a handicapper selecting from his racing program and then drops in the appropriate quarters to make the music play. Through the darkness he calls out, "Found my two favorites." Leaning against the big music machine, he continues, "O man, dig this. First I picked 'Prop Me Up at the Jukebox When I Die' and then 'I'm in the Big *D* and It's Not Dallas—I Get the Jeep and She Gets the Palace,'" Stan twangs in his Texas drawl. We are not disappointed by his choices.

Through two beers each we continue with the musical themes, never knowing how close we may be veering to the truth. Then we decide it's time to eat. Our waitress, as honest as the tunes we just listened to, advises us that we will be better off eating across the street at the Pizza Bar.

The place across the street is packed with townies, campers, and I-75 refugees. The combination of folks seems to work surprisingly well. Everybody is having a good time eating fabulous pizza, shooting pool, and shooting the bull. The sassy, efficient waitress and bartender are keeping everything under control.

After another beer Stan is off into campaign stories from our first congressional election in 1976, when he and my brother Jeff canvassed Harrison Township on Lake St. Clair. They came upon an elderly lady, who was affectionately known as the "worm lady." She had a nice piece of property near the marinas off the Clinton River and sold worms for fishing. Stan and Jeff thought this would be a great sign location, so they asked her if it would be okay to put up a Bonior for Congress sign on her lawn.

"Sure, go ahead and put a sign up here," she said. "I always support Dave Bonior and so does my dead husband. My husband votes for Dave in heaven."

Stan notes that, with Doug Carl's death, her husband's vote will now be canceled out. And so it goes for another two hours. More beers, more stories.

Finally, we head back to camp just before 10:00 P.M., having enjoyed too many laughs and too many beers and memorable pizza. It is a beautiful night with a full moon. Judy is rightly disappointed that we didn't get back earlier so we could sit around a campfire. It

Stan Kemp and Judy soaking up suds by the Rifle River

is now too late for anything but sleep. But, as we approach our tent, Judy points out yet another reason why we should have returned much earlier. We left the flysheet up on the tent, and we are victims of the mysterious dew point. It has not rained, but our stuff is soaked. There are beads of water clinging inside our tent. Fortunately, our sleeping bags are dry inside, but it was a stupid mistake. We never do get a grip on the dew point, but we do learn to always protect our gear as dusk falls and night comes. Of course, the situation is much more annoying to Judy because she had many fewer beers.

Total Walked	146 miles
Walked Today	19 miles
Walking to Do	189 miles

Chapter 10

The Rifle River to Lake George

This morning Judy is not a happy camper. Actually, none of us is too chipper. The irritations are adding up. There were some light showers overnight, which on top of our carelessness in leaving the fly rolled up means that the tent is now wet inside and out. Stan was dry but cramped sleeping in the back seat of his 1984 Chevy. The sky is heavily overcast. The shower is twenty-five cents per minute, and I have only one quarter with me. No time to tarry. I work hard to soap all over before I'm left with no water for a full rinse.

When I get back to our campsite, Stan has brought coffee. Judy is trying to dry things off with an old cotton blanket Stan has given her. Our flysheet, tent, and footprint are draped over picnic tables. Judy is still irked about our damp gear. It takes longer to break camp when things are wet. You want them dry for the next camp. And today we are heading for a campground on Lake George, nineteen miles away.

We head for breakfast at Dave and Kathy's, a restaurant we had seen on Old 76 on our way into Cedar Springs. It's hot, steamy, and busy inside. The convivial hustle and bustle is just what we need to jump-start our attitudes. Stan is going to do us one last huge favor today by taking our backpacks up to Lake George. Our hope is that without the heavy weight of the packs for one more day my feet might improve. Otherwise . . . well, otherwise goes left unsaid because neither of us wants to give up on the walk. As we leave the restaurant, it is beginning to sprinkle. Out come our rain jackets. Stan departs up the road, and we are on our own.

We will stay on Old 76 for twelve miles until we hit Greenwood Road, crossing into Ogemaw County. Old 76 was once the major trunk line north before I-75 was built one mile to our west. Paralleling the road is the Old Lake Shore Railroad. The road runs straight and is bordered by many hardwoods and, now more frequently, stands of pine. Houses are few and businesses even less. There is little traffic and no dogs. Under a leaden sky, in the rain, the silence is almost eerie.

The road travels through the Au Sable State Forest. It is now beginning to feel like "the North." The peaceful quiet of our surroundings starts to feel monotonous. We look for diversions to keep our interest. The usual cast of bird life busies itself along the roadside, paying no attention to us. The natural inhabitants have asserted their domain over what is no longer a busy thoroughfare. We hope to see deer, and I think about the remote chance of coming upon a black bear.

Nothing can long distract me from my pain. The roll of my foot along the stone shoulder reminds me of my torturous arrival into Bay City. But perhaps more serious is the old heel problem. It seems my morning bandage work has left the molefoam edge in an uncomfortable position at the bottom of my heel. It's rather like when your sock has slipped down into your shoe and each step presses the double fold of the material painfully into your heel. Only it feels more like a granite ridge than supple cloth.

There are just too many things going on in my boots. Besides my heavy socks and a thin liner sock, I also have inserted an inner sole as well as a heel pad. All of this is supposed to cushion my step. In addition I have taken to applying the thicker molefoam in order to allow more air around my blisters. These protective measures have thrown my gait off, and I now walk with a limp as we struggle up the road. The pain has become a stabbing numbness rather than a burn.

We stop over and over again to make adjustments, but to no avail. In desperation we try every option and every combination, taking out the inner sole, moving the bandages, removing the heel pad, changing the molefoam to moleskin, putting the heel pad back in. All of this is very difficult because of the rain. Exasperated, I finally blurt out, "Maybe it is time to quit." Judy responds with stunned silence.

Trying again, I add, "Aren't I ruining everything already?"

"Not for me," Judy answers but then rushes to add, "But, I'm not suffering like you are." She is struggling to be understanding but can't hide her huge disappointment.

I continue pressing. "What is the point of this whole enterprise anyway? Just to see how much pain I can take? I'm sick of focusing on my feet. Aren't you?"

Judy quickly seizes the opening. "I don't mind," she insists, "if you can endure the pain."

She knows that I rarely give up, that I normally respond to a challenge. At the same time, this means so much to her that she won't be part of the decision. She is forcing me to make the call. And so I finally ask out loud, "Why is it so hard for me to quit? Why am I so prideful?"

That does it. Judy gives me a consoling pat on the back and says, "I'm sorry sweetie pie—it's just not fair."

We discuss our options. There is little chance of hitching a ride on this desolate road. But Stan said he would check on us after he drops off our backpacks. He could simply take us home. Slowly that idea takes hold. I limp up the road for five wretched miles, the piercing numbness in my right heel my sole focus. The rain falls. Judy and I fall into silence. She crosses the road and disappears into the bushes to go to the bathroom. I plod on. It will be easy for her to catch up with me.

Later we learn from Chris Koch that when Stan saw me with head bowed and shoulders bent, struggling forward, that he thought of Jesus Christ on his way to Calvary. I do not make light of the image. But it was a moment of intense experience and, yes, suffering. Stan has treats for us. I crawl into the back seat, take off my boots, and enjoy every bite of my Strawberry Shortcake Good Humor Bar. Maybe it is the sugar, but I say nothing about ending the walk. Stan leaves me with a handful of butterscotch hard candies, and Judy gets peppermints. I rearrange my bandages, and we wave good-bye to Stan, speeding toward home. Judy turns to me in the rain and asks incredulously, "Why didn't you tell Stan you wanted a ride?" All I can say is that I am still not ready to quit.

We have three and a half miles to the town of Alger. Stan has been waxing eloquently for the past two days over a "dozer" he saw for sale just this side of Alger. He is enamored with this piece of machinery and thinks his cousin Sam in the paving business might be interested in buying it. We are on the lookout for this different breed of cat. There it is. Just sitting out in the middle of nowhere with a For Sale sign hung on it. Looks like a standard yellow bulldozer to us.

A mile farther up the road we pass the Alger Cemetery. We learn in town that the cemetery was located here because of a tall pine tree that became known as the hanging tree. It was a matter of convenience. Outlaws were hung and buried in the same spot.

We walk into the village of Alger at about 1:00 P.M. Wet and hungry, we seek refuge on the covered porch of the old general store. As far as we can see, the town consists of this store, a post office, and a few blocks of neat, modest white houses. This tiny spot was founded in the 1880s as a terminus point of Alger's lumber hauling railroad. It was named after Russell A. Alger, governor of Michigan and town founder. A Civil War general, he became a lumber baron and was elected governor as a Republican in 1885. He served only one term and then expanded his business interests to include banking and manufacturing. He later served as secretary of war during the McKinley administration and was even appointed to the U.S. Senate. The history of this man is far grander than this little town.

But we are as happy as can be that Alger is here at all. There are few way stations for wet walkers in these parts. Inside the store we step back into another time, quite possibly the McKinley era. The wooden floor is worn smooth, pressed tin plates cover the high ceiling, nineteenth-century pictures hang above the shelves. Only the small stock of videos for rent reminds us that it is the 1990s. Even the angelic young woman behind the counter seems to reflect an earlier style. Deanne is actually a descendant of the store's founder. She cherishes the history and character of this old store as well as the special role it plays in people's lives. When a neatly dressed middle-aged woman returns a video, the two chat about the movie. She is respectful of an old man who comes in and then hurries to serve a worker who is on a break and rushing. And she graciously tells us a little history of the area in a soft, melodious, almost mystical voice. Perhaps she is the ghost of her ancestors!

Having been given permission by our new guardian angel, we settle in on the porch to repair my damaged heels. Judy and I conclude that part of the problem may be the thickness of the mole "foam" compared to the thinner mole "skin." So we spend forty-five minutes switching all the bandages.

While I get back into my socks and boots, Judy darts out into the rain to a pay phone to call her son Stephen, who is scheduled to have that job interview today. Judy wants to wish him good luck. When she comes back, I can tell from her face that something is

In rain gear on the porch of the old general store in Alger

awry. "You'll never believe it," she sighs. "Only Stephen could end up in a situation like this." I wait for her to vent her motherly concerns before hearing the story. It seems that Stephen attended an out-of-town wedding over the weekend and probably left his only pair of dress shoes in the hotel. He has discovered that he is shoeless just forty-five minutes before the interview. Judy caught him as he was leaving his house to try to buy a new pair, which for him is not a sure thing. It's not easy to find size 15 shoes in just any store. We don't hold out much hope for this job. But we are struck by a common theme here. Feet are the problem.

Before we leave the porch we put on our rain pants for the last half of our day. The rain is much heavier now. As we cut back across the road to assume our usual position of facing into the traffic, I immediately notice some improvement in my heel. My confidence is lifted. Perhaps I will at least finish walking this day. We joke about our appearance. Judy is in University of Michigan blue and I in Michigan State green. Our visored hoods are drawn tightly to cover our heads and lower faces, leaving only small windows for visibility. We are two otherworldly apparitions moving through a nearly unpopulated landscape. Turning off Old 76 and heading west on Greenwood Road, we see a herd of horses grazing in a pasture. Rather than approaching us as usual, with one look they gallop toward the barn. Not a minute later a bike rider coming toward us on our side of the road exhibits the same nervousness when she moves to the far shoulder and refuses to acknowledge our greeting.

There is no traffic. We can walk side by side. The rain falls steadily, but at least there is not much wind. On our left are stands of tall white pines so characteristic of the North country. Occasionally, there is a vacationer's log cabin tucked back in a clearing. On our right are farms with expansive fields that rise gradually as the land stretches northward. We are all alone.

I have made a big mistake today when I forgot a plastic bag for our map. One of the many tips that Judy took very seriously from her research was the importance of plastic bags. We have all sorts and sizes for every purpose including the protection of our maps, but they are in our gear, which Stan has stowed at the campground. So, our map gets soaked and nearly unreadable as I keep pulling it out of my pocket to check our location. I am very anxious not to miss a turn—my feet would never forgive me. My obsession with checking the map even in the rain, even as it is disintegrating, starts to annoy Judy. It's slowing us down, she claims. At the same time she admits that, since the route is my responsibility, she does not worry at all about it and therefore is less burdened. Her total faith in me, however, does nothing to relieve my concern and fixation.

We are now in Ogemaw County. The name derives from Chief Ogemakegate, one of the Indian leaders who spoke for and signed the Lewis Cass Treaty of 1819, which granted six million acres of land to United States ownership in the territory of Michigan. Since we have passed no other shelter, we decide to rest in one of these acres ceded by the chief. We make our way into a young white pine forest, replanted some years ago and now twenty to thirty feet tall. I sit down on the ground with my back against a tree, and Judy takes the same position against another tree facing me. We are tired, cold, and soaking wet. The boughs offer only partial cover from the rain. In total seriousness I tell Judy that I never expected to be in a situation like this at the age of fifty-two. After an appropriate pause out of respect for this sentiment, we both start to giggle.

"What's funny to you?" I ask.

"Well, just the idea that you could conceive of this moment, given your real life. What's funny to you?" Judy asks in return.

"Maybe that this now is my real life." The natural elements can break down your emotional mask in a way that worldly pressures do not. We are practiced at our usual lives. This walk is full of unexpected, raw confrontations with ourselves—lost youth, the possibility of failure, our mortality. I feel that vulnerability now.

But, despite how pathetic we may be, there is a certain inevitability to this moment. It began in 1976 with a terrible ice storm that destroyed thousands and thousands of trees in southeastern Michigan. I was running for the United States congressional seat vacated by the late Congressman James G. O'Hara. One morning while reading the newspaper a small notice caught my eye. The Michigan State Extension Service was distributing pine seedlings free of charge to anyone who wanted one. The proverbial light bulb went off in my head. Eureka!! I could do that too. I found a tree farm in Allegan, Michigan, and ordered a box of seedlings. In the basement of my house my family, my volunteers, and I separated each little seedling, put the roots in a plastic baggie, added peat moss and a squirt of water, put a twist-tie around the bag, and added a sticker with my name. We bagged seventy thousand trees that year and handed them out door-to-door. I won that election and have won ten more since then. We have continued and expanded the trees. We still bag them the same way, and I have volunteers who have been there every year. We still hand them out door-to-door each year. And we also take them to schools as part of an environmental program.

As of the summer of 1997, more than 700,000 Bonior pines have been distributed in my congressional district over the past twenty-two years. People send me pictures of their trees. They call and ask for new ones when they move. They stop me on the street to tell me stories about their trees. I am known as "the tree man."

So, here I sit with rain dripping off my glasses and down my beard, a middle-aged man in a green rubber suit in a white pine forest. These were not originally Bonior pines, but they are now. Judy and I will never forget that moment together when we laughed, but almost cried, at how forlorn we looked and felt.

We know we have to get moving again. The temperature is falling. We are increasingly colder, wetter, wearier. According to all we've read, we are prime candidates for hypothermia. It is raining harder than ever. We have come seventeen miles but have at least two to go.

The time has come to turn to our last resort.

Judy offers: "Singing in the rain. Just singing in the rain. What a glorious feeling, I'm happy again. With a smile on my face. De de de de de. De de de de dum. Just singing in the rain . . ."

I try: "Raindrops keep falling on my head. And just like the hum, hum, hum, hum, hum. Something's gotta hum. Dumta, da da dum . . ."

All together now: "The rain in Spain stays mainly on the plain. And where's that blasted plain? In Spain. In Spain . . ."

From *The Fantasticks*: "Soon it's gonna rain. I can feel it. Soon it's gonna rain. I can tell. Soon it's gonna rain. What're we gonna do? Da do da do da da do . . ."

We're dancing to "Just walking in the rain. Getting soaking wet . . ."

Judy sort of remembers: "I made it through the rain and kept my world protected. I made it through the rain and kept my point of view . . ."

Or how about "The itsy, bitsy spider climbed up the water spout"? And "It's raining, it's pouring, the old man is snoring."

The inspirational: "When you walk through a storm, hold your head up high and don't be afraid of the dark. At the end of the storm is a da da da da and da dum dada dum dada dee. Walk on, walk on with hope in your heart . . ."

Then the grand finale in unison: "Somewhere over the rainbow, bluebirds fly. Birds fly over the rainbow. Why then, o why, can't I?"

With apologies to all the songwriters and performers who have thrilled us and animated us. Our voices boom and crack, the glorious melodies barely discernible, most of the words lost in our frozen memories, but with hearts full of music the miles do almost fly by.

Still, it is a relief to see the sign for Cook Road. With our heads bowed into the rain, we might have missed our turn. The fields are luminous in the late-afternoon light. Judy thinks this must be what it is like in Ireland or Wales. It is a wet, green, radiant world.

At the corner of Channel Lake Road there is a new log home with smoke curling from the chimney. The promise of warmth and dryness and comfort taunts us as we plod ahead with hardly the strength to avoid the large puddles that dot this gravel road. Slowly it occurs to us that what lies ahead is not sanctuary but further problems. We have been so focused on reaching our destination that we have given no thought at all about what our circumstances will be when we get there.

We had visited Lake George Campground several months ago and have been looking forward to staying there. Lake George is a 120-acre trout lake; the private campground rises gently away from the shoreline. We had been surprised to discover that the owners of fifteen years, Jack and Carol Keller, are from Roseville, a city in the heart of my congressional district. In our imaginations we have been anticipating a few warm, sunny hours after a refreshing dip in the lake, a simple supper, and a beer by our campfire and the stars twinkling over the lapping waters. It was going to be the perfect embodiment of our walk. We would celebrate the halfway point of the journey.

How different is our reality! It is pouring rain. It has been raining steadily for seven hours. There is no indication that it will ever stop. Although our gear will be reasonably dry, we still will have to pitch our tent in the rain. Nothing will stay dry. And we are so cold. What madness is this? Yet, as we laugh hysterically at our predicament, Judy starts to warm to the challenge. To her this will rebalance her personal scale of justice. In return for having the luxury of walking without our packs for the day, we should overcome this additional burden tonight. Anyway, what choice do we have? I cannot argue with that. We entertain ourselves by trying to perfect a strategy for setting up our campsite while keeping stuff as dry as possible. The mental gymnastics of this exercise actually warm us and brighten our spirits.

Suddenly, off to our right, on a slight rise in a meadow, we see an entire herd of deer. There must be fifteen to twenty doe, buck, and fawn feeding. We stand silently thrilled. Then a raised head, a nose to the wind, and one by one they leap off into the woods. In the very next clearing we are greeted by the sight of ten more deer playing in the field. On this miserable day we feel so lucky to have received a wondrous gift. A bit farther up the road we are startled to see an adolescent deer running directly toward us. Obviously, it is lost and confused. Ahead we see the herd crossing the road, and at the last moment the juvenile turns back to join the rest.

After this excitement, the last half-mile into Lake George seems almost easy. The campground appears to be nearly empty. Judy heads directly to the ladies' room, and I go into the office. Inside is Carol Keller, who has been watching the Weather Channel and worrying about us. The temperature is forty-nine degrees and falling. She has our gear, but under no circumstances is she going to let us pitch a tent there that night. The sites are all flooded out. Only a few trailers are still at the campground. The forecast for the night ahead is for even bigger storms. Carol has already made up her mind to call a friend of hers to pick us up and take us to a motel. When Judy walks in just a few minutes later, she is shocked to find that everything has been decided. Carol is in charge here, and I am secretly delighted. Judy, I can see, is struggling to come to terms with this abrupt change in her guilt equation. Rather than the neat trade-off she had earlier calculated, she now has to accept further concessions. I am not having any problem with this.

Carol's friend Diane Burkhart pulls up in a big old black car. The trunk is huge but loaded with bags of cat food. Luckily, the back seat is also large, and the backpacks fit there. Diane is probably about our age and appears to have had a tough life, but, like Carol, she has a generous heart. She tells us that she has eighteen or so cats and will feed anything that comes her way. She refuses any gratuity, and I am embarrassed for having offered. I have no intention of cheapening her natural act of kindness.

Instead of struggling to pitch our tent in the rain, we find ourselves standing dripping in the lobby of the Quality Inn in West Branch. We are a strange sight here. This is a mecca for outlet shoppers, not hikers.

Once in our room we strip off our wet gear and each take a hot shower. With the TV tuned to the trusty Weather Channel and a beer and a bag of chips brought from the campground, we consider tomorrow. Day 11 was always going to be tricky for the simple reason that we have no place to spend the night. We searched the maps, combed the roads by car, and even made some phone calls but never found a campsite, motel, or even a friendly backyard. But we had expected to go ahead anyway and pitch our tent somewhere in Nester Township on public land. To this already dicey situation we now must add two additional complications. The weather forecast is for continued rain through tomorrow night, with chilly temperatures. But more problematic, upon inspection in the motel, it is obvious that my feet are worse than ever.

So we face another moment of truth. So many times we have reached a point where we were prepared to quit only to find reserves of determination somewhere that kept us going. Here we are again.

This time we compromise. We will drive to the motel on Houghton Lake where we had planned to spend our twelfth night. We will rest for one day. We will see if my feet can recover enough that we can continue. A decision has been made.

We have dinner at the Italian restaurant in the hotel. A group of successful shoppers in the corner is in high spirits. We are almost sad. We have walked 165 miles. We could be proud. It has often been grueling. It has also been immensely rewarding. We do smile at the memory of our first night in our little tent. We marvel at the wonders we have encountered that have already heightened our senses, enriched us, and cast permanent imprints on our souls. We have relished one another's almost exclusive companionship, reinforcing our sense of how well suited we are for each other. These ten days have begun the fulfillment of our dream. We are subdued by the realization that it may have ended today.

Total Walked	165 miles
Walked Today	19 miles
Walking to Do	170 miles

Chapter 11
West Branch to Houghton Lake

Thursday, August 21

Last night we made the painful decision to interrupt the walk. Today we will proceed by car west to Houghton Lake and spend an extra night where we already have a reservation for Friday. We sleep late this morning, our reluctance to rise caused somewhat by physical weariness but more significantly by our dread of facing the reality that we are now breaking the integrity of the journey. Such emptiness. It is like losing a championship ballgame. I feel the hollowness in my gut of knowing there is no retrieving a lost opportunity. We have come nearly halfway and always before this have pushed on. But now our options run out. My miserable feet and the equally miserable wet and windy weather combine to waylay us. If only we could just hole up here outside of West Branch, let the weather pass and my feet heal—at least we would keep the walk intact. But then we would be off schedule, defaulting on our reservations and deposits at every campground and motel ahead of us. Furthermore, I had been lucky to carve out three weeks as it was from the competing demands of my real life. To complete our walk by joining the annual Labor Day walk across the Mackinac Bridge means we must stick to our timetable. We have no choice: to gain a day off, we have to give up two short days of walking and drive to Houghton Lake.

I know how terribly disappointing this is to Judy. She is religious about finishing what she has begun. This gap will haunt her. But even she realizes that this decision is our best hope of ultimately finishing the walk. So, with great regret, we surrender to our reality. But it does not come easily, and it does not feel good.

The other disappointing aspect of our decision is forfeiting the most mysterious portion of our journey—the walk from Lake George to Houghton Lake. On our scouting expedition we drove this twenty-eight-mile route, which took us along the scenic cottage-lined shore of Lake George and then on old country roads that followed the timber clearing of one hundred years past. After a few miles of farms the dirt road narrows, becoming little more than two deep ruts as it plunges into dense woods. There we were to have been on our own, pitching our tent somewhere in Nester Township, perhaps on the edge of one of four small lakes in the area—Clear, Spring, Woods, or Twin Lake. With no commercial establishments of any sort and not even a campground, it was going to be our only "wilderness" experience. All this is very alluring to Judy.

I, on the other hand, think only of the black bear, which all our literature admonishes us to treat with "respect." I have convinced myself that in the bowels of Nester Township we will meet our bear challenge. Again, on our scouting trip, I noticed with dread that the few cottages on Woods Lake had heavily fortified private garbage containers. Surely these were not your average "go away raccoon" enclosures. No, all that thick wood and heavy wire mesh definitely looked to me like they were meant to keep out a grizzly. The message was clear, "Bears Hang Out Here."

The Michigan Department of Natural Resources together with the National Forest Service puts out a pamphlet entitled "Understanding the Black Bear." The operative word here is *understanding.* I've never seen pamphlets entitled "Understanding the White Tail Deer" or "Understanding the Elk." The second sentence underscores this ominous tone. "By understanding bear behavior you can co-exist avoiding problems and confrontation." Sure. And there's more. "Black bears have an enormous appetite." Oh boy. But read on. "They are also very curious, thus leading them into an occasional encounter with humans. Black bear do not have to be feared; but their strength, speed, and intelligence must be respected." There's that word *respect* again.

Richard Smith, in his book *Understanding Michigan Black Bear,* dryly observes, "When coupled with the fact that there are more people than ever before in the outdoors and the number of humans is expected to continue to increase, the odds of some one being injured or killed by a bear go up even more." There are anywhere from one-half to three-quarters of a million black bear in North America, some of which can weigh up to 650 pounds. The inescapable conclusion is that a bear could bump into me. Or, as Bill Bryson in his book *A Walk in the Woods,* puts it:

> Black bear rarely attack. But here is the thing. Sometimes they do . . . All bears are agile, cunning, and immensely strong and they are always hungry. If they want to kill and eat you, they can, and pretty much whenever they want. That doesn't happen often but here is the salient point—once would be enough.

So it is in this humbling context that I imagine lying next to Judy in our little tent, nothing but a thin layer of nylon between us and whatever is roaming about in Nester Township. As the powerful haunch brushes against us in the darkness, will I be brave because I "understand and respect" the black beast of the woods? Or would I rather be at the Gas Lite Manor resort? I admit I am a coward. I've endured blitzing linebackers, screaming drill sergeants in boot camp, the last miles of a marathon, appearing on "Meet the Press," but nothing can ever prepare me for an evening in the wild with a bear. I'm secretly pleased to be going to Houghton Lake.

The morning is growing old. We've both been lost in our own thoughts. I'm startled by Judy's voice.

"Turn on the Weather Channel. Maybe there's been some improvement," she says hopefully.

As the traditional male clicker person in our family, I hit the power button, and Weather, the last channel we watched before sleep overcame us, bursts into view. The local forecast is for wet, windy, and cooler weather for the next couple of days. I turn silently to Judy.

"Call her," she sighs.

Chris Koch answers the phone in Mount Clemens. She's been hoping we would call. Of course, she will set out as soon as possible on a rescue mission.

Chris and I have known each other since 1972, when I ran my first campaign for state representative and she was a volunteer for the George McGovern for President campaign. Twenty-five years ago, after my win and McGovern's loss, progressive activists in Mount Clemens formed a group, Locus Focus, emphasizing local grassroots politics. In light of the national drubbing, it was obvious that we needed to rebuild from the ground up. Chris was one of the leaders of our efforts, which have seen handsome results over the years in elections for school boards, county commissioners, township trustees, state representatives, state senators, and me.

Judy often says, and I agree, that Chris is the "dearest" person we know. She is smart and savvy enough to have run my Michigan operations with Ed Bruley since I was first elected to Congress. The hallmark of her personality and character, however, is genuine goodness. Chris is unfailingly kind, thoughtful, understanding, and unflappable, all qualities I have repeatedly tested in her over the years and never found wanting.

Chris, who is our age, was raised in Rock Island, Illinois, where her father was a UAW worker at a tractor facility and her mother a waitress. Chris was the first in her family to graduate from high school (and did so with straight As). As for college, she says, "I narrowed my choices to the University of Illinois at Urbana-Champaign or Illinois Normal [a teacher college and now Northern Illinois]. Both schools offered the financial aid I needed. I chose the U of I because there were more men. I saw nothing 'normal' about the lopsided female to male ratio at Illinois Normal." It worked. She met and married her husband Allan at the U of I. After his graduation Allan found work in Detroit, and they moved to the area in 1965. Chris finished her degree at Wayne State University and began a short career as a high school teacher before starting a family and joining my staff.

Together with Ed Bruley, whose amazing strategic and organizational skills have lifted our political fortunes, Chris has helped to build and mold our coalition. Since our first campaign for Congress in 1976, our lives have run on parallel tracks. In addition to her family and office responsibilities, she is very active in the community, serving on numerous boards as well as representing me in hundreds of public settings a year. She is also a committed and valued member of her church and has raised two wonderful boys, both of whom are Eagle Scouts. But, lest one be misled by all this achievement, it is most important to know that Chris has in her suburban home four dogs, an iguana, a rat snake, a box turtle, an underwater frog, and a ten-year-old newt (acquired before the speaker of the House's rise and outlasting his fall). Chris is a great reader, and one of her favorite authors is Anne Tyler. It is little wonder. Like Tyler's most endearing characters, she is without guile, irony, or cynicism. She can laugh at herself and love the whole world. We cherish her friendship, and right now we need a friend.

"Where are you?" she asks, only slightly incredulously.

Somewhat sheepishly, I answer, "At the Quality Inn in West Branch."

"Oh, I know exactly where that is," Chris responds enthusiastically."It's right next to the shopping outlet—you know, Bugle Boy, Calvin Klein, Liz Claiborne . . ." Her voice trails off, as she suddenly realizes that we are not here to indulge in the great American pastime. She'll be on her way shortly. By car the trip from Mount Clemens should be about two and a half hours.

Checkout is noon, so Judy and I have plenty of time to view the lobby while we wait for our ride. We are in luck because the lobby is a veritable museum of logging in Michigan. We study the displays. Cross-cut saws. Cant hooks (a tapered wooden pole, three to six feet long with a seven- to nine-inch loose, dangling hook near the working end). They were used for loading logs on sleighs and skids. The cant hook man caught the hook on a log, bore down on the handle, gave it a pull, and the log would cant over. Gabriels (long tin horns used to signal meals). Corked boots (boots with sharp spikes to keep the rivermen—riverhogs—from slipping as they drove the logs on the rivers). High above us hanging from the ceiling is a Big Wheel. This ingenious but simple piece of equipment consisted of two ten-feet-tall wheels axled together and pulled by a team of horses. The height of the wheels allowed logs ranging in length from twelve to one hundred feet in length to be chained under the axle.

Enlarged photos and murals of logging camp scenes, most dating back to the 1860s and 1870s, hang on the walls. Here are shanty boys axing and sawing the state's precious resource. (A shanty boy was a logger or woodsman. *Lumberjack,* or *jack,* is of more recent literary origin and was seldom used by workers themselves.) The grainy and distant images remind me of Mathew Brady's civil war photographs. Bearded men lost to the ages.

These scenes bring back memories of my mother's father, John Gavreluk, who labored in these woods as a shanty boy at the turn of the century. My grandfather was born in 1894 in western Ukraine in a region known as Galicia near the Carpathian Mountains. Being from a poor village where his family toiled as peasants, he sought to escape the grinding poverty. In 1912, when he was eighteen, perhaps sensing the coming storm of the Great War that would consume millions of young men his age, he made his way north for

Belgium. He boarded the passenger ship *P. Canon* and made the crossing in steerage from Antwerp to North America, where he arrived in New York Harbor on St. Joseph's Day, March 19. He would need the blessings of the patron saint of workers as he struggled to build a new life. Without family or a friend, speaking no English, and with only a third-grade education, he faced an unknown world. Years later, when Judy and I visited Ellis Island, a vivid quote from another immigrant of that era reminded me of my grandfather's circumstances. "They said come to America where the streets are paved in gold. Well when I arrived in America I found out three things. The streets were not paved in gold. Actually, the streets were not paved at all. In fact, they expected me to pave the streets."

In New York for only one day of medical and civil exams, my grandfather was then herded onto a train for the ride north to the province of Quebec. From Athelstan, Quebec, just across the New York state line, he would make his way to Montreal and eventually to Sudbury, Ontario. After working there in the mines, he later moved on to Sault Ste. Marie and then to the logging camps in northern Michigan. He was a strong man, well built for hard work. His certificate of naturalization papers granting him U.S. citizenship in 1926 describe him at thirty-two years of age as five feet and nine inches tall and weighing 170 pounds, with a ruddy complexion, blue eyes, and brown hair.

As I gaze at the photos, it dawns on me that this was his world. Life had always been hard for him. I recall his bleak description of the lumber camps. "Cold," he would say, hugging himself and shivering at the sound of the word. It was brutal work for little reward. But a big change was coming.

When the woods were just about wasted, along came an entrepreneur who offered shelter from the cold and a decent wage. Henry Ford drew upon this labor pool and offered the unheard-of sum of five dollars a day to work inside and build horseless carriages. Ford's promise drew workers by the thousands down to Detroit, and a new era dawned in the United States.

Bruce Catton, the eminent Pulitzer Prize–winning historian and Michigan native, captures this transition well in his excellent 1976 work, *Michigan, A Bicentennial History:*

The lumber barons, unintentionally but effectively, prepared the way for the men who were going to make autos; by piling up the necessary capital, by stimulating the immigration that created a pool of available factory hands, and by helping to develop industries that could take easily and naturally to the production of autos when the time came. In its beginnings—indeed, all through its lusty youth and beyond—the manufacture of autos was dangerously speculative, frowned on by eastern capitalists and for that matter by middle western bankers as well. The men who made money out of the pine forests were, first of all, chance-takers; they had a good thing going, and they grew rich thereby, but they always knew that a bad turn of luck—a couple of mild winters, for instance—could put them in the red, perhaps put them out of business altogether. They were speculators by nature, their trade was born of the frontier's boom-or-bust philosophy, and to put surplus money into a business that might prove to be no business at all was nothing they were not used to. The deep-wood lumber trade kept the frontier alive in Michigan right into the industrial age, which created exactly the condition in which this new industry could find birth and vigorous growth. Basically the auto industry was a frontier venture. That it grew up in Michigan was wholly natural.

There were side effects. The lumber boom had created a carriage trade—people prosperous enough to ride around in horse-drawn carriages—and it had also created carriage factories to meet the demand created by this trade. These factories clustered about places like Flint and Detroit, where the needed specialty timber was easy to obtain, and when the time came it was simple enough to have them make horseless carriages. The requirements of sawmills, logging railroads, and mining camps had brought machine shops and foundries into being, downstate, and had built up a corps of skilled workers who knew how to operate them. By supplying both the building timber and the paying freight, the lumber trade had developed a ship-building industry along the Detroit, St. Clair, and Saginaw rivers, and as iron and steel began to replace wood in the shipyards, a number of the builders began to turn out small craft; and so there were factories that developed and built the internal combustion engines that would power the small craft. Altogether, the bits and pieces needed for auto production were all in place, ready to be used. (178–79)

My grandfather came a long way in his journey from Ukraine to Canada to Michigan, from peasant farmer to miner, logger, and then automaker. And his hope for a better life was eventually realized beginning with Henry Ford's foresight in paying his workers enough money to enable those making the automobile to also buy one. This simple lesson is one I've always tried to include in our international trade debates. If our current CEOs followed this example, rather than exploiting the productive labor of the poor in developing countries, they could be building markets for their own products.

John Gavreluk brought his bride, Effie Mallenek, from Canada, and together they raised two beautiful and loving daughters, my Aunt Nell and my mother, Irene. With his family by then in Hamtramck, Michigan, my grandfather worked for thirty years in the auto plants, finishing his career at the old Dodge Main plant a half-mile from where we lived.

I am drifting in these memories when Chris and Ruth Gallop, another long-time friend and coworker, walk into the lobby. It is immediately obvious that their mood will be a counterpoint to ours. They are bubbling with excitement about their adventure today. For those of us who live in southeastern Michigan, going "up north" is usually associated with vacation and an escape to the out-of-doors from the usual routine. For Chris and Ruth this is an unexpected adventure. They get to play hooky in a beautiful setting. We appreciate their enthusiasm even if we can't quite share it.

It's time to load up Ruth's minivan with our gear. We each carry our packs out to the parking lot. Judy goes back to the lobby for a large plastic bag filled with our tent, sleeping bags, and other camping equipment. She returns to the van, struggling with this brimming oversized garbage bag, carrying it pressed against her body with her arms wrapped around the awkward load.

Ruth's jaw drops at this sight. "Gosh, Judy, it's surprising you didn't keep tripping, carrying that bag all this way," she innocently exclaims.

Laughter is definitely good for the soul. And, given our amateurish ways, I guess it's not so improbable an image.

A quick turn out of the parking lot puts us on the entrance ramp of I-75, a highway that runs from Sault Ste. Marie across the Mackinac Bridge all the way to the west coast of Florida. It is well traveled by Michiganders seeking sun and warmth in winter or vacations during the rest of the year. Ruth and Chris describe their trip.

They too have had a near-bear experience. They got a bit lost and found themselves on a back road when straight ahead of them they saw a large, dark, moving object. Fearing she was going to hit a bear, Ruth slowed down. As they drew closer, what had appeared to be one large animal turned out to be a flock of wild turkey walking down the road. Earlier they had seen a cloud formation of the entire state of Michigan, not just the mitten shape of the Lower Peninsula but the UP as well.

Judy leans forward between the bucket seats to talk with Ruth and Chris. The happy sound of their chatter warms the van. Laughter rises and falls. They are so engaged with one another, relaxed, at ease. Listening and talking; sharing stories, reactions, excitement; caring about one another's experiences—all the hallmarks of friendship among three people who are important to me. Yet I choose my own thoughts, an observer, not a participant. For a moment I wonder if it's because I'm a male or because I'm the boss where Ruth and Chris work or because it is just my personality. Whatever the reason, I feel the separation.

Out the window, looking northward, I take the measure of the land billowing up the "fingers" of the mitten. The image transports me into the future. I feel drawn to the most picturesque part of our walk. The van zips by stands of birch, pine, and oak. Aspen seems to be more and more abundant up here. Their quaking leaves appear to be talking away to the rest of the forest. My favorite tree man, Donald Culross Peattie captures their character perfectly. "A breeze that is barely felt on the cheek will set the foliage of the trembling Aspen into a panic of whispering." Do I hear amid the leaves, "Why are you riding? We thought you planned to walk among us." The aspen lighten my mood further. "As they rustle they also twinkle," says Peattie, "their lustrous upper surfaces forever catching the light like thousands of little mirrors, flashed in mischievous fingers to dazzle the eyes." Turning to look to the south, I see the woods of Nester Township and all those real or imagined bears who will not dine on us.

As we approach the Prudenville area I reengage my riding companions with a request. "Please help me be on the lookout for the Music Box." When I was in high school (1959–63) the Music Box was the place to go if you wanted to meet girls and dance your feet off. Tucked in a wooded area off M-55 across the road from Houghton Lake, this sprawling Alpine structure with an open-air courtyard served as the teen center for the summer vacation crowds. The young people who swam and sunned by day and ached to explore their awkward social skills at night made this spot their own northern Michigan dancehall, reflecting the adolescent TV dance show rage of the era, "American Bandstand." The rules at the popular gathering place were simple, or so it seemed. Only teenagers. No alcohol. No smoking. You queued up to get in, usually waiting a good while, heightening the anticipation. Once inside the profusion of perfumes fermented by warm bodies mixed enticingly with the beat of Motown sounds.

On a boring Friday evening in the summer of 1962, a few friends—Bill Beels, Mal Batherson, Dave Diegel—and I scraped up a few dollars for gas and cold drinks and headed up north to experience what had become known down below as a hot spot. For two and a half hours we drove to get there and then waited in line for another hour to enter. I remember the dark-brown window shutters and the alternating cut-out patterns of hearts and diamonds. Once we were inside, it was all that had been promised. The night was timeless until the clock struck midnight, the dancing ended, and we were on the street, out of money, and with no place to stay. We drew straws to see who would sleep in the car and who got the trunk. I spent the night with a large tire, oily rags, a moth-infested blanket, and a swarm of northern Michigan mosquitoes. But oh the memories . . .

"There it is on the right." I'm the first one to spot it. To my surprise I find I'm actually excited at the sight of this relic from my past. We pull over and get out to explore the premises. The rambling buildings connected by open courtyards remind me of a California high school campus in alpine dressing. Peeking through windowpanes, I spy a handsome room furnished with wooden tables and chairs and a big old country stove. It looks as if they might open for dinner in a few hours. Yet the door to the main entrance is padlocked. Still standing are the metal poles that guided the queue. We learn later that only ghosts stand in those lines now. The simple rules of my youth became unenforceable. In 1980 the Music Box closed. The owner, Lee Kelly, lives above one part of the building and obviously still takes great pride in its upkeep. A new thatch roof was recently added, and we are told that the air conditioning is kept on during hot summer weather to preserve the old collection of 78 rpm records. He maintains the building and grounds well, possibly preserving his own sweet memories of lost summer nights.

Beyond the Music Box, a few blocks along the developed south shore of Houghton Lake, we spot the Gas Lite Manor, an appealing but simple resort and our home for the next one and a half days. There are two buildings running from the road to the beach, each with six units and parking between. In front of the office there is a posted yellow diamond sign reading "Golden Retriever Crossing." He greets us with tail wagging and a teddy bear held playfully in his mouth.

"I'm going to like this dog," I announce. "And it's the way I like my bears, too—subdued, small, and stuffed."

We learn that the dog's name is Hobbes, after the cartoon character. We need this exposure to Hobbes to readjust our overly harsh attitude about dogs. Hobbes's buddy, a second golden retriever, also shows up frequently, and the two have quite a high time together bounding about the beach.

After quickly checking into our room, we take Ruth and Chris to lunch at a place on the water. We watch the chop roil on the lake and fill them with details of our odyssey. After lunch we take further advantage of our saviors to make a drive up the eastern side of Houghton Lake to the state park on the north shore of Higgins Lake. I have a plan. Even with two days of rest, the really bad blisters on my feet are not going to be cured. If we are to resume our walk and finish it, somehow I still need to build in further relief for my wounded feet. The less weight I have to carry, the better. I will surely suffer a total relapse if on the first day of walking after our hiatus, I have to carry a full pack for twenty-three miles. So I hope to store that big plastic bag full of our camping gear at the park and thereby lighten each of our loads by seven pounds.

In the van I practice my pitch to the park gatekeeper. Just what is the best approach? Should I grovel? Should I offer a simple gratuity palmed in my hand like some politician out of the past, dispensing "walking around money"? Should I tell the person who I am? Or should I do what has worked for better or for worse in my life, just make the case? "We are tired, old, and walking the length of the state. We need a break." That's it.

At the park I walk into the gatehouse. Behind the counter stands the young park registrar, Kevin Coors. He listens passively to my request, his eyes sizing me up. I surmise that for him the summer is coming to an end; he is probably going back to school shortly. He looks like the type who himself might have done some backpack-

Hobbes with his stuffed bear at Houghton Lake

ing. And how many hikers has he seen check in here? In all likelihood, none. On the other hand, he might not care to risk a blemish on his employment record.

"Here," he says abruptly, shoving a piece of paper in front of me. "Write your name and when you expect to arrive." Success. He tells me to bring the bag to the side door, where he takes it in to store it for us. I'm humbled and thankful, repeating my gratitude as I shuffle back to the van, unnecessarily acquiring a slight limp. I suspect what he has done is irregular, but he will do well in life because he is flexible and can use common sense.

We drive back to our motel by way of the other (western) side of the lake and conclude that the least commercial and more interesting walk will be the eastern shore of Houghton Lake and then up the southern and western shores of Higgins Lake. Chris and Ruth drop us off at 5:00 P.M. and head for home. We are immensely grateful to them. Judy goes grocery shopping, and we eat our dinner using the refrigerator freezer tray and a large ashtray as plates. We sit in the window of our room overlooking the windswept lake. Ducks are feeding at the weed bed not far from shore. Small motor boats anchored in the shallows bob like bathtub toys under angry skies.

Total Walked	165 Miles
Walked Today	0 Miles
(Should Have Walked Today	14 Miles)
Walking to Do	156 Miles

Chapter 12
Houghton Lake

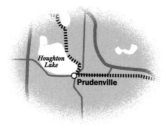

Despite our warm, safe, and dry surroundings, neither of us sleeps well. Judy is bothered by the insane itching of one small blister of poison ivy and also wakens feeling stuffy. It could be a reaction to the weather or perhaps to a pet having stayed here.

I dream that my former colleague in the House, Morris Udall, was doing terrifying acrobatics on the high wire near the top of a circus tent. No net below. Mo Udall was one of the most beloved public figures during his long career in the House and his run for president in 1976. Also in 1976, after forty years of robust health he broke an arm, caught viral pneumonia, suffered a burst appendix, got peritonitis, and was diagnosed with Parkinson's disease, all within eight months. He left Congress in 1992 after serving thirty-one years. At the end of his tenure his motor skills had deteriorated dramatically. To see this brilliant and caring man, whose wit and humor are legendary, succumb to the point where he could no longer physically function on the House floor was heartrending.

One day when I noticed Mo having difficulty sitting down or standing up I went to Speaker Tom Foley and mentioned that I feared he might fall and injure himself badly. We talked about how to handle this delicate situation. After all, Mo was a proud man, the father of so many progressive pieces of legislation, including the most important environmental bill of our era, the Alaska Lands Wilderness Act, which put more than a hundred million acres of federal land scattered throughout Alaska into more than a dozen new national parks, wildlife refuges, and a national forest. These are the crown jewels of Alaska, now protected, thanks to Mo's leadership. Well, we notified his chief of staff, and I made it my job to watch out for Mo when he came to the House floor. It was a very awkward situation, but he had reached such a condition that it was necessary to be near him in case he lost what little balance remained.

Soon after becoming aware of his disease, he dealt with it in his typical fashion by making light of it. At that same time there was a scandal involving Paula Parkinson, a blonde lobbyist who kissed and told about her affairs with several congressmen. Mo would joke: "There are two kinds of Parkinson's disease: the kind discovered by an English doctor, and the kind you get when you go to Florida with a blonde lobbyist. There are no similarities between the two afflictions, except that they both cause you to lose sleep—and they both give you the shakes."

I guess I am still watching over Mo in my dreams.

Judy arranged last evening to get a ride to the laundromat from the motel owners. She meets Lowell and Barbara Souder at 8:00 A.M., and they drop her off on the way to their morning breakfast. For me the goal is to stay off my feet. I lose myself in reading about where we are.

Every child in Michigan grows up learning about Houghton Lake in school. It is our state's largest inland lake. Measuring seven miles wide and sixteen miles long, covering some twenty-two thousand acres of sandy bottom and nearly seventy-two miles of shoreline, it is twenty-two feet at its deepest and has an average depth of only eight feet. It is well stocked with walleye, northern pike, large- and small-mouth bass, and, in its weed beds, perch, bluegill, and crappie. Today, with fifteen to twenty mile per hour winds, this shallow body of water looks foreboding. "All sailors ashore." The lake is also the source of the Muskegon River—one of the principal logging rivers in the state. Intense commercial and resort development lines the south shore in what is known as "nine miles of opportunity." A bike and hike asphalt trail starting near our resort runs the length of the strip. Along this route, if you look carefully, you can find several old log structures among the newer buildings. The Shea Lodge, Pine Moose Theatre (which boasts a live organ), and the wedding chapel in the old village are all historic originals. They are the few remaining vestiges of the past.

In 1877 the village of Houghton Lake had a population of a mere twenty people. The lake's name was changed from Roscommon to Houghton in honor of Michigan's first geologist, Dr. Douglass Houghton. Houghton, along with William Burt, surveyed a good part of the state, including the Upper Peninsula, where they discovered a treasure of metals, namely iron ore and copper. In the fall of 1845 Houghton drowned when the boat he was sailing in to pick up other surveyors smashed on the rocky coast of Lake Superior in a storm.

In the early years large-scale fishing was a popular enterprise on Houghton Lake, with prodigious amounts taken. But, as in the rest of the state, lumbering became the main industry of the area. When railroads made their way into the region, sawmills sprang up. Eventually, the same railroads that were built to haul out the white and red pine became the transportation for folks traveling from urban areas to this vacation land.

Today the population of Houghton Lake is eleven thousand and swells to thirty thousand between Memorial Day and Labor Day. Billboards leading into town advertise Houghton as the "Tip-Up Town." This designation evolved from a contest to name the annual winter festival on the ice that began in 1951, when folks realized that the lake provided fantastic ice fishing. The name derives from the action of the red signaling flag on the ice-fishing rig indicating that a fish has struck the baited hook lowered into the hole drilled through the ice. During Winterfest, celebrated annually on the third and fourth weekends in January, the town attracts some forty to fifty thousand visitors. The frozen lake becomes a village on ice catering to the needs of ice fishermen, snowmobilers, and other winter enthusiasts. One local wag suggests the purpose of the festival is "to promote bigger lies, hilarity, tomfoolery, and goodwill."

Our local historians and hosts are Barbara and Lowell Souder, a handsome couple in their early sixties. Thirty years ago they started vacationing each year here with their children from their home in Fostoria, Ohio. Lowell worked as an over-the-road trucker and Barbara as a medical technician. Finally, after ten years of visits, when Mark was ten, Diane fourteen, and David seventeen, they moved up here permanently in 1977 and bought the resort. The family loved northern Michigan, the hunting and fishing, the people. At school the boys ran track and played football, and Diane was a cheerleader. The parents immersed themselves in the community. Barbara has served on the hospital board and as secretary of the Rotary. Lowell has always been active in planning and development in various business groups and was president of the Lions Club.

Together they run the resort. Lowell reminisces about their start twenty years ago. "When we began we had linoleum floors, no phones, and black-and-white TVs." He sounds nostalgic but also very proud of the way they have upgraded and changed with the years. Today 75 percent of their guests are repeats. "It's like family," Barbara says. "You get to know the folks who come up year after year. We have seen four generations of the same family. Kids come to see how their parents and grandparents used to vacation."

"Now it's changed," Lowell interjects with regret in his voice. "The younger generation demands more action. They want to be entertained and don't like to stay in one place for a whole week. And, with single moms, there is no one to teach the kids hunting and fishing."

"So, do you have any funny stories you can share with us about any of your visitors—no names, of course?" My question is innocent.

The answer is cautious. Even now, near the end of their years in the business, they are protective of their guests. No foolish antics will be revealed. Anonymity is insufficient disguise. "Well," says Lowell slowly. "A couple of people did not heed our warning and sank through thin ice near the mouth of the creek." Twenty years of guests have been well served by the Souders.

They are apprehensive about the future. Barbara shares her fears that the "chains" will eventually replace small family resorts such as their own. A Holiday Inn Express and Travel Lodge have designs on the Lake. Here again is the refrain of our walk and our history. Time yields to change, and in Michigan that has often meant rapacious change, which has depleted our most precious resources—furs, trees, metals, the water, and the land. Not all change is progress. A chain society, devoid of individuality, is not appealing to me. Chain hotels, chain restaurants, chain banks, and chain stores have homogenized our experiences and often destroyed many a productive family business. The Wal-Mart phenomena has sucked life out of small-town America and contributed to our sprawl problem, which eats away at a sense of community while destroying prime agricultural land and leaving older, more historic areas to languish in neglect. It is a vicious and destructive cycle that is finally getting some attention. It is sad to think that the Gas Lite Manor may well be a victim of this new wave of change.

I next turn to two short stories from the *New Yorker* that Judy's mother sent to us in Bay City—"That Was Me" by Michael Chabon from the June 16 issue and "Us or Me" by Ian McEwan from May 19. They are each very haunting in quite different ways. I feel lonely and restless but steel myself to stay put and turn to writing in my journal. My thoughts are jumbled. The walk has been good despite, and in some ways even because of, our troubles. After all, it was intended to be about challenge. I like the small improvisations, such as using an ashtray as a plate. We've been reasonable about making adjustments. It has divorced us from our "real" lives. I admonish myself to be more insightful and introspective about my real life. Instead, I just stare out the window at the wind-blown lake. My bare feet are propped up on the coffee table with silent orders to heal.

Judy, on the other hand, eagerly laces on her boots again this morning. She is prone to stamping on the ground or floor when she gets them on and proclaiming, "I love my boots." Sometimes when people ask if she too is getting blisters, she exclaims, "Oh, no. I have happy feet." I try not to take any of this personally. During the years when I suffered from debilitating back pain, I struggled with how to accept that reality with grace. Being forced to lie on the floor during meetings of the Rules Committee in the chairman's ornate Capitol office is a profound lesson in humility. I am now earnestly hoping, however, for a miraculous foot cure.

Hours later Judy returns with clean clothes. She tries to entertain me with stories of her day. Judy is quite shy about attending many of the events that we are invited to in Washington and has often suffered from almost phobic reactions. But she has a fine time at grocery stores and laundromats. This one is clean and pleasant—an excellent place to write postcards and chat with the other customers. One puzzling feature is a sign in large red letters instructing, "Hunters Please Use This Dryer." She carefully avoids that machine and is glad she did when Barbara Souder explains to us later that hunters often just throw their dirty, sweaty, wet clothes directly into the dryer without washing them. An older man offers her a ride to the post office, but she wants to walk. She enjoys the three miles back to our room and laughs that she was carrying the laundry in a plastic bag in just the ungainly manner that Ruth had envisioned.

Near the end of the afternoon we venture out for a few supplies. In line at the Hub Supermarket, the cashier recognizes Judy from yesterday. She turns to me and announces knowingly, "You're the husband with the bad feet." Some reputation.

In the parking lot our attention is drawn to a line of people waiting to get ice cream cones even in the cold and drizzle. We join the
line and watch in amazement at the size of the scoops. I order one
sugar cone and one cake cone, both with black cherry ice cream.
"Single or double?" asks the young woman. I have often noticed
over the years that certain ice cream dippers are very generous. Perhaps it is the act of making people happy. Surely there are few
things in life that make people more pleased for the moment as an
unexpectedly big cone. Of course, all dippers have themselves probably stood in line as kids hoping for the same generous scoop. The
choice here is easy. "One scoop for each cone, please." By any
stretch of the imagination, these are the biggest scoops either of us
has ever seen. Each is a veritable mountain precariously balanced
on the relatively tiny cone, a full meal of ice cream. They cannot be
making a profit.

Back in our room we check in with our kids. Judy reaches only
Stephen's machine, so we still don't know how his job interview
turned out. Julie too is considering new job opportunities. At
twenty-seven my lovely daughter is exploring life's possibilities.
After high school she went to work full-time at a trade association
answering the phone. She was quickly promoted but eventually
realized that without a college education her advancement was lim-
ited. So at twenty-two years of age she entered Florida Atlantic University and lived in the dorm with eighteen-year-old freshmen, not
an easy thing to do. I admire her determination. With a degree and
a major in sociology, she returned to the Washington, DC, area and
landed a job at an information services company. Although she has
made friends there and has again been quickly promoted, she gets
no personal sense of satisfaction from the work. Julie has always
been a deeply caring person and is especially sensitive to interper-
sonal relations. She yearns to connect those natural traits and interests to her working world.

Two possibilities have emerged for Julie. We discuss the pros
and cons of each situation. As always, her enthusiasm is contagious.
Our conversation is fast paced, far ranging, and punctuated by
laughter. I am confident that she is asking the right questions and
exploring good options. Even if these two particular jobs do not
work out (and they don't), Julie is clearly defining her choices
appropriately. Later, when she goes to work at the Peace Corps, it is
a reflection of her positive attitude and strong values.

Now it's finally bedtime. The long day is over at last. It's as if I have been holding my breath for forty-eight hours. Tomorrow we will try walking again. How far will we get? The question goes unspoken. But, as I try to sleep, I feel the same anxiety as I did the night before our first day.

Total Walked	165 Miles
Walked Today	0 Miles
(Should Have Walked Today	14 Miles)
Walking to Do	142 Miles

Chapter 13

Houghton Lake to Higgins Lake

Saturday, August 23

Jacques Cousteau and *National Geographic* have stamped Higgins Lake one of the most beautiful lakes in the world. Our journey today takes us along the eastern shore of Houghton Lake and then up the southern and western shores of Higgins. The 5:00 A.M. weather is not encouraging. No surprise here. Cold, fifty degrees, overcast, with fog rolling in. The big moment of the early morning is hoisting on our packs again after not carrying them for three days. Even without the actual camping gear, each of our packs is about thirty pounds.

By 7:00 A.M., as we are leaving, Lowell is already working on the beach, raking the sand. The two golden retrievers are bounding about with morning energy. We've developed some affection for these dogs, but now when they see us they react aggressively. Hobbes drops his teddy bear and starts barking as if we might be sneaking off without paying our bill. It is our packs that have alarmed them. Lowell hushes them up, and they take their cues from his disposition towards us. After final thanks and good-bye to Lowell we are on our way.

Judy is elated to be on the road once again—thrilled at how good her pack feels on her back. Her enthusiasm is contagious, and we stride briskly in the cool morning air. Across the road we catch the last glimpse of the Music Box through the foliage of stately old oaks. Even the Michigan Highway litter cleanup sign is upbeat, proclaiming, "This stretch patrolled by Mutt and Jeff." At the intersection in the road we follow Yogi Berra's famous advice, "When you come to the fork in the road—take it." We choose the shoreline road, leaving M-18 to run north without us.

Ahead on the left is a gas station and mini-mart. Experience cautions us to take advantage of such amenities. Inside I engage the cheerful, elderly clerk in conversation. After I tell him that our destination is Mackinaw City, he tells me about his daughter, who lives to run and competes every year in the Crim, one of the most famous ten-milers in the country, held every year in Flint, Michigan. Bobby Crim was once the speaker of the Michigan House of Representatives. I had the pleasure of serving with him from 1973–75. Speaker Crim at one time carried over 250 pounds on his five-foot, seven-inch frame. He then lost over one hundred pounds by watching his diet and running. He turned his personal success into something special for our state by founding a great running event that has attracted some of the best runners in the nation.

The fog begins to lift and burn off, opening views of the east bay behind a charming string of log cabins. There in the midst of this inviting settlement, I notice a small trailer with Monitor Sugar painted on its sides parked in front of a cabin adorned with the name LEACH in wooden block letters. "That must be Dick's place," I exclaim. We had dinner with Dick Leach just a month ago in Montana at their national sugar convention and shared our upcoming adventure with him. It's too early to knock, so I leave a note on his car window, thanking him for a nice evening in Montana. I suspect he'll be tickled to hear from me this way.

We walk the shoulder of our quiet road, following fresh deer and raccoon tracks, which beckon us into the woods across the road. Ahead, as far as we can see, stretch birch and aspen set against cedar, spruce, and white and Norway pines, with occasional stands of oak and black walnut. The whites and grays are luminous among the greens, and the blacks and browns add dimension and texture. The forest is bewitching in the morning silence. All at once Judy speaks, softly but urgently. "David, a bald eagle!" I instinctively look up, but she grabs my shoulder, pointing down across the road to the ditch that runs along the shoulder. There it is, gliding, just dipping ever so slightly, hunting for mice, muskrat, or rabbit. Flying low, snow-white head lowered, its telescopic eyes scan the ground. We watch in awe as our national bird, its white tail growing faint, vanishes into a patch of remaining fog.

I recall for Judy the trip I took to Alaska in 1981 after having worked on the Alaska Lands Wilderness Act. Flying over tracts of cottonwood along the Chilkat River, I witnessed pairs of bald eagles along a ten-mile stretch feeding on salmon. The Chilkat is fed by thermal hot springs in this area and does not freeze in the winter. At their peak in mid-November three to four thousand eagles congregate here to feed on dead or spent salmon. Even the hundreds I saw that summer was a sight I shall never forget. The sheer numbers of this exquisite bird actually made me feel gluttonous—there were too many to behold at once. Better that such magnificence be dispersed and shared in other habitat.

It has only been recently that the bald eagle has made a resurgence from being on the endangered species list. During the 1950s and 1960s the number declined slowly in some parts of the United States but at a catastrophic rate in others. The population of this impressive bird, like much of our natural heritage, was being threatened in Michigan and throughout the country. The causes were many: the loss of nesting trees, shootings despite their being protected by law and heavy fines, human occupation of waterside habitat, the use of pesticides, and the effect of chemicals such as DDT on reproduction, which caused the eggshell to thin. Banning DDT and other chemicals along with a strong enforcement program and a national awareness campaign have made a huge difference in the bird's revival.

"It's 9:30," Judy announces with evident satisfaction. "So?" I ask. Judy remembers a story told to her by Barbara Souder. Barbara has a friend who lives near here on the lake. She makes sure that her two miniature schnauzers are in the cabin at 9:00 A.M. and 4:00 P.M. every day, the times the eagle flies by. The eagle was on time today. I recall on our recent trip to the coastal plain of the Alaska Wildlife Refuge that Fran Bauer, the fish and wildlife biologist, informed us that a mature eagle will weigh up to fourteen pounds and has been known to prey on newborn caribou. So we understand worrying about schnauzers.

Two miles beyond our sighting, we come to the Cut River. The name of this twenty-three-mile long panorama of beautiful waters befits its function of connecting Higgins and Houghton Lakes. Some say it is an artificial outlet blasted by dynamite during the lumbering days of the 1870s. Others, like Bertha Carpenter, whose family was around at that time, believe that was not the case and that the stream was just dredged deeper and the course of the stream changed at certain points. In the heyday of lumbering, logs were piled up along the shore of Higgins Lake in winter or were hauled out on the ice to remain until spring. After the thaw the logs on the banks were rolled into Higgins Lake and sent down the Cut to Houghton Lake and then down the Muskegon River to the city of Muskegon on Lake Michigan, where sawmills prepared them for market. Over the years a series of dams was built on the Cut for various purposes, prompting the inevitable conflict between the riparian rights of the waterside home owners and those engaged in commerce.

We also find ourselves on sacred ground. Indian mounds are located near where we watch the meandering river run its course to Houghton Lake. Native Americans were attracted to this area because of the ease of transportation by water as well as the excellent fishing and hunting. Once the land had been deforested, the lush primary growth became ideal feeding for deer, bear, and other species. Lowell Souder shared with us his own sighting of a black bear just east of where we stand overlooking this historical tract. Bears! Time to move on.

We head four miles north to Sharps Corners and the southern shore of Higgins Lake. The temperature is climbing; the sun emerges to brighten our way. Judy stops ahead to examine the wildflowers. Milkweed. One of her favorites. The plant contains a milky juice, which gives it the name. Growing between two and five feet high, milkweed is most commonly recognized by its graceful, gray pods that split when dry and send its seeds flying on tufts of white fluff. Now, in the flowering stage, we are treated to a profusion of clove-scented clusters of tiny purple trumpets. The sweet fragrance and violet color remind Judy of lilacs, the flower that evokes her childhood in Northfield, Minnesota. I have bought several lilac bushes for her, and we have them in our yard. Now she plucks several of the milkweed clusters to sniff as we walk.

Sharps Corners is a community of cabins on the south shore of Higgins Lake near the southern end of the State Park. The park, one of two on the lake, was created in 1924 and is one of the state's most popular vacation destinations. We find the shore road and eagerly approach the "Queen of Inland Lakes." Of the more than eleven thousand inland lakes in Michigan, this is one of the most stunning. We strain to catch our first sight of the ravishing blue through the great pines.

Bertha Carpenter, writing fifty years ago in the local newspaper, the *Roscommon Herald News,* recalls her mother-in-law's description of her first visit to the lake in 1874, when she was but a child of seven.

> She [Mae Robbins] stood there on the shore and marveled at the beauty and splendor about her. Never had she seen a sight more impressive. Here was a gem of a lake in a magnificent setting of virgin Norway and white pine. All around the lake as far as the eye could see were these tall pines. Not a cottage or a building of any description was there to be seen anywhere.

The lake is ten thousand surface acres, our state's tenth largest. The depth reaches 135 feet, with over half having a depth of 50 feet. Named after Sylvester Higgins, the state topographer in 1939, the lake is spring fed. The crystal clarity of its water is legendary. It has been described as having "water so clear that a dime could be seen at a depth of forty feet." Before the popularization of refrigerators, its winter ice was valuable for drinking water and for use in iceboxes. It once was common to see workers on the frozen lake cutting and spudding blocks of ice for sale.

Standing on the shore, we understand what Mae Robbins might have felt 120 years ago or what Jacques Cousteau recognized on his visit 100 years later. This is a special place. It's not too hard to imagine its virgin beauty. Nature's colors, from darkest purple and shades of blue to green, depending on light and sky, and depths enthrall us. The shimmering surface is a jumble of jewels—amethyst, lapis, turquoise, emerald. A troubled mind or soul can surely be soothed here.

We tear ourselves away from this beautiful sight and begin the second half of our day's walk, up the southwest shore along the beach road. Glacial moraines, which carved the bowl of the lake, also created a hilly terrain here. It is actually a nice change from what has so far mainly been a flat journey. Elevated, we are treated to views of the lake through the wooded and cottage-lined shore. For three miles we walk, up and down but mostly up. At Birch Road we head west, avoiding a protrusion called Detroit Point, in search of the northern neck of the lake. Birch Road becomes a dirt road and then a little-used seasonal road running into the woods. Deer tracks are everywhere. "Good," I whisper, "maybe we'll see more wildlife in here." The ground is a soft sandy loam and feels like the beach. Our footsteps are muted, all the better to surprise the natural inhabitants.

We walk quietly but alertly. Time passes. No sightings. And we're lost. From time to time we have passed what might have been other seasonal roads, but we think we have stayed on the main rutted trail. Still, according to my estimates, we should be to the village of Hillcrest by now. I worry that we have missed our turn or perhaps have gone too far west. Our map has no markings in this area. Just then we emerge into a group of homes. Whew! Ahead we spot a trim, elderly man clearing his property with a weed whacker. I try to get his attention without scaring him. He cuts off the motor and stares at me. "Excuse me," I say apologetically, "I'm sorry to have interrupted you, but we're looking for Hillcrest on the lake." He continues to stare. I briefly tell him our story and that we are from Mount Clemens. He volunteers that he lives in Clinton Township and his name is Zigmond. We figure out that his home is one block from Chris Koch. Zigmond is still staring at me. Finally, he says, slowly: "You're Bonior. You're the one who represents me." Pause. This is always a chancy time. When people recognize elected officials, often they either like you or hate you. But I think I can tell by the way he said "You're the one who represents me" that I actually do. Pointing down the road, he says, "The lake is there, just a little ways." We both thank him. We couldn't quite tell if he really believed us, but already having covered fifteen miles today we look appropriately trail worn.

At the lake's edge once again, we travel a picturesque road with neat cottages set above the road on our left and the water at our feet on the right. The rays of the noon sun are splayed by the branches of the remaining shoreline pines as we walk west. We strain to spot the State Park miles up the shore, but the distance is too far. Closer to us is an island in the center of the lake, Flynn Island.

Lake legend has it that a hermit named Israel Porter Pritchard hid on the island most of his adult life. Reputed to have been a "bounty jumper" during the Civil War, he supposedly accepted money paid by seven separate states for enlisting and then would desert in search of another pay-off. As a deserter he was a fugitive from the U.S. government. Escaping to the island, he remained there for most of his adult life, until he was found dead in a dug-out in 1902. If you don't like that story, you can believe the one about him hiding on the island because he killed his wife.

Our lake road runs for only a half-mile and then turns north one block to the main road. It is 12:30, and we have come nearly sixteen miles. This would have been an adequate distance and a good time to stop for a full day. But we still have seven miles ahead of us. This will just be a lunch break. A small roadside store painted red with an attractive deck and picnic table offers a good stopping place. A sign in the window advertises London Ice Cream, a local dairy in Port Huron, at the northern end of my district. Oddly, the store is closed this Saturday afternoon in August. We see no reason not to take advantage of their picnic table. Just as we are finishing food and drink we had with us, a young woman pulls into the parking area and with keys in hand proceeds to open up the store.

Judy suggests, "Maybe we should buy something . . . like an ice cream cone." After we make our purchases, the young woman joins us on the deck. We ask her about the business.

She tells us, "I've been coming up north to Higgins Lake with my family for many years. My mom and I run the store during the summer season only. It's too cold up here except in the summer. During the winter I go down south."

And where, we ask is down south?

"Port Huron," she says with no sense of irony.

Port Huron is a terrific little city in the beautiful Blue Water Area, but it is usually not considered an escape from winter weather. We learn more about Tara Elliot. She attends St. Clair County Community College, better known as SC4, in Port Huron. Tara lauds the beauty of this area and especially Higgins Lake, calling it the sixth most beautiful lake in the world, echoing all the literature we have read. Of course, we talk about what we're doing. Finally, getting up her nerve, she blurts out, "You look so familiar. Am I supposed to know you?" Hers is a common question. The answer is more complicated. We make a final purchase from Tara of marshmallows to roast in our fire tonight. Then it's time to say goodbye, hoist our packs onto our backs, and head off.

Our muscles are stiff now and slow to warm up. Thank goodness we got such an early start this morning. If it were late in the day already, we would feel mentally fatigued as well. But guess what? I've hardly thought about my feet. Oh, the blisters are still there, but the improvement is significant. I begin to believe the worst is over. The bright sun with rays piercing the tree-canopied lake road makes it seem as if the day is still young. The sight of the lake at the end of each little road or driveway heightens our desire to get to the beach at the park.

A little way up the road we pass a small bed and breakfast. The handsome, carved wood sign reads, "Pop's Legacy." We know there is a loving story behind this affectionate name. Rustic log cabins nestle in a stand of hardwoods. The neat grounds are accented by a roadside flower garden. Baskets of pink petunias hang from the tree trunks. It looks so inviting. Clearly, this too is a family business like the Souder's. Meticulous attention has been lavished on every detail of the property. A lot of heart and soul has been poured into this place—and the love shows.

Four miles up the road we break for a rest at the Lakeview Market, which is the last store before the park. I buy a bottle of wine and a newspaper. Outside Judy chats with a couple about our age from Flushing, Michigan, who has been coming here for thirty-five years. The husband built the cabin with his father, and now they are preparing to retire and live year-round in what has been their vacation getaway. It is a familiar pattern. The lure of the north teases folks over the years, and they yearn for the slower pace and natural beauty. The day can't come soon enough for this couple.

They are fascinated by our story. The woman jokes that the exercise would be good for them; her husband laughingly points out that they have just driven over here to use the pay phone, a distance of about one-quarter mile. On second thought, they'll look for us on TV in the coverage of the bridge walk, from the comfort of their couch. They are very jolly together and should have a happy retirement.

Although my feet are fine, the next three miles to our campsite are difficult for me for a more frightening reason. My upper back muscles are giving me the same trouble I had walking into Bay City. Nothing panics me more than back pain. It can lead to near total paralysis, which would obviously end our journey. In order to ease the strain, I reach back with both hands and lift my backpack while walking. Theoretically, the pack is supposed to rest on the hips, but over a long haul there is burden and stress on the mid-back muscles. I think about taking a muscle relaxer but decide to wait until we get where we're going.

Judy is captivated by the small wooden signs linked together with chains that hang at the entrance of each road down to the lake. Printed or engraved on each sign is the name of a cottage owner. Sometimes there are as many as thirty names. Here are people insisting that they are not just numbers. These are friendly announcements of communities. In each case a dream has come true. The owners have worked hard and saved to buy a vacation or retirement home. Maybe they have even built the cottage with their own hands. These are small properties. The cabins are very modest and built close together. The simplicity is appealing.

At 3:40 we enter the campground at North Higgins Lake State Park. It is Saturday, so we know the camp is full. We are anxious about our reservations as we approach the check-in building. I have my receipt ready, anticipating problems, but we need not have worried. Two pleasant college students start our paperwork and retrieve our bag, which was in the back with a nice note from Kevin Coors. The sight of his name reminds me of how thirsty I am. The young women ask which we prefer, "woodsy" or "grassy." We are momentarily stumped. I decide to go for a nice carpet of grass. Our site turns out to be at the edge of the woods and what grass there ever might have been has been worn to dirt from a full season of use. We do have a fire ring and a picnic table. Around us are the sounds and smells of campers enjoying a last fling with summer before work and school call them back to the routines of life.

Off with my pack. Off with my boots. A little rest before we put up the tent. We swig the last of our warm Diet Squirt from our water bottles and survey our new neighborhood. After we pitch the tent we walk through the woods a few hundred feet, and the lake shimmers before us. We can see how this jewel seduced even such a world traveler as Jacques Cousteau. It is stunningly beautiful. But it took one hundred years to recover from the devastation rendered during the nineteenth century.

It is now late in the afternoon, but there is still much lake and beach activity. Family and business picnics are clustered in and around the shelters. The clank of horseshoes and the *oohs* after a thrown ringer punctuate the dull groan of small craft motors on the lake. The high-pitched shouts and squeals of children create a general mood of gaiety. The beach front is fifteen hundred feet of soft sand.

The late summer sun still warms the air. I've brought my towel. It is so tempting to go for a swim. But I remember my surgeon's admonition: "Do not subject your back to sudden temperature variations." Already in spasms, I wisely resist. The last time I made the opposite decision, in 1992, I ended up with a thirty-day stay at Walter Reed Hospital and my third lower back operation on a herniated disc. So I settle for a nice patch of grass next to the beach, spread my towel, and enjoy young and old frolicking in the shallows, envious of their play.

Occasionally, at moments such as this I do indulge in some regrets about my back problems. No running. Only tedious, repetitive exercise. No team sports. Oh, I play in a couple of charity basketball and baseball games a year but cautiously. No heavy lifting. Only standing by uneasily as others are helpful or handy. No cool shoes. Just sturdy, plain styles. No carefree disregard for my health. No endless summer of golden youth.

Except, in a way, that's precisely what I have right now.

Judy walks over to the nearby concession stand and brings back two double cheeseburgers and two large lemonades, which we devour. Afterward we mosey over to the wood cage and buy a three-dollar bundle, eight pieces, of dry wood. Judy has to lug them back to our campsite and requires three rest stops to make it. She is a willing Sherpa, but I feel wimpy about not carrying my load. I'm sure just one piece of wood now would put my back into severe spasm. I make a mental note to take a pill when I reach the tent.

At our site we gather kindling, which is a rare commodity by the end of the summer. Soon we have a fire blazing, just in time to warm us as the evening air starts to cool. We each find a long stick and start toasting marshmallows while sipping our wine. The fire is three hours of entertainment. Across the road from us is more entertainment. A large gathering of family and friends is celebrating an eight-year-old's birthday. It is easy for us to learn his name from the nearby festivities. Alex revels in the song, cake, and attention. Alex has spent the late afternoon racing about the camp with eight other youngsters, all on bikes and speaking into walkie-talkies. Apparently, they do not actually run into anyone, though there are numerous close calls. Watching this community of campers is more fascinating than any television show, except for the weather, of course.

Through the darkness voices rise and fall. Around each campfire there is a special and enduring bond being exchanged. Televisions, cell phones, pagers, Game Boys, laptops, CD players, and all other technological distractions of daily life now abound in campgrounds. But we come believing, hoping, that there is more.

At 9:30, our wood running low, we decide to call it a day. We crawl carefully into our little tent, seal ourselves in, and assume our mummylike positions pressed closely side by side. Then trouble

Toasting marshmallows at our campsite at Higgins Lake

strikes. The zipper on my sleeping bag gets caught. I'm trapped just like I was as a child. I recall zippers being caught my whole life on jackets, pants, luggage, and now my sleeping bag. It is just as frustrating to me now as it was then. Fixing it requires only patience, of which I have none in this circumstance. After making it worse by pulling and yanking, I turn the whole mess over to Judy. Thirty minutes later my sleeping bag is zipping just as smoothly as can be. Mothers and wives have lots of practice with this zipper thing.

Total Walked	188 Miles
Walked Today	23 Miles
Walking to Do	119 Miles

Chapter 14
Higgins Lake to Grayling

Sunday, August 24

The intermittent splatter of raindrops wakens us. "We can't get a break from the weather. Packing up a wet tent in a wet campsite stinks," grumbles my groggy wife. The campground is still, quiet enough for a church service on this Sunday morning, except everyone seems to be asleep. Nothing is stirring, not even the dogs. Only the chirps of a few birds greet us as we crawl out into the cool, damp morning air. By the time we have returned from the bathrooms, the rain has stopped. We spot smoke and hear the crackle of small fires. A whiff of bacon hangs in the air. Most of our neighbors will be packing for the trip home. As people start to move about, the mood is subdued. Another summer is nearly over.

I build a fire with our two remaining pieces of wood, while Judy breaks down the tent. Working from the inside out, she stuffs the dry items in their own bags and then uses our camp towels to dry the tent, flysheet, and ground cover. The smell of coffee is tantalizing. We must be content with stale cookies and toasted marshmallows washed down with water. Ugh. Huddled near the struggling fire, in hushed tones we sing the praises of Chris and Ruth. Lucky are we that they are our friends. Lucky that they enjoyed rescuing us this past Thursday. Lucky that they are willing to do it again this morning and move our tent up to the state park at Otsego Lake, our next campsite. Lucky that they are vested in our adventure and seem genuinely enthusiastic about helping us. Our walk today is sixteen miles, so a later start works logistically for them and us. With the morning ours, we hike the half-mile to the Civilian Conservation Corps Museum on the site of the old state nursery.

I immediately feel a bond with this place. My years of public service have been devoted to the twin ideals of the integrity of the land and the dignity of all workers. The CCC was established during the Great Depression in 1933 "to save the land and the men." Our two most precious resources are our people and the land we inhabit. Central to a just and livable society is the protection of our natural resources and the protection of the value of work. This place blends those two ideas in a moving tribute to those who preceded us.

Judy and I are what might be called Roosevelt Progressives— that is the descendants of those three twentieth-century giants, Theodore, Franklin Delano, and Eleanor. In my office in Mount Clemens rests a bust of FDR. Likewise, in my personal office in the United States Capitol hangs a poster of a jaunty FDR in profile, in porkpie hat, teeth clenching a long cigarette holder, with a quote that reads, "I see . . . an America where the workers are really free; and through their great unions . . . the dignity and security of the working man and woman are guaranteed by their own strength and fortified by the safeguards of law."

On the first day of the Gingrich Congress, January 4, 1995, Judy taped to her desk just outside the door to my office in the Capitol this simple declaration from Eleanor. "I have spent years of my life in opposition, and I rather like the role." Always in the forefront in the fight for civil rights and dignity for all, Eleanor never shied from her cause because it might be controversial or unpopular.

Earlier there was Theodore, FDR's cousin, who made a career of taking on the special interests. His sensitivity to the relationship between man and the natural environment started a movement at the turn of the twentieth century to save the land from continued destruction. TR sought to halt the exhaustion of timber and mineral resources by private interests. He added millions of acres of land to public ownership.

These Roosevelts pursued their battles for justice with vigor and enthusiasm and are linked to us by another "happy warrior," Hubert Horatio Humphrey, senator from Minnesota and Lyndon Johnson's vice president. Like the Roosevelts, Humphrey was revered in our homes, and in Judy's case actually known. Before entering the political arena, Humphrey taught briefly at Macalester College in St. Paul, Minnesota. His office mate was Samuel Manasseh Struminger (aka Strong), who had immigrated to the United States from Romania (via Canada) in 1928, married Mary Prower Roth Symons in 1940, and in 1944 was about to become the father of Judith Naomi

Strong. Similarly passionate, ebullient, and smart, Hubert and Sam became fast friends. Though her father was raised an Orthodox Jew and her mother is the daughter of an Episcopal Canon, Judy always says she was born a Democrat.

My father to this day has a framed picture of Humphrey on his bedroom dresser. I too grew up a Humphrey Democrat. Like Humphrey, who left academia to become mayor of Minneapolis, my father left his trade as a printer to become the mayor of East Detroit, Michigan, and then chairman of the Macomb County Board of Commissioners. He also was an ardent advocate for the positive role of government in each of our daily lives. Why should he not believe this? After all, it was the government that cared enough during the Great Depression to sponsor jobs through the CCC. It was the federal government that organized the effort to defeat Hitler and Mussolini and Tojo. And, when the war was over, once again it was the government that created the GI Bill that educated a generation of veterans. It was FDR and Congress who established Social Security, which has lifted millions of our elderly out of poverty. And, of course, it was government that set aside land for national and state parks as well as our forests, wildlife refuges, and state and national seashores. National laws allowed workers the right to organize unions and bargain collectively, which led eventually to the largest and most prosperous middle class in recorded history. Hubert Humphrey helped lead the national fight to pass civil rights and equal rights legislation that fairly included African Americans and then women and the disabled and all of us regardless of our faith or heritage or sexual orientation in the promise of our country. Led by Humphrey, the government established Medicare, which further decreased the poverty rate among seniors from 33 to 11 percent.

The sweep of government's positive role within my lifetime on my family and my constituents is clear and undeniable. This is the will of the people as expressed through their elected representatives in the form of their government. It is truly our government "of, by and for" our people. It is not an anonymous evil force or menacing enemy, as some claim. It makes me very sad to hear people talk this way. We are a democracy. Our government is us. I will always be grateful to the vision and boldness of positive leaders such as the Roosevelts and Humphrey, who inspired many to enter public service.

I had the chance to work with Hubert H. Humphrey in Congress before he died of cancer in 1978. With the help of the hunger organization "Bread for the World" I had adopted in the House of Representatives an amendment to an agriculture appropriations bill requiring a hunger impact statement from countries that were receiving our agricultural assistance. Senator Humphrey worked the amendment for me in the House-Senate Conference Committee. He was kind and gracious, helping a fledgling freshman on the first piece of federal legislation I would pass. He did it with such joy that I then knew personally why he had acquired the moniker the "Happy Warrior."

Even Humphrey apparently had his petulant moments. The story goes that one evening Hubert was complaining bitterly to his wife, Muriel, that he was sick and tired of going to fund-raising events. Finally, Muriel said, "Hubert! If you don't want to go, you should think about another line of work." Caught up short, Humphrey went into the bathroom to straighten his tie. Shocked by his scowling image in the mirror, he changed it to a smile and, lecturing himself, said, "Hubert, you are going tonight, and you are going to have a good time."

Now when I would rather be reading a good book, watching a movie, taking a walk, or enjoying a ballgame but must instead attend many of the same kinds of events, I try to remember Hubert Humphrey's lesson. I don't always succeed, but it has made a difference in how I approach my work.

I am often reminding people that their government is there in so many ways to protect them throughout the day. Whether it's the police and fire fighters, the quality of the food in the market, the safety of the planes we fly, or the purity of our drinking water. Our nation works best when the private and public sectors work together, each recognizing and supporting the contributions of the other. Government through its public policy is the expression of our collective will and in the end requires us to share and come together as a community. And it is through community that as a nation we achieve our greatness. We enter the memorial site honoring these values.

This was once the world's largest seedling nursery. In 1903, during TR's presidency, Filibert Roth, the new head of the Forestry Department at the University of Michigan, was made the state forest warden. He had the prodigious task of trying to reclaim the state's rich forest heritage. Roth had his work cut out for him, the state having been plundered by ax and saw. The fires and erosion that followed left a bleak landscape. On an abandoned farm site

Roth and Ed Zettle experimented on four acres to determine which trees would grow on a pine plain. They planted hedges around the plots to keep the rain from washing out the seedlings. They tried blue and white spruce, black spruce, Scotch pine, and red, white, and Jack pines.

Ed Zettle was appointed the first superintendent of the nursery in 1921 and served a total of thirty years there. During his tenure several buildings were erected, including the pinecone barn, where the cones were heated in ovens to remove the seeds. We walk into the restored barn. It's overwhelming to think that the seeds from the cones heated here reforested the entire state. The seeds were planted in plots the size of an ordinary house door. When they sprouted, the seedlings were packed so tightly together that the plots were said to look like "a lot of green rugs laid out in an orderly fashion on the brown earth." At its height the nursery produced as many as twenty million seedlings annually, until it was phased out in the late 1960s, when the land was turned over to be incorporated into the state park.

Fifty yards beyond the cone barn is the museum, housed in a replica of an original CCC barrack. Inside we meander through a series of simple but moving displays, each telling a part of the Civilian Conservation Corps story in Michigan. Established by FDR in the 1930s, out-of-work men aged eighteen to twenty-five and unemployed veterans were eligible to join. The men were paid thirty dollars a month, of which twenty-five dollars was required to be sent home to their families. They were provided with clothing, board, and room, though often the room was a tent, until more permanent barracks were constructed.

The walls are decorated with photos and testimonials of those who served.

> I was a city boy. I came from the east side of Grand Rapids, a Polish neighborhood . . . I was a young man 17 years old and I went into camp to get something to eat. I was pretty hungry. In fact I weighed 102 pounds and the minimum was 107 pounds. So the doctor added five pounds to help me out and get me in.
> —Joe Krzeminski, Camp Hale #2686

From 1933–43 there were ninety thousand young men in Michigan who served the CCC in 125 different camps, including Bloomer

State Park camp, which we skirted on the first day of our walk. The social structure at the camps was developed around both work and play. Each camp organized athletic teams, which competed against one another in swimming, football, baseball, basketball, and boxing. During World War II the camps were used for maneuvers, work-places for conscientious objectors, and, in five instances in the Upper Peninsula, for prisoner-of-war camps.

At this very site the CCC workers, along with the nursery staff, were able to accomplish something quite extraordinary. They established a process that would eventually lead to the planting of more trees in Michigan than in any other state, over 484 million. The state ranked second, New York, had a mere 500,000 trees. In addition CCC workers in Michigan built 504 bridges, 33 airplane strips, 221 buildings, and 7,000 miles of trails, and they stocked 156 million fish in our lakes. Through these good works the glory of the state was restored, recreating an outdoor Eden.

Fighting fires was another job of the corps.

My first forest fire—half of Marquette County was on fire at one time. We didn't get back to camp for days. Driving to the fire, after dropping off my crew, the fire jumped the fire lane and I lost my truck and almost me.

—Albert Cuellette, Polack Lake #688

Outside of the museum barrack sits the state's first iron fire tower, a wobbly structure reaching no higher than thirty feet. This three-legged contraption looks as if it needs someone to steady it lest it tip over.

The CCC and its successors, the Michigan Civilian Conservation Corps and the Michigan Youth Corps, served the state for over five decades. Today the park service has a daily interpretive program that recalls the history of the nursery and life in the CCC camps.

Unfortunately, time does not allow us to tarry any longer at the museum, but we have felt the enormity of what happened here—the struggle to recapture the land and an effort that gave hope and sustenance in a time when there was precious little of either.

At 10:00 A.M. Chris and Ruth meet us. We invite them for a real breakfast at Harold's Silver Dollar Restaurant, a log cabin structure we had noticed on our walk into the park yesterday. The place is packed with families out for Sunday brunch. There is a great buzz of activity, conversation, laughter, children darting about just barely missing the table corners with their heads, the wait staff calling out food orders, dishes crashing, all innocently festive but a startling contrast to the quiet of our walk. The four of us share fantasies about retirement cabins and reminisce about earlier visits we've made to these lakes.

Ruth is not too adventuresome on her own, but she is enjoying these mini-expeditions and her part in our experience. Try as I might, I cannot get her to accept even gas money for the trips she is making. But this is not really surprising. Ruth, like Chris, is the sort of friend you pray to find in life. She has an overflowing heart, rock-solid values, and excellent judgment. Quiet and unassuming, she also possesses a very good sense of humor. Her brother Steve has been part of my office in Mount Clemens since the beginning. Ruth joined us early in 1986 and juggles phones, mail, visitors, and case-work with kindness, patience, and efficiency. Ruth and Diana Wheatley, who has been with us since late 1985, between the two of them, I really believe, know every single person who has ever called our office.

Following one of our few commandments, No Steps Shall Be Retraced, we have Chris and Ruth drop us off on Old 27, where we turned to walk into the park yesterday. This deserted two-lane road cuts through the reseeded pine forest of the Au Sable State Forest. It is almost noon, and even though our walk is shorter today we are feeling guilty about our late start.

The silence is unsettling. Planted mature pines stand in uniform rows like soldiers waiting for morning inspection. The hand of man is too obvious here. Rather than nature's grace, this arboreal formation appears to be the work of a mathematician constructing a geometric equation. All is strictly ordered, the casualty of the demise of the virgin tracts. The undulating gray road ahead of us strikes me as oddly similar to elephant hide in color and texture. Our map shows a grid of trails covering about ten square miles, a hiking, cross-country skiing, and snowmobile haven through a forest of red pine and quaking aspens. Miniature stop signs at the edge of the woods are posted to alert snowmobilers of Old 27, deserted as it may be. Low ferns carpet the pine forest floor.

In the distance we eye a moving speck on the road. My first reaction as always is, "Bear!" but too many false alarms and embarrassing exclamations have tempered my tongue. As we draw nearer to

Our rescuers, Chris Koch and Ruth Gallop

each other, the form becomes a cyclist, our first human sighting in thirty minutes. Obviously happy to see us, he stops and says he's looking for Pere Cheney Road. He is lost. I dig into my pack and haul out my maps, but I'm not able to find any such road. I suggest the park might be a source of information. He heads on. For some reason I feel such disappointment that I couldn't help him out. These fleeting personal encounters are of more consequence in our current circumstances. I can still see him pedaling up to us and within minutes disappearing from our lives.

The cyclist reminds us of our own vulnerability. During the planning stages of our trip a number of people expressed reservations about our safety. Many of these concerns were easy to discount, but there was one significant exception. The Michigan Militia had recently gained notoriety as a result of the Oklahoma City bombing. My staff was particularly worried about the Thumb region, where much of the membership is concentrated. I am an opponent of assault

weapons and a supporter of the Brady Bill, the law requiring a waiting period before a gun sale is made so a check can be run to see if
there is a criminal record or any mental instability.

Also provocative in this region is my emergence over the previous two years as the leading critic of Speaker Newt Gingrich. I ques-
tioned his signing of a $4.5 million book deal with a publisher
whose owner had pending business before Congress. Likewise,
there was the speaker's highly controversial misuse of tax-exempt
organizations (charities) for his own political benefit. Ultimately, the
speaker faced a reprimand by the full House of Representatives and
a $300,000 fine for misleading the ethics committee. Over the two-
year period of 1995–96 the speaker's conduct became a contentious
and bitter battle. As the leader of the opposition, I was vilified by the
Far Right, attacked nearly daily by Rush Limbaugh on radio and television as well as by other right-wing radio talk shows and political
pundits. During this period the House sergeant at arms had been
pressing me to accept security protection due to physical threats I
was receiving. My own mail and phone calls substantiated this hostile atmosphere. At the same time, there was an outpouring of support for me around the country. That mail and the generally positive
reception at events bolstered my spirits. Nevertheless, my profile
has risen and for the first time I am being recognized in airports and
places outside of Michigan and Washington, DC. Now, if people
don't like me, they probably know what I look like. Still, I was not
inclined to worry about this until I had cause to worry.

Cause came. Four nights hence we will be in elk country, where
the stretch from one place to another is longer, and we had problems
finding anywhere to stay. Finally, we were lucky to find a place in
Vanderbilt, where our reservation was initially accepted. When we
called back weeks later to confirm, however, the chilling response
was, "We don't want his kind around here." Certainly, we will avoid
Vanderbilt, but in the meantime we need to get to Grayling.

Several miles farther on our side of the road in a clearing is a
run-down deer hunting lodge. There are old vehicles, tires, auto
parts, and other junk scattered about the property. Not fifty yards
from us is a cluster of four men, perhaps in their thirties. My first
reaction is a generalized sense of trouble. My second thought is
guns—they probably have them; we don't. I try to maintain my composure, but it sure looks to me as if they are trying to hide some-

thing—maybe drugs or guns—and are surprised by our sudden appearance. I can feel Judy tense as she moves closer to me. Eight eyes follow us as we draw even with them along the road. Maybe I'm overreacting. No.

Breaking from the pack, one fella trots out, angling his way to join our walk. Matching us stride for stride, he walks too close to us.

"What're you doin' out here?" he challenges.

"Taking a walk," I answer.

"Where you comin' from?"

"The state park," I answer.

"You always walk this fast?"

"It's good exercise," I say. Only when I'm scared to death, is what I'm thinking.

"Where you goin'?"

"We're meeting friends," I lie. His tone is growing increasingly snide and angry. And now he picks up speed, moves ahead of us, turns, and, walking backwards, looks me straight in the eye.

"Hell!" he snaps, "You sound like a damn politician."

My pulse is racing. Can that comment be just coincidence? He drops back, and we keep moving. I strain with every degree of my peripheral vision to gauge his position. Are the others joining him? Are they all following us?

"Is it time for Chris and Ruth yet?" whispers Judy.

"Nearly so." I say.

"Do you think those guys know who you are?" Judy asks.

"We're only forty-some miles from Vanderbilt," I say.

Ten very long minutes later Chris and Ruth pull up along the shoulder of the road. We are so relieved to see them. They have good news. We are happy to turn our attention elsewhere. The state park rangers at Otsego Lake have accepted our tent and sleeping bags. When we have calmed down, Ruth and Chris head home and we set out again.

Continuing on Old 27, we pass a stretch of rural country homes, a small motel, and then a sign heading up a hill to the Skyline Ski Lodge, elevation fifteen hundred feet. From here the road angles straight north running parallel to I-75. Along the next two miles we notice signs for three of ten locations on an auto tour of Michigan forests. Indeed, the swoosh and roar of traffic on the superhighway is the soundtrack for this touch of tourism.

Site 7: Oak/Pine Forest. Pure oak forests thrived after the white pine was cut and burned. In the shade of those broad oak branches, natural white pine is regenerating in the understory. It will take another hundred years, however, for these trees to match the majesty of their predecessors. Site 8: Red Pine Plantation. Red pine is the most commonly planted tree species in Michigan because it does well in sandy soil. This area was planted in 1914 by the Department of Conservation. Information gathered from research conducted on this stand of red pine was used later by the CCC. Site 9: Jobs from the Forest. The Grayling area is still home to a lumber and forest products industry, as are many other parts of Michigan with estimates claiming 150,000 jobs statewide and over nine billion dollars contributed annually to the economy. Our part of the tour ends as Old 27 merges with I-75.

The only route into Grayling from here is either the divided highway or a vague series of trails. We decide to try our luck at linking together the markings on our atlas. It certainly is possible to get lost here, but we're anxious to escape again from the intrusion of traffic. Interestingly, the trailhead is also the halfway point on the established and fully marked Horse and Hiking Trail that covers 240 miles and stretches from Lake Michigan to Lake Huron. This east-west passage across the state had been one route I considered when we were thinking about our walk.

A mixture of oak, aspen, and birch line the trail with an undergrowth of what look like clusters of raspberry bushes. Grasshoppers accompany us. A half-mile into the woods we emerge into an open corridor that appears to have once been a railroad but is now a powerline. A sign nailed to a pole advertises "Windbreaker 4 miles →" with the arrow pointing toward, we assume, Grayling. The sign is probably intended for snowmobilers, and the Windbreaker is likely to be a restaurant or bar. We follow the trail guided by this lone sign. The soil, sandy loam, has the texture of a Lake Michigan beach. Our boots twist and turn as we plod doggedly up the dunelike slopes. We echo Shakespeare's Richard II when he observes, "These high wild hills and rough uneven ways draw out our miles and make them wearisome." I recall a trip to the Rio de Janeiro beaches where deeply tanned, muscular men, some in their fifties, with calves the size of footballs, carried thirty-pound metal water coolers strapped to their backs, the contents hawked to the thirsty sun worshipers. I now truly appreciate their labor as sweat pours off my brow and the salt burns my eyes.

Finally, we wind down into oak and pine woods again. Then a meadow opens before us where deer are feeding. This is a chance for us to catch our breath and again admire these enchanting creatures. The reddish-brown coat is soon to give way to the gray disguise of winter. Before long they sense us, and their heads rise. We can see the soft white hairs around their gentle eyes and lining their twitching ears. Off they bound.

We seem to have descended into a shallow crater. Perhaps it is a sinkhole or a dry lake that is now overgrown. We keep crossing what may be other paths and have a growing sense of foreboding about where we are or, more to the point, where we are not. Climbing up a winding trail, out of the bowl, we enter what feels like a primeval woods with twisted branches overhead and clean dirt underfoot. It's a little spooky. Abruptly, we emerge again into an open corridor, a ridge line with woods on either side. There is no sign of civilization, not even any traffic noise. I am now genuinely confused, not sure what direction we are headed. The clouds are heavy, so I can't tell where the sun might be.

Again, I quietly curse myself for not bringing a compass. What sort of fool would walk the state without one? We're hauling all this weight on our backs without the single instrument that at this moment would be such a consolation. I try to make some rational calculations. We have been walking at a pretty steady twenty-minute-per-mile pace. Just where might that put us on our map if we are headed in the right direction? As I look down to make this calculation I spy a horseshoe. And at that exact moment a ray of sun bursts through a crack in the otherwise leaden gray sky. Good luck. I can now tell that we are headed north, where Grayling awaits us.

A mile farther along the ridge of the sandy dune we see the sewage disposal facility marked on our map. It is safe to say that this is the first time either of us has ever actually been happy to be in the proximity of such an operation. Such is the joy of confirming our location. Soon thereafter Judy spots another doe with a cute spotted fawn. They watch us but do not bolt. I wonder if the fawn will mature fast enough to survive the coming winter.

Railroad tracks leading into the center of town present us with a chance to try what we have until now avoided. Once we get the rhythm, it is easier than we had imagined. But we definitely must pay attention to avoid stumbling on an elevated or decaying tie. The track looks old and abandoned. The rails are rusty, and spikes are missing. We feel safe. There was a time in this country when walking the live rails was common. Recently, I reread Wallace Stegner's terrific novel *Joe Hill*. Now I can almost hear the legendary Wobbly bard singing as he bummed the rails in the West.

> I took a job on an extra gang,
> Way up in the mountain,
> I paid my fee and the shark shipped me
> And the ties I soon was counting.
>
> The boss he put me driving spikes
> And the sweat was enough to blind me,
> He didn't seem to like my pace,
> So I left the job behind me.

Judy and I enter Grayling in high spirits, singing boisterously and off-key "I've Been Working on the Railroad." Like all smart hoboes, we jump the tracks in town. Returning to reality, we walk the half-mile to Penrod's on the Au Sable River. A few blocks before our destination we pass the Church of the Tabernacle. Three basketball hoops, each netless, stand in the churchyard with the words "Hang onto Jesus, not the hoop" printed on each backboard. I love that sign. As a youngster, I played a lot of basketball. Two things annoyed me—no net or, worse yet, a bent hoop. Part of the joy of a fifteen-foot jumpshot is to see the net dance into itself and to hear the swoosh as the ball whips through. The rhythm of the game is compromised without a flat, netted rim. I think when I retire I'll carry boxes of nylon nets and a stepladder in my car and dress all those forlorn hoops we see across America.

At 4:30 we arrive at Penrod's. Fourteen small log cabins are set along the river on the seven-acre site. The banks of the Au Sable are anchored by large split willow trees that shade the clear, running river. At the southern end of the property is the canoe and kayak livery. There is a large, covered patio and a private island that are used for picnics by visiting groups. We approach the cabin that is marked as the office and are greeted by an attractive, older woman. Barbara Humes helps her son Jim operate the resort. They have been expecting us.

In the late spring, when I made our reservation, I got into a political discussion with Jim. He volunteered that the Republican Party had just solicited him for a big contribution. He seemed taken aback by how brazen the request was, and he wondered if this is standard operating procedure. I confessed that, yes, it is, for unfortunately both parties. This turn in our conversation made me worry that he might have doubts about my expectations. Whether he did or not, I assured him that I was just a regular paying customer. Now Mrs. Humes gives us our cabin number and seems pleased to have hikers our age staying with them. She even offers us the use of their car if we want to go shopping or visit the nearby attractions.

Our cabin is captivating. Built in 1939, the logs are painted a dark brown on the outside and varnished on the inside, creating a rustic but finished authenticity. Rather than closets and drawers, there are hooks and shelves. The tables and chairs are constructed of pine, and a handsome quilt covers our bed. On the lawn, just beyond our screened porch overlooking the river, are a grill and two old-fashioned metal lawn chairs, one painted pastel yellow and the other pastel green. Except for the television, it is easy to imagine another time here.

We are charmed by Penrod's and thrilled that we will have two nights and a full day tomorrow in which to indulge in this atmosphere. I unpack and organize our stuff, while Judy walks into town for food. When she returns we enjoy a cold beer on our bench by the river, dangling our bare feet in the cool stream, feeling the four-mile per hour current rush up over our ankles. We drink a semi-serious toast to my feet, which apparently really are healing. I have done better than I expected the past two days. The sky has cleared, and the late afternoon sun filtered through the willows casts dappled light. Kingfishers swoop among the trees, occasionally diving to the river for fish. After dinner we read on the porch until dark and then head early for our real bed. I am looking forward to a good night's sleep.

As we are about to drift off, a familiar whistle moans in the night. Judy turns over and says, "You said that was an abandoned railroad line." I thought it was.

Total Walked	204 Miles
Walked Today	16 Miles
Walking to Do	103 Miles

Chapter 15
The Au Sable River

We have been looking forward to this day, when we will try canoeing and give our feet a rest. After breakfast we walk over to the livery, where Jim outfits us with cushions, life vests, paddles, and backrests. He also lends me an eyeglass holder, explaining that glasses are the most often lost item on the river. Judy takes the bow, and I climb into the stern of our green, seventeen-foot aluminum canoe. Her job is to watch for submerged logs and low-lying branches and limbs, while mine is to navigate our meandering course. A private put-in channel between the dock and a picnic island allows us to engage the river easily. The island, a thirty-foot by one hundred-foot spit of land is accessed by a low, arched footbridge, which we duck under as we blend easily into the confluence of the gently moving currents.

The Au Sable, like Houghton Lake and Higgins Lake, holds a special place in the imaginations of adventurous boys and girls growing up "downstate." Friends, relatives, neighbors, and scouts are forever talking about their experiences on the Pine, Manistee, Rifle, or Au Sable Rivers. Now, for the first time, I am on one of these almost mythical rivers. It is nationally recognized as such a special place that through the leadership of my colleague and friend, Dale Kildee, we were able to get the Au Sable designated as a wild and scenic river.

Our trip today will take us a modest eight miles. The river will continue another 110 miles, until it empties into Lake Huron. The current runs between three and five miles per hour, a nice leisurely pace. There are no rapids or rocks to worry about, only submerged logs in the shallow water, which averages eighteen inches in depth for the first twenty-five miles.

We stroke rhythmically, almost in slow motion, as we glide by our cabin and the overhanging split willow trees, which form over us like the arches of a great cathedral. The dip of the paddle creates upon its return a sprinkle of water much as a religious blessing anointing this a holy place. The deep serenity I feel harks back to my early religious experience.

As an eleven-year old, I would rise at 5:00 A.M. and trudge the mile to St. Veronica's Church in East Detroit to serve Mass. Like our river ride now, the quiet of the morning seemed to be all ours, my partner then, my guardian angel. Inside the sacristy I donned my cassock and began my ordered rituals. First, I would light the altar candles, then I would fill the crucibles with water and a red wine so dark and pungent that I am reminded of my child's place in this most solemn of religious expressions. With our hands palmed together and fingers pointing to the heavens, the priest and I together enter the altar from the sacristy. The half-dozen elderly parishioners slowly rise out of respect, wanting ever so much to be close to their maker as their own time draws near. High in the choir loft at the rear of the church Mrs. Lenhardt plays the organ and sings in her angelic morning voice, which falls like soft snow over the empty pews.

The priest stands at the foot of the altar and crosses himself, reciting in Latin, "In nomine Patris, et Filii, et Spiritus Sancti. Amen. Introibo ad altare Dei." Kneeling beside the priest, I respond in my newly acquired language, "Ad Deum qui laetificat juventutem meam." The God of my gladness and joy. And so it continues for the whole Mass—the priest praising in Latin and I in turn reciting my scripted lines, likewise in Latin. The climax of the Mass is reached during the transubstantiation, when the bread and wine of the Eucharist are transformed into the body and blood of Christ. So profound is this moment that the altar boy is privileged to ring the altar bells as the celebrant lifts the host and chalice of wine high above his head for all to witness—the miracle of the Mass.

For me this honor of serving Mass with its rituals and responsibilities and new language was a seminal experience. As an altar boy, I participated on Sunday before a thousand members of our church. I assisted at baptisms, weddings, and funerals—witness to the full cycle of life—the joy and grief poignant and rich in the rituals of my faith. From a safe place, windows opened to a bigger world, I learned understanding and built confidence. It was to be both an anchor and a lighthouse for my life.

Relaxed and lost in reverie, I'm startled by Judy's voice rising in alarm. "David!" The stream's current is swinging the canoe toward a low-hanging limb protruding from the bank. Judy just barely slips under the branch, but at my end the branch is too low, and I'm about to be knocked over. Instinctively, I straddle both my legs over the sides into the cold, shallow water and try to brake with my feet, using my hands to fend off the heavy limb. The canoe tips, and we take in some water before I steady it. I've slowed our movement enough so we are able to swing back out to the middle of the river with little damage except to our pride. Daydreams will have to wait for another time. My attention is now fully on the river.

Only the occasional thump of our paddles against the sides of the canoe interrupts our peace. The winding river passes cottages with inviting decks perched high on the banks and tie-ups on the water's edge. A hammock swings lazily between two trees with gnarled roots exposed by rain and wind. A bird that looks like a woodpecker, but isn't, follows us, flitting ahead to the next large tree as we make our way downstream.

We are nearing the east branch of the Au Sable. It is here that one of northern Michigan's legends settled in 1876. David Shoppenagon was the son of a Chippewa Indian tribal chief. He was also reputed to have been at one time a chief of his tribe. Shoppenagon moved to the junction of the Au Sable and its east branch when deer became depleted at Swan Creek near the Saginaw River. He was a great trapper and marksman, whose reputation as a hunting and fishing guide was widely acclaimed. David Shoppenagon was familiar with practically every stream between Saginaw and Mackinaw City. His name appears frequently in the historical records of Higgins and Houghton Lakes. Today his memory lives on in northern Michigan, and his name is honored by Shoppenagon's Inn in Grayling.

About a mile downstream another navigational challenge presents itself. A fly fisherman in hip-high waders is casting in solitude ahead of us when we round a bend. After our earlier mishap, I am fearful we might hit him. That would certainly ruin his day—not to mention ours. Fortunately, we glide by, looking, we hope, as if we might know what we are doing.

"Morning! Catch anything?" I ask.

"Just a sun tan," he teases.

We suspect he will catch his share today. The Au Sable is rated as one of the best trout streams in the Midwest. But its history has not always been so glorious.

The lumbering industry plus overfishing left the grayling trout extinct. Wise conservation measures and the stewardship of the Department of Natural Resources and folks like Trout Unlimited, which was founded in Grayling, have helped the river recover. Regretfully, it was too late for the grayling and almost too late for the rainbow and brook trout. In 1891 the now-flourishing German brown trout was introduced to the river. When the mayfly hatches in late June, the river becomes crowded with fly-fishing enthusiasts.

The shore along the river is home to deer, mink, muskrat, beaver, and duck. Around another bend Judy spots a large blue heron, gracefully stalking along the south bank. We silently slide to within ten feet of this slender creature, and I snap a picture. The click flushes the great bird away; its dusky wings bend slowly and majestically, its head pulls back into its shoulders, and its long, skinny legs flow behind in flight as if they are an afterthought.

Cedar becomes more abundant along the shore. Thriving in damp ground, it is often found with tamarack. Also known as arborvitae, or tree of life, the cedar lives two to three hundred years. This resinous beauty has a heavy, nearly fireproof bark. That unique bark keeps it free of insect pests and fungus, and the damp, spongy ground protects it from forest fires. All the old lumber camps in this area had cedar shingles because the wood resists decay. The cedar grows in soggy, springy ground, in the deep and ancient humus of decay where, as Thoreau said, "The woods are all mossy and moosey." The distinctive aroma of cedar is, for me, the scent of the north.

Near a cluster of cedar and spruce Judy spots a doe with her fawns. At this moment we feel that we truly are in the "Heart of the North," Grayling's motto. The juveniles continue feeding, while the doe nervously eyes our passage.

A month ago on this very stretch of river, the fiftieth annual Au Sable River Canoe Marathon was held. The genesis of the present race was the annual Grayling canoe carnival begun in 1934, when about one hundred canoes made a 50-mile trip on the river. Now the race begins at Ray's Canoe Livery in Grayling and runs 110 miles to Oscoda on Lake Huron. It is the longest and richest marathon of its kind. The fifty thousand dollar purse attracts canoeists from all over the country and Canada on the last full weekend in July to navigate the dark and winding course in two-person teams. Sixty teams competed this year, and the winner, Serge Corbin, crossed the finish line in fourteen and a half hours. The competitors begin at 9:00 P.M. and must fight the darkness as well as the river and exhaustion on this grueling race. It is not uncommon for participants, who usually include some half-dozen women, to be felled by protruding branches. And of course there is always the fear of hypothermia when temperatures drop at night into the upper thirties. Team helpers, called "feeders," are positioned along the river to assist the canoeists. Traditionally, Canadian teams do very well.

Two hours out we pass a canoe camp equipped with tables, water, toilets, and, according to our map, good swimming. Paddling another thirty minutes, we reach Burton's Field, where we are to be picked up by Jim. We overshoot the landing by twenty yards and now find ourselves struggling to keep from floating downstream. We do not have the strength to paddle against the current. The canoe spins 180 degrees, and Judy ends up holding onto a tree trunk to keep us from being swept away. Neither of us has any experience at this, and we panic trying to figure out how to exit. Finally, Judy's weary arms give way. Relying instinctively on what we know, we step out into the shallow running water and just pull the canoe back to our pick-up spot. The uncertainty of what to do causes us to argue, releasing some built-up tension over being on the water. We seem to do better on land.

We drag the canoe ashore and spread out our wet stuff, including hooking our shoes over fencepost stumps, as we had learned from the migrants. Still smarting from the unsatisfactory conclusion of our river trip, we separate to regain our composure and soak in the sun while we wait for our ride. Soon Jim appears with his truck and trailer. We load the canoe, tying it down with cords, then pile into the truck. On the way back we pepper Jim with questions about how the Humes family came to northern Michigan.

There was a Mr. Penrod, who built the cabins in 1939. The livery was added in the early 1960s. After Penrod there were three other owners before Gale and Barbara Humes bought the resort in 1969. Leaving behind a career as a mechanical engineer in the automobile industry, Gale and his wife brought their five children up north from Bloomfield Hills, Michigan. Jim, the youngest child, was twelve when they moved here, and he now runs the resort with his mother. His two sisters and two brothers have moved away from this quiet place. Gale Humes passed away in 1994.

Jim is not easy talking about himself. Nice looking, with brown hair and blue eyes, trim, and five foot, ten inches tall, he is very much at ease, however, with the awkward boats. It has been hard work and lonely, but he is proud of the business. He has four or five full-time employees and adds students during the peak summer season, when the staff grows to thirteen. Like the Souders, the Humes rely on repeat visitors. Seventy percent of their business is folks coming back year after year. Often they are youth groups, scouts, or church organizations. Occasionally, a tradition is forged, such as the group of men from Ohio and Tennessee who have been gathering annually for twenty-five years. Anywhere from twelve to twenty of them make it back each year to renew the bonds of friendship.

Or there is the middle-aged woman from Detroit who told Jim she was "tired of going to Cancun with my girlfriends and complaining about our ex-husbands." She decided to canoe by herself the forty-nine miles to the Mio Dam. Camping was a challenge she had never before undertaken. She was so satisfied with her experience that she returned the next year to try again. She sounds rather like us.

Jim notes with justifiable pride that they are now into the third generation of family members as guests. He is convinced that appealing to families is the best strategy. "We've been through the drugs of the 1970s and the alcohol of the 1980s. Now it's settling down. Family business is much easier," he says. The season ended yesterday, so only three cabins are presently occupied. Jim will now turn his attention to repairs and maintenance.

Before we part he has some information for us. This morning I had asked about the best route to Otsego Lake. Jim said he has a friend who might know. True to his word, he's made the call and has a suggestion. "The Roberts Road turns into a trail north of town and will take you straight north to Blue Gill Lake. You'll go through the western edge of Hartwick Pines State Park. The only drawback is that there are bears in the area and north of Forbush Corner there is an eccentric fellow who might hassle you. Dogs shouldn't be a problem because there are very few homes along this trail." Wow, some decision! We don't like the idea of another remote personal confrontation or the possibility of bears, but the lure of the virgin white pine forest is enticing.

In the parking lot one of the student van drivers reminds us that we can use one of their vehicles if we want to do any shopping. Judy explains that she really wants to walk everywhere if at all possible. At that response his eyes light up, and he says, "I read a great book that I think you would really like, *Walking Across America* by Peter Jenkins." The van guy is obviously a kindred spirit.

Back at our cabin we relax on the riverbank, basking in the afternoon sun, writing, reading, and napping. Judy stakes out the bench by the water, and I opt for the cool green grass beneath a large crack willow tree. These giant trees are prone to splitting. Consequently, they can be dangerous overhanging the river or elsewhere. Jim worries for the safety of his guests and watches closely to keep the trees trimmed.

After a while Judy stirs herself to walk over to Barbara Humes's cabin to see if we have mail, and indeed we do. My artistic sister in New York sends a personally designed postcard. In the center is a stamp of an Alaska Brown Bear. Is this sibling telepathy? She writes the card in a crisscrossing grid so it is visually arresting but difficult to read. She once saw a letter that had been written like this during wartime. She also mentions the movie *Shall We Dance?;* her daughter Eva; Anthony Quinn; the song "Rock around the Clock"; the Journal Writing Exhibit with entries by Thoreau, Hawthorne, Hugo, and Emerson; red Michigan gladiolas; and *Alice in Wonderland.* Nancy's mind is a wondrous thing.

There is a letter from Judy's mother that includes more clippings from the *New Yorker.* She also mentions that her older brother Gil, Judy's uncle, loved to hunt and fish in Grayling. A postcard from the Michigan staff pictures thousands of people on the banks of the Clinton River in downtown Mount Clemens listening to one of our summer concerts. Our condo is visible in the background. The note reads, "Had a few people over to the condo while you were gone. We cleaned up after we left. Chris has the key back." Just a little joke. And finally there is a care package from the same staff including packets of foot soak, Band-Aids, Tylenol, a comb, Handi-Wipes, hard candy, and a bag of dried fruit. We are bemused and touched.

Late in the afternoon we stroll into town. The early history of Grayling is somewhat clouded. Some folks say it was first called Au Sable; others mention the name Forest. But, when the Jackson, Lansing, and Saginaw Railroad (JLS RR) "laid a grade and iron" through town, they tagged it Crawford Station. Crawford was the name that the state geologist Douglass Houghton attached to all of northern Michigan and portions of Wisconsin, then part of the Michigan Territory. By 1873–74 the locals felt Crawford was too common a name, so they voted to change it to Grayling in honor of the local species of trout that was then so abundant in the river. The 1875–76 gazetteer contains the following entry: "This is a new town having been settled in 1873. It is situated on the Au Sable River which affords good water power. It is surrounded with pine woods and it ships venison, furs, whortleberries, and grayling fish."

By the early 1880s the grayling became overfished and overrun by logging. The species dwindled in number and soon disappeared. A character in early Grayling and Michigan sportsmen history, Reuben S. Babbitt (1859–1932), led the effort to plant brook trout in the river to replace the grayling. Rube, as he was known, is also credited with designing the Au Sable riverboat, a twenty-two-foot long, narrow craft seldom exceeding twenty-four inches in width and tapered at both ends. They were operated with a pole, or punt stick. These boats are still on the stream today, part of the legend of the river. The idea is to run the boat with one hand poling while fishing with the other. Rube Babbitt, beloved by outdoors people throughout the state, went on to become a guide, historian, and the first conservation officer in northern Michigan.

The first sawmill was located here in 1876, beginning a familiar pattern. The Grayling Mills expanded and soon became the largest employer in the area. In 1903 Grayling was incorporated as a village, and by 1920 the population had swelled to over four thousand, with the mills dominating the area both economically and physically. Then, as quickly as the logging grew, it was over. The last great mill closed in 1927, marking the end of the lumbering era.

Now there was no choice but to restore the scarred land and damaged rivers. Eventually, those efforts led to the development of a tourist industry. Today this quaint town has a population of about two thousand. Ironically, it is the hundreds of miles of logging and CCC trails in and around Crawford County that make this a paradise for outdoor enthusiasts. Snowmobiling and cross-country skiing are popular winter sports on the maze of trails. Hunting and fall color tours also attract tourists as well as the excellent fishing and boating on the rejuvenated river. Now the life of the lumbering era exists only in the village historical museum located in the restored railroad depot.

One other vestige of the early days remains. In 1913 village pioneer Rasmus Hanson gave a gift of land on Lake Margrette to the Michigan National Guard. Camp Grayling was developed into one of the finest and largest National Guard training facilities in the nation. Its 147,000 acres are also used for hunting, fishing, snowmobiling, and other recreational purposes. Today it is one of the area's largest employers, with over two hundred full-time jobs. Caravans of camouflaged vehicles winding their way to and from the maneuver sites are a common sight on I-75 and other roads in Crawford County.

These military exercises have aroused deep suspicions among people inclined to conspiracy theories. I have been asked in public meetings about secret camps of Russian forces in Michigan preparing to overrun us. My office also from time to time receives calls and letters reporting on "black helicopters" preparing to attack. The level of alienation rises and falls depending on the economy and other circumstances, but, as we know, these fears are no joke. People who feel threatened can be dangerous to themselves and others.

After windowshopping both sides of the main street, we walk the few blocks back to our cabin. Preparing the grill for our hot dog barbecue, I am surprised to note on the bag that Henry Ford invented charcoal for commercial use. I guess combustion was his thing. How have I missed that Michigan fact all my life?

No escaping Michigan mosquitoes, though. As darkness falls, they force us to seek refuge on our screened porch, where we read in the dim light. The quiet sounds of night barely pierce the darkness. And then there it is again—the mournful notes of that train. Our eyes lock for just a moment.

Total Walked	204 Miles
Walked Today	0 Miles
Walking to Do	103 Miles

Chapter 16

Grayling to Otsego Lake

Tuesday, August 26

> *The rule is, jam to-morrow and jam yesterday—but never jam today.*
>
> —Lewis Carroll

The raspberry bushes along the trail leading into Grayling teased my tastebuds. As a treat, Judy bought a small jar of raspberry jam when she shopped that day. Now I spread thick portions of seedless raspberry jam on my morning toast. Today will be our longest walk, and any extra energy will be helpful as we also hike the most hilly day of our journey. Our trek will eventually take us to an elevation of thirteen hundred feet before we end the day at Otsego Lake.

The Weather Channel confirms what we already see, thick fog, and a temperature of fifty degrees. We complete our packing, even stuffing the leftover cooked hot dogs wrapped in their wrinkled buns into our packs. At 7:00 A.M. we walk out into the cool, soupy air. Last night we considered the three choices for our route today. We can follow the uninteresting Grayling Highway up to the village of Frederic. Or explore the winding Au Sable River trail, an old Indian route, to the same destination. Or take the Roberts Road, which turns into a trail just outside of town, north thirteen miles to our lunch stop at Blue Gill Lake. The Au Sable trail may have been more of an adventure, but we choose the third option because it skirts the heart of the Virgin White Pine Tract in the Hartwick Pines State Park. The path in the old-growth forest has been described as "one of the most memorable short walks in the state."

We will miss our homey cabin. I am drawn to the notion of building a simple cabin in quiet woods on the edge of water. This place captured my heart. Perhaps that was inevitable. A year and a half later I will finally learn the meaning of my family name. Bonior is neither shortened, Americanized Polish, nor a French mutation, as many have surmised, but rather a true Polish name. As a location, it means deep pool in a mountain stream. As a characteristic, it means reticent.

After casting a fond last glance back at Penrod's, we walk up Michigan Avenue into the rain. Under a large tree across the street from Mercy Hospital we put on our slickers. At the edge of the city we pass the Grayling Fish Hatchery, which was opened in 1916 in an unsuccessful attempt to save the nearly extinct grayling trout. Today it is stocked with brown, rainbow, and brook trout.

On Roberts Road we pass portions of houses visible through the fog that shrouds the neighborhood. The road quickly degrades from asphalt to gravel to dirt and eventually to two rutted trails. The rain stops, and we pause to remove our slickers. It feels good to shed our nylon uniforms and feel the invigorating morning air. We move on at a better pace. Bushes, ferns, blackberry vines, and tree branches occasionally reach out into our way, but for the most part the trail runs straight and flat. A large raptor flies overhead. Our footpath is stamped with deer prints. At the five-mile point we enter Hartwick Pines State Park.

The park is a magnificent effort at recapturing the last glory of these once virgin tracts while preserving several tracts of old-growth forest. The largest state park in the Lower Peninsula, it encompasses a rectangle five miles long and three miles wide, ten thousand acres in all. Ancient glacial deposits formed the hills overlooking the valley of the east branch of the Au Sable River, one of the premier trout streams in the Midwest. Within the boundaries are four small lakes, numerous trails, a handsome visitor center, and a logging museum located along the old-growth foot trail.

The park's reputation rests principally on the unique timber lands, which include old-growth virgin pine, old-growth eastern hemlock, and old-growth jack pine. The original eighty-two hundred acres were donated to the people of Michigan in 1929 by Karen Hartwick, who purchased it from the Salling-Hanson Lumber Company for fifty thousand dollars as a memorial to her husband, Major Edward Hartwick, a forestry engineer who died of spinal meningitis in France in 1918. In November 1946, on Armistice Day, a fierce windstorm struck the park and destroyed nearly half of the old-growth pine. Today only forty-nine of the original eighty-five acres of old growth remain.

Designated nature trails lead to Bright and Glory Lakes less than a mile to our east, in the southeast corner of the park. These "kettle" lakes were formed as the Wisconsin Glacier retreated northward across Michigan more than ten thousand years ago, depositing large blocks of ice in the outwash material left behind. Today these two remnants of the Ice Age are designated as trout lakes. In early spring they are stocked with five hundred rainbow trout, which swim among the bass, perch, sunfish, and bluegill. Patches of northern white cedar surround the lakes. The cedar in turn provides the whitetail deer with an important supply of winter browse. Winding around the lakes, the nature trails are lined by a host of edible plants, ranging from the bracken fern and their fiddleheads to sweet-fern leaves, perfect for steeping into a soothing tea, to a summer abundance of blueberries and wild strawberries. The local DNR brochure advises to "be careful not to bump into a bear" on these berry-laden trails. It goes on to say that, if you do, "prepare to share." Wise counsel.

Beyond the trails is the Michigan Forest Visitor Center, the gateway to the virgin pines. The center is actually a fantastic treehouse artfully designed to appear to be suspended among the tall trunks. The approach through the trees is along wide, gently inclining boardwalks that rise to meet a huge deck encircling the center. We are here too early to enter, but we read that inside is a fifteen hundred square foot exhibit hall with hands-on exhibits, dioramas, and a talking, living tree that reportedly delights children of all ages. The center also houses a classroom, bookstore, and auditorium, all of which are intended to set the scene and provide information that will enhance the experience of walking the old-growth trails and visiting the lumbering museum.

Standing on the deck at the rear of the building, we are overwhelmed by the mystical view of the dark primeval forest. We crane our necks, and our eyes behold the long, straight, bare trunks. My mouth is agape, and my ears are tuned to the whispers of the winds as they brush through the ancient canopy, 150 feet above the needle-carpeted ground.

This place reminds us of Muir Woods National Monument just

outside of San Francisco, in Marin County. Named for the great American naturalist John Muir, the 553 acres preserve a grove of virgin redwood trees. Our visits to the San Francisco Bay area usually include a trip to Muir Woods, often with our friends Harley Shaiken and Beatriz Manz, professors at the University of California at Berkeley. Like Muir Woods, Hartwick Pines confronts us with a sobering sense of perspective. We feel profoundly respectful. Our hurried, self-important lives are a mere blip in nature's time line. Yet even our very brief stewardship of these magnificent natural monuments has all too often bitterly betrayed our responsibility. We are grateful to those who had the wisdom to preserve these special places for us. We walk reverently into the midst of the woodland giants. This is indeed a place to renew the soul.

The old-growth trail is a short mile and a quarter walk with twenty-two stations along the way describing the natural evolution of this unique tract. Our walk is like a visit to the Detroit Institute of Art. We move solemnly from one site to the next. A brochure explains our first station, a Beech Maple Climax Forest. We take turns reading the text aloud but find ourselves speaking not much above a whisper. We read about the process of forest regeneration. Beech and maple sprout after logging, fire, wind throws, or glaciation. Here this process occurred after logging and then fire about one hundred years ago. The slow-growing and thin-skinned American beech grows in the shadow of the neighboring virgin pines. The sugar maple also finds a home. After a time there is a relatively stable natural adjustment to a new environment. Regretfully, as a result of industrialization, the sugar maple today is undergoing a long decline. This autumn beauty contains the largest concentration of sugar in its sap of any tree. Interestingly, maple sugar syrup is North America's oldest agricultural crop. Now a combination of factors—including air pollution, acid rain, and changing climate—bode ill for the sugar maple, and for us.

A few steps farther up the path, and we are transported into the presettlement primeval Michigan forest. The virgin white pines ahead reach 150 feet skyward, with 80 feet of trunk standing straight, thick, and free of branches. Where the branches do begin, the tree is pagoda-like in outline, its limbs growing in tiers as if forming successive platforms of a tower. The giant white pine is often found with its mate, the red pine, red for its colorful bark of armorlike plates. At the present site of Dartmouth College in New

Hampshire, a 240-foot white pine specimen was once measured, rivaling the Douglas fir and redwoods of the West.

Before us a dying white pine is honored with a station stop. Time and the elements are slowly ravaging this great tree, which has until now somehow been spared man's assault. Appropriately named the Monarch, this 300-year-old giant did rule the forest at 155 feet tall prior to a windstorm in 1992 that took 30 feet off its top. Large wounds in the aged tree now provide an avenue for insect and fungal invasions. This venerable natural wonder seems to be struggling to maintain its dignity. We feel uncomfortable staring. It is sad to see any great beauty fade. Born in the 1690s, before the birth of our nation, this tree conquered the centuries, but the end is not merciful.

The story of the white pine in the American Revolution is an interesting sidebar often overlooked by historians. The particular combination of the great strength and light weight of its wood made the white pine one of the most prized resources of the colonies. Its strategic and military value to England and its enemies alike could be seen in the straight trunks of prodigious length used for masts on their seagoing vessels. The Royal Navy saw this resource as critical to its defense of England. Our colonists believed that these lands and their resources belonged to them and most certainly not to the mother country. And, of course, Native Americans had the most legitimate claim to what was naturally and historically theirs, though they were the least successful in defending their due.

To assert the right of England to the trees, King George III went so far as to appoint a surveyor general of His Majesty's Woods in America and sent him off with the authority to mark with a blaze every great pine. This naturally infuriated the pioneers as the Stamp Act and Townsend Act had enraged the merchants and as the tax on tea had angered the city dwellers. When the Revolution broke, the Americans foresaw that their very own white pine might well come back as a mast on an enemy ship bringing armed men.

In the earliest days of our nation's history the pine tree was a popular design on banners. A white flag with a green pine tree and the inscription "An Appeal to Heaven" was the familiar ensign of ships commissioned by General Washington. Later a coiled serpent at the foot of the tree was added with the slogan "Don't Tread on Me." After my first election to Congress, Judge Tom Bullard and his wife, Jane, friends and supporters presented me with this flag in honor of the seventy thousand white pine seedlings we had distributed door to door throughout the district. At the time I saw only the symbolism of the tree. But perhaps the Bullards were also prescient in foreseeing the battles ahead in my congressional life.

In the three hundred years of its exploitation the white pine more than any other tree was the basic building material of our nation. Although public awareness came too late to save the virgin white pine, the conservation ethic made itself felt just in time to preserve some of the great forests of the western states and to support Theodore Roosevelt in his battle for timber conservation.

Today in Congress, a century after TR, the battle continues. The fight is waged to save the old growth in the Pacific Northwest and Alaska. The threat of clear-cut and road logging is always before us. Whether it's saving the Tongas National Forest in Alaska or the Headwater tract of virgin redwood in northern California, the debate is passionate. Through the leadership of Congressman George Miller of California, in the tradition of other fine environmentalists in Congress such as Morris and Stewart Udall and John Seiberling, we aim to protect our national antiquity.

Our trail ends at the logging museum, which was built at the request of Karen Hartwick when she donated the land. This camp was built by the CCC in 1934–35 as a museum to preserve the history of an era that had only recently ended. Typically, those logging camps would contain six or seven buildings, housing sixty to one hundred men. The bunkhouse, mess hall, and office would each have been contained in separate buildings. Much of the property within this park was heavily logged during the 1880s and 1890s. The red and white pines now growing were planted by the CCC in the 1930s as part of its massive reforestation effort. This forest is described as second growth.

Other trails in the park are used for cross-country skiing and mountain biking. Some, such as Deer Run and Aspen, describe what they behold. We exit the heart of the park via the aptly named Weary Legs Trail. At an elevated clearing we stop to catch our breath and ponder the experience of visiting this place. Sadly, when we lost the virgin tracts of white pine, we lost more than the trees. Gone with the trees were the woodland caribou, fisher, pine marten, gray wolf, and the grayling. Although some of these still exist in places other than Michigan, each year species are permanently lost because their habitat has been destroyed. It is difficult to determine the extinction rate accurately, though it is generally agreed that the vast majority

On the Roberts Road Trail

of species that have ever lived on earth are now extinct. Species of plants, animals, and insects that potentially could improve the quality of life for future generations become extinct sometimes before we even are aware of them.

Linked once again with the Roberts Road Trail, we turn our attention to what lies ahead. In all likelihood we will have to climb over fences in order to cross the interstate highway. Our map also indicates another fence eight miles farther north. But before we reach I-75 we are confounded by a fork in the trail that our map omits. Puzzled, we decide to stay west, to our left, selecting the better of the two rutted possibilities. Soon we become aware of the sounds of the interstate to our right, the east. Also we now note that every two hundred yards or so there is a yellow pole about waist high marked "Michigan Consolidated Gas" in mid-trail. We are walking a utility pipeline. We have taken the wrong fork in the trail.

The pipeline follows the true lay of the land. We are now walking steep inclines and declines largely on beach sand through pine forests. This rollercoaster effect challenges our legs and lungs. Judy asks in breathless bewilderment, "Where on earth did all this sand come from?" We surmise that we are walking on an old lake bottom or perhaps through part of the glaciation process we read about in the park. Nevertheless, it's unexpected and disorienting. In the woods, midway between Lakes Michigan and Huron, we are traversing dunes.

Suddenly there is a clearing on our right that leads us to a rest stop along I-75. Approaching as we are on foot through the bushes at the back, we feel a bit like unauthorized interlopers at this creation of the automobile culture. But it serves the same purpose. Lucky for us, it appears just in time for a civilized bathroom break. The glass-encased map of the local area confirms what we have recently figured out. We did leave our designated trail. I buy two cups of coffee from the vending machine, and we sip our unexpected treat while taking stock of our uncertain situation. We indeed may have stumbled upon a fortuitous trail—fortuitous, however, only if it runs north all the way to Blue Gill Lake and does not abruptly end in another climax forest. Feeling lucky, we decide to take the chance and proceed north on our unmarked trail. Besides, avoiding all the fence crossing is appealing and worth the risk of the unknown and the possible need to retrace our steps.

Our trail takes us through woods of aspen and pine and then a variety of hardwoods. A mature beech forest abruptly envelops us, heightening our sense of mysterious adventure. The thin-skinned, gray-barked trees create a deep, dark, sinister atmosphere. In our present state of uncertainty we are overcome by foreboding that something threatening might emerge from these woods.

Then, shockingly, we spot real bear tracks and soon after fresh bear scat. Tension mounts. I am oddly comforted by the distant sounds of the interstate on my right. We are both very alert, which in itself is an exhausting state. Following all the advice we have read on how to scare away bears, we talk incessantly. It is inane chatter, intended just to fill the air with our voices. I have my fingers tightly wrapped around my pepper spray in case we come upon a berry-hungry bear. Up and down we march, our boots twisting with each step we take in the shifting sand. Where is this trail headed? Will it veer west? Will it suddenly just end? Our imaginations are spinning

wild, highly improbable scenarios, but we can't seem to stop ourselves from ratcheting up the suspense.

Over the crest of a dune we spot what looks like a blue utility
truck about a quarter-mile ahead of us. Judy is concerned that we
might get in trouble for being on private property. I am hopeful that
they might be able to allay our worries about bears and give us some
clues about our route. We try to pick up our pace to catch up with
the truck but cannot make any time on this terrain. When we finally
reach County Road 612 there is not a vehicle in sight in any direction. Maybe that truck was merely a mirage in the sea of sand.

We find ourselves at the Michigan Consolidated Gas Frederic
Transfer Station. Around it they have actually planted grass, so we
take advantage of this spot. I take off my boots to fix the Band-Aids
that all shifted during the twisting walk through the sand and cover
a new set of blisters with moleskin. No traffic passes on the road
behind us. To our west a mile and a half is the town of Frederic,
which was founded on the rail line in 1874, about the same time as
Grayling. Once a lumber center, it only exists today as a small village outpost amid pine forests on the middle branch of the Au Sable
River. The town now serves the trout fishermen who frequent the
river. Before we proceed north, I take a picture of Judy in front of
the MichCon Gas sign to send to our friend Rense Hoksma, who represents the company in Washington, DC.

Our trail continues for a short distance through sandy hills
before yielding to a flatter and firmer terrain. We are four miles from
Blue Gill Lake and lunch, an interval punctuated by a changing forest. From pine we blend into beech and maple, the maple already
beginning to turn colors. Before we have time to decide if we have
entered a climax forest, similar to that which we experienced in the
park, we are presented with a large stand of gently quaking aspen.
We enjoy the variety but are confused by the changes and wonder if
we are reading the woods correctly.

For the first time in many miles we come upon a house on our
right that would appear to be abandoned were it not for a red-and-
white checkered tablecloth on a picnic table. On our left, tucked
into the woods, an unfamiliar subculture is slowly revealed to us.
Small trailers and cabins dot the woods. It dawns on us that we are
walking through an area of hunting lots. It is not hunting season,
and there is no sign of another living soul. Our pace quickens along
the trail, which is now wider and graded to accommodate this com-

munity of hunters. The walk is easier, and our legs welcome the flat, solid earth.

At the intersection of a gravel road with our dirt road, we pause to get our bearings. Since the trail we are walking is not on our map, we are still fearful that it will abruptly end, leaving us nowhere. Interrupting the silence is the unmistakable grind of a colossal engine. Over the crest of a hill, bearing down on us, chugs a massive front-loading road grader. With my hands I signal to the operator that we need assistance. He slows his giant machine as I approach. Looking up into the cab, I immediately have second thoughts about this strategy.

The greeting on the fellow's cap reads, "Make My Day You Son of a Bitch." This was not what I had in mind. But my fears are unfounded. To the contrary, before I can even speak, he yells down, "Can I help you?"

I shout back, "How do we get to Blue Gill Lake? Will this trail get us there?"

Nodding yes and still yelling over the rumble of the engine, he advises, "Just stay on the trail another two miles. It ends at a road that takes you to the lake. Don't pay any attention to the fence at the end. Just walk around it." I tip my Habitat for Humanity hat in appreciation. He smiles and waves, leaving us in a cloud of dust.

Our confidence regained, we walk toward our lunch destination. Along the way we pass many more hunting sites that actually seem to be part of a planned hunting township plat. Lucky for us, we were forewarned about the fence. It's high and imposing and prominently posted with a sign declaring "Private Property." But bearing in mind our instructions and taking courage from the motto on the hat, we find a way around the gate, dash across the property of what appears to be a lodge, and happily find ourselves on the road to Blue Gill Lake.

The little lake is nearly a perfect oval. Cottages border half the shore. An opening in the bushes beckons us toward the lake, where we drop our packs and sink to the matted grass by the water's edge. Oh, it is heavenly to rest. But we are also hungry. The leftover hot dogs and crumbled potato chips are delicious washed down with tepid water. Judy stretches out with her head pillowed on her backpack and savors the sweet juice of a plum for dessert. She looks great, her long tanned legs crossed at the ankles. By birthright Judy is half-Bessarabian, a people noted for their long and graceful limbs.

Coupling long arms and hands with a Mediterranean temperament lends itself to considerable expressiveness but also plenty of spilled drinks. Judy is irrepressible in debate. Her face radiates her joy or pain or fury. Her smile is open and full and as free as her gesticulating arms and hands. But now we are both at rest.

After lunch we walk up the gravel road past several other small lakes, Horseshoe Lake, Lake Marjory, Big Bradford Lake, and finally Little Bradford Lake in the village of Waters. As we trudge up Old 27 into Waters, on our left is the railroad line, and a snowmobile trail follows the same course between the railroad bed and the road. Over the last century the conveyances for travel up here have evolved from rail to auto to snowmobile. It's not the information superhighway but the industrial/recreational highway. For each of these modes of locomotion we pass signs of various shapes and sizes and codes announcing proper speed limits, stop and go warnings, and directional signals. It is all a jumble of instructions trying to bring some order to an increasingly crowded and quickened world. Nothing seems to be speaking to us.

Not surprisingly, as we walk into Waters, it starts to rain. I am not making this up. We do our best to jog, with our heavy packs bouncing up and down, and duck under the overhang of an old general store just as the hard rain starts to fall. Waters, formerly known as the village of Bradford Lake, was once another busy sawmill town. With the passing of the timber harvest, the mill shut down. The town's most renowned citizen was a character by the name of Henry Stephens, Waters's last wealthy lumberman. His unusual legacy is a "bottle fence." This fence made of beer, wine, and whiskey bottles, of which Henry contributed his share plus some, was originally four feet high and two hundred feet long. Portions of it exist today as a remnant of a hard-working, hard-drinking past.

Thirsty ourselves, we purchase water in the store and chat with the animated sales clerk while we wait for the rain to let up. She recounts for us how the fence made it into *Ripley's Believe It or Not* and how it also, believe it or not, made it into the National Historic Register. I try telling the clerk about our walk and query her about who buys all the lottery tickets. But my topics are anticlimactic after her astounding revelations about the fence. We adjourn to a bench on the porch. My gaze drifts down my outstretched legs to my boots. Slowly, I recognize a condition so ordinary that it almost passes unnoticed. "My feet are not killing me." We watch the rain. The peaceful rhythm of the falling drops and the fresh scent of the washed air lull us into a pleasant trance. How easy it would be to just stay right here for the night—it has already been a long walk today. But we dutifully rouse ourselves, don our slickers and rain pants, and hope the rain will seem as kindly while we are walking through it for the four-mile finale up Old 27 to the campground.

Otsego Lake is five miles long and a mile across at its greatest width. The melting of ancient buried ice blocks formed the depression in which the lake now rests. Residual moraines bound both sides of the lake for most of its five miles. As we slog the last mile, I recall for Judy what few details I can of my visit here as a boy of twelve. Still vivid is my memory of swimming in the crystal-clear water. Perhaps I can visualize the long, narrow course of the lake. Forgotten is the contour of the land created centuries ago by the glacial passage. Even in the rain I am happy to return to this place some forty years later.

Inside the park we are greeted warmly by the park personnel. They have been expecting us. We are their only walkers this year. The park is nearly empty, with only 24 of 220 sites occupied. Unfortunately, their one and only cabin, which I have been secretly hoping might be available, is not. The park rangers offer us a lift on one of their golf carts to our site, and we eagerly accept the luxury. Retrieving our tent bag left by Chris and Ruth three days ago, we load it on the cart along with a few groceries we bought before we entered the park and zip down to our site. After twenty-six miles of walking, the speedy cart feels wildly out of control. It is a relief to have the ride, but, curiously, it is also a relief to get back on our own feet.

Our campsite is gorgeous. There are occasional tall pines to provide some cover from the rain as well as a soft floor of needles. Through the trees we can see seventy-five feet to the lake. The sites on both sides of us are occupied. It seems a little crazy to be squeezed together when there are sixty-two acres available and so few people here. On our left is a large modern camper, but no one seems to be home. On our right is a pop-up camper, obviously owned by an experienced outdoors person. As we take stock of our surroundings and appraise our neighbors, we realize we too are being watched. Tethered to a stake near the pop-up is a regal animal with X-ray eyes. We are locked in his stare. He is still and silent but very alert. Wow! For a moment we wonder if it is a wolf but then

One of six Michigan state forests

realize it is more likely a dog. After slowly exhaling, we begin war-
ily to pitch our tent. The good news is that the rain has stopped.

We work quietly together. I have my back to the camper. Judy is
bent over the tent. Then she straightens and with a look of total dis-
belief says urgently, "David, look behind you." Bounding out of the
camper are three full-sized collies! What is going on here? Dogs are
everywhere. And any one of these dogs could crush our little tent

with one leap. We don't even want to think about what they could do to us.

The message is coming through very clearly to me. Dogs are definitely a significant subplot of our walk. And we need an attitude readjustment. This is obviously the perfect opportunity for us to mellow out over the dog issue. Time to try again. "Think positively," I suggest helpfully to Judy. I can't quite make out what she mutters in response.

I am saved by the sun. The sky is clearing, and the late afternoon sun backlights the trees on the western shore. In another time Chippewa and Ottawa Indians would come to gather food on these shores among the tall pines before the railroads and loggers forever changed this place in the 1870s. We drag a bench from our campsite down to the water's edge in anticipation of a great sunset. We are not disappointed. The water laps gently near our feet. We can almost imagine that we are those early Indians savoring this moment of serenity in harmony with the natural world. Enchanted, we watch as the great golden globe dips below the treetops, which form a lacy skyline across the darkening water. Behind us, an interesting evening awaits. We prepare to meet the dogs.

Back at our campsite we build a fire and get to know our new neighbors. The pop-up guy offers us some paper for our fire. His remarkable dog is a Siberian husky named Jake. At night Jake's eyes are two round white lights in the dark. Jake and his master are from the Upper Peninsula. Years ago the pop-up guy was a newspaperman "down below." In his mid- to late fifties, quiet and thoughtful, he seems content with his spare lifestyle and happy with Jake as his only companion.

Just as we are falling under the spell of the leaping flames of our healthy fire, the campground "host" appears and introduces himself. The subculture of campground hosts is an interesting study in the evolutionary structure of informal communities. Originally a casual, voluntary phenomenon, it has become a competitive, paid position. The host typically meets and greets new campers, offers some assistance, organizes programs, and is generally a permanent, friendly presence in a transient setting. This host, however, is a provocateur. Somehow he knows I'm a congressman, and he is aching to challenge me. "So, we're not too good at building a fire, are we, sir?" he says mockingly, as the smoke blows directly into my face, bringing tears to my eyes. "Doing the best I can," I answer lamely. I hardly want to get into an argument with this guy.

Calmly, Jake's master helps me out. "Been a lot of rain, you know. Wood's pretty wet." He pauses and then adds with perfect timing as he rises from the log he's been sitting on, "Time to say good night." Mercifully, his strategy works. Without another word, the campground host leaves as well, riding off on his bike into the darkness beyond our small circle of light.

Our other neighbors, the Blanchards, now join us around the fire. They introduce us to the three collies, Brandy, Reggie, and Chester. As we talk, both husband and wife are constantly attentive to the dogs, brushing and grooming them with obvious affection. We talk about our families, our children, our lives. The conversation is so easy with strangers. When the fire dies down, all five of the Blanchards retire to their camper. It's 10:00 P.M. At the end of our longest day we should be tired enough to sleep even in our little tent.

Total Walked	230 Miles
Walked Today	26 Miles
Walking to Do	77 Miles

Chapter 17
Otsego Lake to Circle S

It is as if we are tucked into tight berths on a tiny boat. The sound keeping us awake all night is like a sail luffing in the wind. We did not stake our tent tightly enough, and the flapping of its sides further reminds me of my mother shaking out the area rugs on our back porch. Obviously, we should brave the dark and repair our mistake. But the idea of rousing Jake, who stands guard not twenty feet away, deters us. Someone had Jake in mind when they coined the phrase "let sleeping dogs lie." In all likelihood he would have been quiet and well behaved. Only our imagination of what he might do imprisons us in our noisy nest. At times the flapping is so intense that I am certain a major storm is blowing off the lake. We wait for the rain. Sleepless, I check my watch at 1:30, 3:30, 4:30, hoping the night will end. Finally, the added racket of the *ka ka ka* of the crows drives me out of the tent.

To my amazement the day is as gorgeous as the night was hours ago beside our campfire. Only a gentle breeze kicks up from the lake. Our tent and campsite are bone dry, and the temperature is a pleasant sixty degrees. Breaking camp is easy, since nothing is wet. The collie owners emerge from their spacious camper rested and refreshed. I am envious. Jake's master builds a fire, and I offer him what is left of our wood.

Judy takes our tent equipment up to the park gatehouse for storage. A friend, Julie Matuzak, will retrieve it and move it up to Indian River for us. Luckily, she will be passing this way to visit her family at their cottage on Lake Huron. The two rangers on duty are full of talk this morning and both soon tell Judy their life stories, which are almost mirror images of each other. The senior of the two, a thirty-nine-year-old man, decided to become a park ranger after working at a sporting goods store. Now he is happily living what he had only worked at. The much younger woman, on the other hand, dreams of leaving the park service and opening her own craft shop.

While Judy is gone, I work on my feet, which have acquired new blisters from yesterday's long walk in the shifting sand. Though my feet still need regular tending, I have no doubt now that I can finish the walk. Or, dare I say, I can take it in stride now. This is a vast improvement from those wretched days not so long ago.

When I'm finished I notice Judy is deep in conversation with our UP neighbor. He's telling her all about Siberian huskies. It occurs to me that this interests her because of her lifelong fascination with the arctic. Indeed, everything about these dogs is connected to that extreme environment. The dogs have a weather-resistant double coat composed of a dense, downy underlayer and a medium-length, very dense, soft outer coat. Of course, huskies were originally bred to pull Eskimo sleds and to guard the home. In those lonely lands they were also raised to be companions. Jake is clearly that to his master. No doubt quite aware of our fears, this sensitive man also assures us that over the centuries huskies have developed a strong sense of devotion to their human families, a gentleness even.

Our musing on dog gentleness is rudely interrupted when our other neighbors release Chester, Brandy, and Reggie from their night's confinement in the camper. Spotting a small poodle being walked by a diminutive lady, the three unleashed collies attack. We fear it will be all over for the little poodle and maybe even for the small woman, who is trying desperately to save her tiny pet. Loud barking and frantic squealing fill the air. Mother Blanchard makes a mad dash to rescue the poodle and scold her three naughty collies. She apologizes profusely to the flustered, frightened woman. Throughout this scene my eyes shift back and forth from the attack to Jake's observance of it. The husky remains calm, its steel blue eyes trained on the commotion. Those eyes. Silent condemnation of such misbehavior.

With quiet restored, Judy and I walk down to the lake's edge for a final appreciation of this idyllic spot. The first American to study the Indians of Michigan was Henry Rowe Schoolcraft, who was appointed Indian agent in 1822. Schoolcraft, an ethnologist and author of many books about Indians, may have been responsible in 1842 for giving the Otsego Lake area its original name, Okkundo. This Native American word means "sickly" or "stomach pains." Lost to history is what unhappy circumstance prompted this appellation, but it was hardly appropriate. The legislature changed the name in 1843 to the Iroquoian word *Otsego,* meaning "meeting place."

First it was Native Americans who traveled here to gather food. Then in 1872 the railroad was built along the eastern shore of the lake, and the village of Otsego Lake was established. The Homestead Act passed by Congress after the Civil War entitled veterans to 160 acres of land to cultivate. The growth of the lumber industry, the arrival of the railroad, and the development of farming combined to form the dynamics for a community. The village even became the county seat until it was moved seven miles north to Gaylord in 1881. Then, in 1942, there occurred perhaps the most unusual of meetings on these very shores on the beach by our campsite. Dr. Arthur Compton and Dr. Robert Oppenheimer met here and discussed the atomic bomb they were developing. From native people fishing and gathering berries to veterans homesteading to physicists developing weapons of mass destruction, we have come full circle to a peaceful place.

We say good-bye to our neighbors-for-a-night and to our four four-legged acquaintances—we've tried hard but already calling the dogs friends would be stretching it. This has been a good "meeting place" for us. We enjoyed the people, and we met some of our dog fears head on. Today our destination is the Circle S campground on the edge of elk country. Our walk northward up the lake is along Old 27 and beside the railroad tracks, which opened up this land 125 years ago. Along the way we catch glimpses of the lake as we pass through communities of cottages named Arbutus Beach, Oak Grove, and the village of Pearll City.

The problem today is that the traffic is heavy and loud. As much as I am obsessed with bear encounters, Judy is obsessed with my inattention to the oncoming traffic. "David, pick your head up and don't wander into the road," she admonishes—over and over again. She insists on walking behind me so she can monitor my attentiveness. Her concern is not wrong, just annoying. I do walk lost in thought with my head down, a lifelong bad habit my father could never break me of and that now terrifies my poor wife. I know how worried she is and promise to be more vigilant. I am quickly rewarded for good behavior. Above us the phone wires are lined with hundreds of doves. And in the thistle along the roadside goldfinches feed on wildflowers, bringing to life C. C. Abbott's lines.

> Whose wary flight and cheery whistle,
> Adorn the waste o'er grown with thistle,
> No field or foul with noisome weeds,
> But there the dainty goldfinch feeds.

At the very top of the lake our road veers northeastward, and we can see that ahead of us is an overpass crossing I-75. Judy will remember this seven-mile stretch into the heart of Gaylord as the worst portion of our journey. And the overpass is the worst of the worst. It certainly focuses me. I don't like this one bit, but there is no alternative. The bridge over the interstate is narrow with absolutely no shoulder. Clearly not meant for walkers. There is only a three-foot-high cement barrier wall separating us from the heavy interstate traffic thirty feet below. The wind is strong, and we both approach this crossing with trepidation. We are not very mobile with our packs nor very well balanced. The draft of a sixteen-wheeler rushing by just inches away could send us over the bridge to disaster. Now how would that look? "Congressman and wife blown over bridge onto I-75 while walking to Mackinac." Talk about losing faith in your government!

As we descend down the slope on the far side of the bridge, relieved to have survived this nerve-wracking passage, we come face to face with sprawl. Our northern Michigan experience is now four lanes of gas stations, fast-food establishments, new and used car dealerships, dilapidated buildings, snowmobile repair shops, new businesses and old of every sort in every style, all one right after the other, all the way into Gaylord. You just want to scream, "Why can't they plan this better? Why can't they plan at all?" Now thoroughly fed up with how this day is developing, Judy punctuates our walk with, "This is so ugly" so many times that I have to tell her she is becoming part of the problem.

There is one saving grace along the way. Busia's is a Polish restaurant in the heart of a Polish community. Poles immigrated to Otsego County from the 1870s to the early 1900s. The first arrivals came straight from Poland as well as indirectly by way of the eastern United States, attracted by newspaper ads offering inexpensive land. The climate and soil in Otsego County is well suited to potato farming. In the winter many of these Polish immigrants worked in the lumber camps, earning between ten and eighteen dollars a month plus their room and board.

I am drawn to this name, Busia, *grandmother* in Polish, because of my own *busia,* born Frances Postelnick in Poland on June 16, 1889. She was a sweet lady, not five feet tall, who migrated to New York and married Frank Bonior, who also came from Poland about the same time. Together they moved first to St. Louis, then Chicago, and finally to Hamtramck, Michigan. Frances bore five children and never spoke English. But she communicated her love to her children and grandchildren with hugs, kisses, good food, and warm smiles. Her husband, Frank, worked at the old Ford Rouge Foundry, at what was then the world's largest industrial complex. Tough work. A tall man with a handlebar mustache, my grandfather eventually left the foundry and established a printing business in the garage in his backyard. I fondly remember watching my grandfather, father, and uncles feeding paper by hand into the large-wheeled printing presses, the pungent smell of ink heavy in the air.

Unfortunately, the restaurant does not open for another thirty minutes. I try bargaining with Judy to hang around for half an hour, but she doesn't bite. Perhaps I would have been disappointed. So we continue up the road into Gaylord. The town center is a different world, thank goodness. Here there is evidence of both thought and planning. The water tower announces the theme, "Gaylord the Alpine Village." The buildings are adorned with carved shutters, balconies, shaker shingle awnings, and new flower boxes filled with edelweiss flowers. Many of the special features are painted bright colors. The main street, almost too wide for the scale of the village, has been given a recent facelift, now popularly called a streetscape. New lighting, bricked sidewalks, and benches near the curbs in front of the quaint shops combine to create a freshly scrubbed and friendly ambiance. Even if many towns are sprucing up in similar styles, it is an invigorating improvement. To my eye they are still more interesting than malls. I'm glad to see the towns fighting back. The singular feature in town is the glockenspiel centered in the alpine A-frame of Glen's Market. Every fifteen minutes between 8:00 A.M. and 10:00 P.M. the music plays while two figures of children dance, one on each side of the large clock.

Gaylord made the transition from lumbering to light industry by manufacturing wagons, sleighs, and for a few years even its own automobile, the Gaylord 30. Farming also played a key role in sustaining the town. Today tourism is the main engine of the local economy.

Located sixty miles south of the Mackinac Bridge, Gaylord can make several distinctive geographical claims. It is the most elevated town in the Lower Peninsula, at 1,350 feet. All rivers drain away. The Sturgeon, Pigeon, and Black Rivers flow north, while the Manistee and north branch of the Au Sable drain south. Gaylord also sits on the Forty-fifth Parallel, exactly halfway between the Equator and the North Pole.

Famished from our morning exertions, we walk into Arlene's Cafe. On the walls are pictures of Humphrey Bogart, Marilyn Monroe, Elvis Presley, and the famous Walker photo of John and Bobby Kennedy deep in thought. We can be comfortable here. We settle into a booth by the window. Judy is already rejuvenated by this place. She can hardly wait to ask about the history of Arlene's.

"Oh it's been open about three or four years," our waitress tells us.

Disappointed, Judy tries another tack. "Well, what was here before?"

"Busia's," is the answer.

Now it's my turn to be incredulous. "The same Busia's that we passed on the way into town?" I ask. "Yup," she says. I order the Polish omelette with Egg Beaters.

In the booth next to us a father and his twenty-something son are also talking about Arlene's.

Dad: The trouble with you is you never eat real food in real places. This is a real place.

Son: I like McDonald's better.

Dad: How can you like it better if you never try anything but fast-food joints?

Son: I just like it better.

And so it goes. There doesn't seem to be any bridge over the generation gap here. Maybe that's why Busia's moved.

After lunch we stop in next-door at the Historical Museum, which opened in 1992. Once a cigar factory, then a pool hall, and finally a printing establishment, the ninety-year-old building now houses relics of the past. Inside I find a nice chap who patiently answers my questions about the best road to travel north. I am determined to avoid what we encountered coming into town. He assures me that Old 27 is the right choice and that the traffic is 70 percent less headed that way. Next we stop at Nelson's Pharmacy for a camera and some Tylenol. Around the corner is Nelson's Funeral Home, which prompts Judy to quip, "They can help you either way." We pass beautifully restored, large Victorian houses as we leave the village.

We are feeling rested and cheerful. The sky is blue, and the sun is warm. What a day. We forget about the morning. But there is trouble ahead. A dog with no apparent owner is trying unsuccessfully to cross the traffic. It's an awful sight to watch as it is nearly hit. Cars are slamming on the brakes and careening to avoid it. The dog continues to wander on and off the road. We don't know what to do. Before we can make a plan the sad, skinny dog has attached itself to us. Collarless and disoriented, this poor pup has probably been abused and abandoned. Doesn't it just make sense—we who are not dog owners, who have been terrorized by dogs for days, are now responsible for a sick, confused animal? Why didn't one of the legions of dog lovers out there stop and help before we happened along? Where is Chris Koch, the savior of the mistreated? We can't let him follow us out of town, and we cannot shake him. At this point it's hard to know who is more pitiful, us or the dog. We're all useless.

Judy decides that she will find a phone and call the Humane Society, but this is easier said than done. In the meantime the disoriented dog keeps wandering back into traffic. Now people are honking and screaming at us, assuming we are the owners. We are calling to the dog to stay with us and off the road at the same time as we desperately try to figure a way out of this bizarre situation. Finally, we see a little business. Judy goes in, and the dog follows her to the door. Inside there is no sign of a phone or of an employee, but there is another customer at the counter—a tall, beefy guy in his mid-thirties wearing a baseball cap and work clothes. Reduced to babbling, Judy blurts out our dilemma and asks him if there is a Humane Society in Gaylord.

Looking at her in total disdain, the guy says disgustedly, "Just tell the dog to get the hell out of here." Before we know it, he strides outside and starts yelling at the poor dog, who skitters away, yelping and moaning.

We are free. But we don't feel very good about it. As we walk out of town, we turn back once or twice and can see that the dog made it safely across the road and is hanging out in front of a family-style restaurant. We hope that someone better equipped than we are to rectify this problem will come to the aid of the dog.

Emerging into the countryside, we are greeted by spectacular vistas. On each side of the road, as far as the eye can follow, the land lies like a counterpane piled with earthly pillows. Among the swells are picturesque old barns, plots of cultivated fields, and charming farmhouses. There is virtually no traffic. We walk by a field of golden-headed sunflowers cheerfully standing with faces all turned to the sun. Judy takes a picture of me hamming it up, pulling a great flower head down close to my own face. The sight of an entire field of these sunny flowers is joyful enough to lighten any burden. Up another hill we spy the Alpine Center, which opened in 1937 as a tuberculosis sanitarium, became a mental health institution in the 1960s, and today serves as offices for the county and school district. Along the side of the road is a large yellow warning sign, "Watch for Pedestrians."

"Who are they kidding?" Judy remarks. "We are the only two hikers anyone has seen on our entire walk!"

Between Gaylord and Vanderbilt our map notes a place called Irontone Springs. We find this natural spring in Wilkinson Roadside Park, a shady, cool glen. We cross the road and go directly to the spring, which bubbles up into a fountain and catch basin constructed of stones and mortar. Judy is hesitant but goes first and swallows. "Ugh" The mineral taste is too strong for her. The iron in the water leaves a rust color on the stones as it flows into the basin. Anxious for a cold bottle of "fresh" water, I dump my water bottle and attempt in vain to refill it. The water flow is too low, and the angle of my large bottle under the spout will not allow more than an inch of water to accumulate. Judy gets the last laugh at my impetuousness.

The roadside park is a pleasant retreat. Someone has sculpted a toadstool from a tree stump. The grass is dark green from all the August rain, and several picnic tables dot the area. I approach a middle-aged man who is enjoying his lunch at one of these tables and ask the distance to Vanderbilt.

"'Bout four and a half miles," he answers amiably. "Where you headed?"

A sunflower field beyond Gaylord yields sunny faces all around

"Mackinac."

"Well, just across the road is an old railroad bed that will take you there. Goes into Vanderbilt, up to Wolverine and Indian River, then up to Cheboygan along Mullett Lake. Pretty along the lake. From there up along US-23 and the Straits of Mackinac to Mackinaw City. Never walked it, but it's great in the winter on a snowmobile."

Eureka! I have been under the impression that this stretch was still a working railroad. But what Cornelius Vanderbilt built over one hundred years ago is now a spur of the "Top of Michigan Rails to Trails."

Our park companion and his wife are from the Traverse City area and are avid snowmobilers. Judy's ears perk up. She is thirsty for information about this culture after passing all the markers. This man owns a six thousand dollar snowmobile. He and his wife travel up to 150 miles a day during the winter—around northern Michigan and the UP, where there are extensive trails. Judy is fascinated.

She loves the winter and snow. I can envision spending our retirement years in Marquette, Michigan, rather than Fort Lauderdale. Before we part he mentions that his service club will be hosting a barbecue charity fund-raiser at the bridge walk the night before and perhaps he will see us there.

What good news to learn of the trail just across the road. After this morning, the idea of avoiding traffic and noise is appealing. But before we can get on the trail we must first connect with Julie Matuzak. Julie indeed is related to Allie Matuzak, whose obituary I read in the *Bay City Times*. She attended her grandmother's funeral this morning and is now searching for us, after picking up our camp gear at Otsego Lake. Since Julie is planning to visit relatives up this way, it is convenient for her to rescue us from Vanderbilt. Everyone we've consulted agrees that Vanderbilt is too small a place, and we are too obvious a target to chance an encounter if there is real hostility. A call to Chris Koch back in Mount Clemens sends us hustling out to the road. Julie has already left the park and should be nearby. We hope we have not missed her.

Judy offhandedly suggests that we walk all the way to the camp-gound. She is loath to break the walk yet again. But the message left at my office by the motel people, "He is not welcome here," reverberates in my head, making a persuasive counterargument. As we hike north and get closer to town, I believe that a detour around Vanderbilt is the prudent alternative. This tiny village, established in the early 1870s on the northern spur of the Jackson, Lansing, and Saginaw Railroad and named for Cornelius Vanderbilt of the New York Central Railroad, does not feel welcoming to me.

About a mile south of the village, we spot Julie's blue Dodge minivan heading toward us. She pulls onto the shoulder and films us with her camcorder as we walk up a gentle hill toward her. Of course, we express our condolences about her grandmother and inquire about the funeral. Julie has been a political and social activist for many years in our organization. She directed the Northeast Center for Racial Justice before joining our staff in 1987. Julie has also chaired our political organizations in the Tenth Congressional District.

In the fall of 1996 she applied through an agency to adopt a child from China. We were all very excited for her and waited with anticipation for her to move up on the waiting list of applicants. The process of being "chosen" took nine months before she was called

Don't break my stride

to go to China and receive her little girl. As a fierce critic of China's human rights policies and trade and environmental practices, I was concerned that my views would negatively impact Julie's ability to adopt. So, during the waiting period I lowered my profile and attacks on the Chinese government, trying not to be a burden to Julie at such a sensitive time. Finally, in December 1997 Julie was notified that there was a child for her. She and Ed Bruley traveled to an orphanage in Changde, Hunan Province, where an adorable one-year-old was waiting for a loving mother. Mother Julie, daughter Allie Shui Matuzak, and Uncle Ed came home on Christmas Eve. Allie is now part of our extended family and one of our youngest Democratic activists.

We pile into Julie's van. She treats us to Michigan blueberries and peaches bought this morning at the Farmers' Market in Mount Clemens. Feasting on fresh fruit, we drive into Vanderbilt, known as the gateway to elk country. Vanderbilt consists of no more than a crossing in the road with just a few stores. At the intersection we turn east onto tree-canopied Sturgeon Valley Road leading into the heart of the Pigeon River Country State Forest, the 98,000-acre home to Michigan's only elk herd.

The Pigeon River Country was logged between 1860 and 1910. During this period the area suffered disastrous, uncontrolled forest fires. Unsuccessful attempts to convert the land to agriculture resulted in returning it to state ownership. In 1919 the state forest was established, and tree planting began. The CCC became active in the 1930s, planting and developing forest recreation. In the young forest the small wildlife population thrived and expanded naturally.

Resuscitating the once widespread elk would be a greater challenge. Overhunted and with the natural habitat destroyed by lumbering, elk largely disappeared in Michigan. In 1916 twenty-four elk were imported from Wyoming but did not survive. Between 1918–19 eight elk collected from parks and zoos were released along the Sturgeon River near Wolverine. Miraculously, these few elk did live and multiply. They moved east to the Pigeon River Country, and by 1926 the herd was thought to have reached three hundred animals.

By 1964 the Department of Conservation estimated that the elk herd had grown to number thirty-five hundred. The first open hunting season on elk was declared. It was later determined, however, that the estimate of elk had been overly optimistic. The hunting season was then closed when new figures revealed drastically lower numbers. The 1970s brought a new concern for the elk range. Oil and gas deposits were discovered under the south-central portion of the forest. Exploration and development followed with deleterious impact on the recreation and wildlife habitats. Illegal elk shooting was also taking a toll on the herd, with a record-high loss of forty-five animals in 1974. By 1975 the numbers had once again slipped to a low of only two hundred elk.

As a new member of the Michigan legislature, I remember well the heated debate that raged through the state. The *Detroit Free Press* did an outstanding job in publishing articles and editorials to alert the public to the destruction of this fragile and important environment. Eventually, a combination of citizen and environmental concerns, court cases, and legislative and administrative initiatives led to a development plan that has protected the elk herd. The herd has recovered nicely to about a thousand. On our way to the campground we pull over to an elk-viewing area hoping to see the Wapiti, another name for elk. As a member of the deer family, the elk is smaller than a moose but more graceful and noble in appearance. Like deer, elk are usually seen at dusk or dawn. There are none in sight, but just the knowledge that they are out there creates a sense of anticipation and an appreciation of the efforts to restore our natural heritage.

"Clean, Friendly, Reasonable" announces the sign welcoming guests to the Circle S campground. We are not disappointed. After we check in, Julie drives us up the road thirteen miles to Indian River and Burt Lake State Park, where we hope to drop off our tent bag. After some hesitancy, the park ranger seeks out his supervisor, who agrees to let us store our gear. On our return we buy some groceries at the IGA supermarket in Indian River before thanking Julie for her help and sending her on to her relatives.

Now we take time to look around. This is the very sort of afternoon that we had expected. The sky is clear, and the sun is hot. Lounge chairs await us by the swimming pond. We write in our journals, while the warm rays work their curative magic on our bodies. We nap and write and chat. Beyond us one of the owners cuts and rakes a huge grassy field. I imagine playing soccer there or football or just being young enough to tumble around on that soft green expanse.

Circle S is meticulously maintained, showing all the signs of hard work and care and thought. There are eighty-three acres here on the fast-flowing Sturgeon River. Half of the people who visit come to see the elk. The others come to fish the river or fish out of Rogers City on Lake Huron or visit Mackinac Island. Some just leave their campers and trailers up all summer and return for relaxing weekends. For children there is freedom and room to roam, the swimming pond, the river, a volleyball court, a playground, and a deer feeder at the far end of the property by the river. At the appointed times, when the feeder drops corn on the lawn, the animal kingdom's ballet dancers perform. The great thick carpet of grass covers the entire campground, unlike the state park sites, which are worn down to dirt, particularly at this time of year. Even though it would be an agreeable extra cushion under my sleeping bag, I'm still relieved that we have one of the two small cabins for this night. I shall actually be able to turn over!

Before dinner we explore the river walk that the owners have designed to take advantage of the special magic along the banks of the Sturgeon. They have cut a winding six-foot-wide swath through the bushes, undergrowth, reeds, and wildflowers. This path, too, is thick grass. Deer leap off, and rabbits hop away as we approach. Birds sing in the rushes. The rippling, rushing water and fragrant, summer-scented air engage our senses. Occasionally, a small clearing reveals the clear, fast-moving river. This idyllic creation stretches for a mile. At the end, as we turn away from the river through some trees, we are surprised to find ourselves at the far end of a driving range. These enterprising owners have even tried to please golf fanatics.

Back at our cabin Judy prepares a salad, and I build a fire in the outdoor grill for hot dogs. We sit together on the same side of our picnic table enjoying the solitude as dusk falls. And then the show begins. Five adult deer gracefully approach the feeder for their evening snack. Two fawns chase each other like two children just released for recess. To no avail, the parents try to nuzzle the fawns toward the food. They continue to scamper, jump, and hide, while the wiser adults fatten up for the coming winter. Several adolescents, tempted by the young ones, join in the frolic. Their leaps are dazzling.

Lost in admiration, we are startled by a voice. "I wanted to make sure you saw the deer," says Jean Gendron proudly.

Jean and her husband, Robert, bought the property in 1989 from an elderly couple. The place had fallen into disrepair but Jean and Robert had dreamed of owning their own resort. With vision and hard work they have brought Circle S back to life. They are rightfully proud of what they have accomplished. They have one child, Angela, who is a student at Central Michigan University, studying to be a teacher. It's now too dark to see her face, but we can hear in Jean's voice her pride in her daughter. We say good night, and Jean heads toward the one speck of light in the vast outdoor blackness.

Total Walked	245 Miles
Walked Today	15 Miles
(Driven Today	9 Miles)
Walking to Do	53 Miles

Chapter 18

Circle S to Burt Lake

Now that we have the days down, our nights are getting worse. I dream of nuclear disaster, kicking Judy hard as I respond to some emergency. Judy tosses and turns, imagining a horrible case of poison ivy. We awaken with relief at 5:30 A.M. to the distant sounds of traffic seeping through our open window. On the way to the campground bathrooms I spy the deer playing and feeding in the low fog that has settled on the field. In the soft light of dawn the deer darting in and out of mist are a bewitching vision. I would rather watch, but the early morning chill chases me to the showers.

We leave quietly by way of Trowbridge Road, which will take us three miles to the village of Wolverine. A trail parallels the road, but we decide that the sights are more interesting on this deserted road. The gurgling river accompanies us. Dotting the roadside is a fine sample of native trees—aspen, birch, cedar, spruce, and maple. In an overgrown apple orchard several deer are feasting on dropped fruit. Across open meadows fog still fills the hollows, and dew shimmers on the grass. Goldfinches peck at the roadside flowers and weeds for their morning breakfast. It is an excellent morning and a pleasant beginning of what is to be an easy day.

Then the spell is broken. Rounding a curve in the road, I'm certain that I see a bear. Abruptly, I stop.

"Judy, there's something dark on the road ahead."

She calmly asks, "Where, honey?"

With no credibility left on the matter of bears, I still can't help myself. "Up there," I say urgently and point to a black blob in the next turn of the road.

"David, I think it's a black mailbox extended over the road at the curve."

"Ah, of course," I humbly respond. Still I doublecheck her judgment by taking a look through the binoculars. Yup, it's a mailbox alright. There is simply no end to my embarrassment about this matter.

Just before entering the village, we pause on a bridge overlooking the river. Now it's Judy's turn to be flustered. She exclaims, "The river is running backwards." No amount of explaining on my part will convince her that it is an illusion. We're even. If I'm entitled to my bear sightings, then I guess she can have her water current theories. For all our love of the out-of-doors, we cannot be entirely stripped of our city ways.

We have Messrs. Burt and Mullett to thank for the location of Wolverine on the Sturgeon River. Two beautiful nearby lakes were eventually named in honor of these two state surveyors who worked in this area from 1840–43. Soon after, a seemingly endless supply of pine began moving down the river. Lumber mills sprang up, business swelled, and the population increased. The railroad made its way north from Gaylord and Vanderbilt, and the present village was platted in 1881 and called Torrey. In 1903 it was incorporated as Wolverine. Legend has it that during this time one George Richards was carrying mail on snowshoes along the west branch of the Sturgeon River and was attacked by a pack of vicious wolverines. He killed several until his ammunition was exhausted and then drove off the others with his hand ax. As a result of these heroics and a request put to the postmaster general, the town was fittingly renamed Wolverine, and Richards became its first postmaster.

I say "legend has it" because there seems to be a running debate about the wolverine in Michigan. Some say it was once abundant, while others doubt it ever lived in our state at all. There is agreement that there are none here now. In addition, although wolverines have a voracious appetite and are described as vicious, they will attack and challenge almost any animal except humans. Whatever the facts, the naming of Wolverine is a good tale.

Wolverines are actually the biggest member of the weasel family though they more clearly resemble a small bear. The wolverine is the official state mammal of Michigan, a nickname for the state, and the mascot of the University of Michigan athletic teams. It is a fitting animal to describe the toughness of U of M football. At the same time it is also a reminder of how we have over the last 150 years altered the ecological balance in our state by exhausting some of our precious resources.

When the lumbering era ended, the economy of Wolverine and the surrounding area was hit hard. The population, which peaked at a little over 1,000 at the turn of the century, dwindled to 270 by 1940. A fish hatchery built in the early 1930s by the CCC in cooperation with the State Conservation Department became a tourist attraction. With the construction of an interstate up to the bridge, more tourism helped the village regain its stability.

Still, the town is composed of little more than a few stores. The library is located in the old railroad station, which was built in 1906. Eager for a cup of coffee, we head for the general store. The owner tells us that the handsome wood floor is over one hundred years old. Obviously interested in preservation, he is also gathering a number of old photographs of the area, which hang in his office. A mixture of old and new, the store maintains the flavor of another era but incorporates the modern necessities of town and tourist life. Our proprietor tells us that most of his business comes from the locals. He attributes some of his success to a nearby meat factory, which delivers fresh cuts of meat a couple times a day. "A nice selection that brings 'em in," he says.

Tiring of our questions, he asks how we keep at it "day after day."

"Persistence," I answer. "Have you heard the story about the duck that waddles into a store and asks the proprietor if he has any soap?" I ask.

"Nope," he shakes his head.

"Well, the duck asks the proprietor if he has any soap. The proprietor says no. Next day the duck waddles into the store and says to the proprietor, 'Got any soap?' The proprietor says, 'I told you I don't have any soap. Now get out of here!' Third day the duck waddles into the store, sees the proprietor, and says, 'Got any soap?' 'Listen, I told you three times now, I don't have any soap. If you come in here again, I'm going to nail your webbed feet to the floor.' Next day the duck waddles into the store, sees the proprietor, and says, 'Got any nails?' 'No," says the proprietor. 'Got any soap?' says the duck."

By this time I've gathered a bit of a crowd, who have been giggling at my wiggling each time I waddle like a duck. But that's okay with me, and they laugh appreciatively at the end. One of the great gifts given to me by a former staff member was the capacity to make people laugh. Bob Lehrman wrote jokes into my speeches and encouraged me to use them. It opened up a whole new world to me, and I shall forever be grateful to Bob. We all love to laugh, and a good joke or funny story can illustrate a point far more effectively than just the facts. I'll never be one of those who can spontaneously keep an audience in stitches, and I still blow a joke from time to time, but being funny sometimes has made my public life a lot more fun. It has undoubtedly improved it for my audiences too!

It's time for us to demonstrate our persistence by moving on. Not far from the store we pick up the trail, which runs near the road for a short distance and then veers north along the river. The trail is flat and clear. It is part of the Top of Michigan Trails system, which connects five counties from Mackinaw City and Charlevoix on Lake Michigan to Gaylord and Cheboygan on Lake Huron, with a spur running south down to Hawks near Rogers City on Lake Huron. In all the system is about two hundred miles of scenic trails. Like the Paint Creek Trail in Oakland County, our straight path crosses back and forth over the river at several points.

Because this was originally a railroad line, the natural contour of the land has been altered. Much of the trail is actually a raised, flat ridge through the meadows, wetlands, and forests. The good thing is that we do not have to slog through any swamps or up any hills, but the downside is that we are not aware of the true terrain. It is an adventure, nevertheless, to cross the railroad trestles over ravines and water. There are no sides to these bridges. Furthermore, there are spaces between the ties. Though certainly not wide enough for either of us even to force our way through, much less slip between, Judy still traverses these stretches gingerly.

Along the way we pass yellow and white wildflowers cascading down the sides of our ridge and tempting paths into cool forests of hardwoods. Of all the trees we enjoy on our walk we conclude that the cedar is our favorite. The tree appears to be almost primeval and in any numbers creates an enchanted atmosphere. The allure of its fragrance evokes wonderful images and memories of log cabins, wood stoves, fireplaces, coziness, snow gently falling, and deer nibbling the foliage.

Trepidation on a trestle over the Sturgeon River

I find two rail spikes to go along with the horseshoe from the trail leading into Grayling. They will make a nice set of souvenirs of our walk, though they are a bit heavy to add to our packs. It is getting warmer, and we are getting sweaty. The bugs begin to bite, so we take turns spraying each other. It usually does the trick but leaves us sticky and chemically contaminated. We appreciate that it works, but have you ever read what is in the stuff? It's a wonder that the epidermis survives a dose.

A DNR boat launch with steps leading twenty feet down to a platform dock along the river is an appealing place to sit and read or fish. Just beyond this access to the water we pass rustic Haakwood Camp Ground. It would have been nice to try one of these facilities at least once so we could have had a more wilderness camping experience. But that would require carrying more water and food, which, of course, would mean more weight. We will have a number of regrets about our walk. This is just one. But we have to push it out of our minds and appreciate the experience as it is. And this morning we really are happy. Never do we see another soul. There is plenty all about us to keep our attention, and we can walk safely side by side, unmindful of traffic or dogs.

Michigan has six state forests, three in each peninsula. We are now walking through the Mackinaw State Forest. In total the six forests provide seven thousand miles of canoeable streams, thirteen thousand miles of trout waters, five hundred miles of Great Lakes shoreline with access/camping on Lake Michigan, Lake Superior, and Lake Huron, fifty-two hundred miles of groomed snowmobile trails, and 150 campgrounds with 3,000 campsites. That's pretty impressive.

Oh, oh, another dark blob ahead, moving on the trail. How many times can I put us through this drill? Alert now, we continue cautiously forward. It would be a small bear, if it is a bear. But that would mean that a big bear could be close by to protect it. There is no one and nothing close by to protect us. It would be fine if someone else appeared on the trail now or even an entire troop of folks. But, wait, isn't the blob moving in several different directions? Safe again. The bear is a flock of wild turkeys walking up the trail just as we are.

John Muir is quoted as saying, "Bears are a peaceable people, and mind their own business, instead of going about like the devil seeking whom they may devour." Now I admire Muir immensely so I must take his words seriously. In defense of bears I have come to learn, albeit belatedly, that they are endangered. So I should stop worrying so much about myself and start worrying about them. The burgeoning trade in animal parts and products has already endangered the elephant for ivory, tigers for skins, and rhinos for the supposedly sexual benefits of their horns. It now seems that the eight bear species across the globe are also threatened. The combined population of bears in the world is less than one million, according to most estimates. These bears, including our elusive black bears, are protected by international treaties from trade exploitation for their parts.

A variety of factors have contributed to a decline in the worldwide bear population, including land mines in Croatia, which have killed European brown bears. Sun bears in southern China and Southeast Asia have been exploited by the pet trade, while polar bears are threatened by environmental pollutants. Yet the greatest risk to the bear population comes from international trade in bear parts and products.

Bear paws are an expensive culinary delicacy in Asian restaurants. Even more threatening is the consumption of bear gallbladder and bile for medicinal purposes, according to traditional Asian culture. The bile is believed to relieve stomach pains, diarrhea, kidney discomfort, and headaches. In fact, bile does contain ursodeoxycholic acid, which has genuine medicinal applications. In 1984 China started "farming" bear for their bile. By 1996 there were 7,642 bears on 481 farms across China. In the United States bear carcasses have been found with only their gallbladders and paws missing.

All of this, ironically, has prompted me to cosponsor a bill that would prohibit the import or export or interstate commerce of bear gallbladder and bile. If bears could only read, I'd wear a sign around my neck announcing "I'm on Your Side." It's just a bit confusing, however, to figure out who the victim is—me (protector/dinner) or the bear (endangered/attacker). That's so often the problem with the facts—they differ depending on whose point of view you're considering.

As I wrestle with these conflicted feelings about our dreaded bear friends, we come upon the dark, wobbling pack of wild turkeys. There are five adults, one with a bad leg, and eight young ones. Baffled and frightened, they continue upon the trail, scurrying just ahead of us. The one with the bad leg glances back at us as they gobble and move in a confused state of frenzy. Judy suggests, "Let's just stop. We're torturing them." They seize the opportunity to scramble down the embankment into the woods. For a moment, seeing that wounded turkey, we thought we might be replicating our dilemma with the lost dog outside of Gaylord. God help us if we really come upon a bear!

The walk along the old railroad bed is similar to our experience on the Paint Creek trail on our second day out. The river is always at our side. I take a picture of Judy walking over a trestle. Her wide smile radiates with delight and warmly expresses her joy. Seven miles from Wolverine we exit the trail at White Road and climb the steep grade for a half-mile to Old 27, which takes us the two miles to the state park.

It is not yet noon when we reach Burt Lake State Park near the village of Indian River. Check-in time is 3:00 P.M. Walking around the perimeter of the park, we come upon a scenic tower. This is an irresistible invitation to a great view. Three floors up we reach a wooden platform and peer into the park and at the lake beyond. Burt Lake is the state's fifth largest and one of the most picturesque. It is part of a chain of lakes, rivers, and streams that make up forty miles of inland waterway.

Thousands of years ago glaciers scraped and gouged the area, melting and creating the basin and lake itself. In the early seventeenth century a tribe of Ottawa Indians settled here and named the lake Ja-Bo-Ga-Ning, meaning "passage through." Over the years, as early pioneers filtered into the region, the federal government settled land disputes through assorted treaties that virtually extinguished the Native Americans' title to their lands.

The state renamed the lake for William Burt, one of Michigan's great historical figures. Burt lived in Washington village near what is now Romeo, Michigan, in my congressional district. From his small shop originated an astonishing array of inventions. In 1829 he patented his "typographer," which was the first writing machine, a forerunner of the typewriter. He invented the solar compass in 1836 and the equatorial sextant in 1844. The lumbering industry benefited from his design of sawmills. Being a man of many talents, he was a member of the territorial legislature and a judge. Burt is most often associated with surveying. With Douglass Houghton he surveyed the Upper Peninsula. While surveying near Marquette, he noticed the wild fluctuations of the magnetic needle, thus discovering the region's great iron deposits. After Houghton's death, Burt alone completed the compilation of their historically important reports on the geology of Michigan.

To our west stands the Cross in the Woods, the world's largest Crucifix. In 1954 the Cross, made from a fifty-five-foot Oregon redwood tree, was erected. The bronze seven-ton image of Jesus created by sculptor Marshall M. Fredericks was raised into place in 1959. The Cross is the centerpiece of an outdoor sanctuary, which also includes a statue of a kneeling, beseeching Saint Francis of Assisi (1181–1226), the patron saint of all who work for peace and justice and also to protect creatures and our environment.

With still more time to spare we have a leisurely lunch at Wilson's Family Riverfront Dining. Judy has Nutty Batter Toast, which, believe it or not, is bread dipped in pancake batter and walnuts then fried. It is scrumptious but can only be justified by taking a 335-mile walk. Finally, at 2:30, with some trepidation, we walk into the park. Because I had difficulty getting them to accept and store our gear yesterday, we imagine the worst. Our stuff will be gone; actually, no one will even acknowledge having ever seen it. To our surprise we are greeted with "Welcome, Senator" by the genial park attendant. I decide to go with the "Senator" since it seems to be working and immediately ask if we can again leave our gear tomorrow until the next day, Saturday, when Jenny Anderson will be driving our car up to Mackinaw City to participate in the Bridge Walk with her union, the Seafarers. "No problem" is the cheery reply. No wonder so many people would rather be in the Senate!

Our luck continues when the park's one rustic cabin is available. I'm elated. Imagine—a small, cozy cabin in the woods by the lake. After paying an extra eight dollars for our lodgings, we collect our gear from the storage barn and walk into the campground.

A large drawing of the Inland Waterway is posted near the parking lot. Described by many as one of the most beautiful water routes in the country, boaters can navigate forty miles from Lake Huron at Cheboygan inland through Mullett, Burt, and Crooked Lakes and the Indian, Cheboygan, and Crooked Rivers to Conway, just a few miles from Lake Michigan. The waterway was used by the Indians and traders to travel across the northern tip of the Lower Peninsula, a shorter and often safer route than the rough water of the Straits. During the logging era the waterway transported lumber products and camp supplies. In the nineteenth century steam-powered boats carried passengers and picnickers between Conway on Crooked Lake and Topinabee on Mullett Lake. Today this enjoyable excursion is still a vacation favorite. The scenic river portions meander through resort towns and marshlands filled with waterfowl.

We wish we had time to explore the waterway. With three campgrounds along the way, we fantasize about canoeing the route and camping—with a larger tent. But we were not that great at canoeing during our most recent foray on the water. Besides, we are not free to wander off on another adventure. First we must finish our last two days of walking.

Our lone cabin is at the edge of 345 campsites. Tucked in the corner, we have woods to our rear and the lake somewhere beyond. We unlock the door and enter the single room. The walls are knotty pine, but the floor is concrete, and a single bulb dangles over the small table and two chairs. Most of the space is occupied by two squeaky, sagging metal bunk beds, which appear to be surplus from a correctional facility. This is not exactly our notion of rustic. To solve the bed problem we pull two of the mattresses onto the floor. Oh well, at least we'll have plenty of room for sleeping tonight. But this is not a place where we want to spend any time.

We each have chores to do. My responsibility is the evening campfire. First, I must clean up the area around our fire ring, which is littered with garbage. Still flush with energy after only a short walk today, I next stride off to the other side of the park to purchase wood at the camp store. On my return I find that the bundle is heavier than I expect. Worried about my back, I hug the wood close to my body and rest every forty yards. The last thing we need is for my back to go out. Judy's admonitions are on my mind. It is a tedious process to stop so frequently, but at least I am still erect when I reach the cabin. Sometimes the simplest undertaking can be surprisingly challenging.

It's a relief to grab my journal and a sweatshirt and head down to a picnic table by the shore. The beach is beautiful, stretching some two thousand feet to the Sturgeon River. Overhead clouds of interesting shapes scuttle across the sky. A stiff breeze blows off the choppy lake. It is a raw but invigorating day, with temperatures only in the low sixties. The beach is empty. The elements are in charge. I enjoy the solitude. Several hours later I'm startled by two beautiful arms wrapped around my shoulders and warm lips nuzzling my neck. Judy has returned from doing our laundry, bubbling over with stories. She has a knack for getting herself involved in the strangest situations. I prepare to enjoy an entertaining tale.

The Indian River Village Laundromat is about a half-mile outside of the park on a dirt side road. It's a simple place, but there is an attendant who also has her son, Spanky, with her. Spanky is helping to wipe out the washing machines after they are used by hanging his little body nearly upside down into each machine. He is very energetic. Judy asks when he will start back to school. "Not till the day after Labor Day," sighs his mom.

An older, cranky woman is also doing her wash, complaining all the while about this and that. As she empties one of her washers, thousands of small seeds spill on the floor. There are thousands more in the washer. In quiet desperation she tries furtively to stuff them back into a small cloth bag, but it is hopeless. Judy finally asks her what it all is, and in a clearly frightened voice she says she doesn't know. Then Spanky draws his mother's attention to the mess, and she starts yelling over and over again, "Wacky tobaccy! Wacky tobaccy! Wacky tobaccy!" There is total panic. Judy has no idea what is going on until she hears Spanky's mom screaming, "There was two parts, the grass and the seeds. Seeds, seeds, them's all the seeds." It dawns on Judy that they think it is marijuana. The older woman is now nearly in tears, explaining, "It was the kids. They were visiting me." But Spanky's Mom replies, "Yes, but they're your kids."

Meanwhile, there is mad sweeping going on, and Spanky is hard at work on the machine, and there is a lot of commotion and words flying about "fault" and "police" and "funny smells." Then it occurs to Judy that "the kids" probably had a sachet to freshen up their mom's old house. It got caught up in the laundry and exploded when soaked in water. Judy tries to explain this likelihood to the two women, but they've never heard of a sachet and are mistrustful of the idea. No ill effects develop from the "wacky tobaccy," and normalcy slowly returns.

Then it is time for the dryer incident. As Judy is preparing to take her clothes from the washer, she asks a man who has just emptied two dryers if they had both worked. "Yes," he says. So she loads one of the dryers, at the same time explaining that she asks rather than risk getting one that doesn't work. After a long pause, the man says, "Oh, if you want the one that works best, it's the other one." Regretting that she had ever spoken to this guy in the first place, Judy nonetheless switches her clothes. But he has warmed to her and continues, "You seem to be a lot like me." Ah, the ultimate compliment! (Judy at this point interrupts her story to say to me, "I hate it when daft people say that to me, and it happens more often than I should admit.")

But he's hot now and goes on, "My doctor says to me, 'Vern, don't ask so many questions. You read too much.' But I say, how can anyone accuse you of reading too much? If there were only ten books in the world, maybe you should slow down because you will finish them before you die. But, as it is, there's enough to read for a lifetime."

Judy considers herself lucky to escape with no more of a harangue than that. She's had far worse. Laundromats are like buses—there is always a story. Judy's favorite experience, when she has found herself in conversation with a not quite balanced person,

Hamming it up over simple pleasures in Burt Lake

ended when the man started yelling outside of a grocery store, "Don't talk to her—she'll drive you crazy." The good thing about Judy is that she laughs at herself for getting into these situations. They can also be provocative. Once she saw a homeless man staring at footprints in new cement. She stopped too. He looked up at her and said in awe, "I knew I'd been here before."

Back at our cabin, if I do say so myself, I build a picture-perfect tepee fire. Judy takes a snapshot of my best-ever effort. We heat two cans of chili in the fire for dinner and roast marshmallows for dessert. My plan is to keep the fire going as long as I can to keep the bugs away, so we can stay out and watch the camp come alive. I carefully schedule the addition of each log and get us to 10:00 P.M. We see a great show.

It's the weekend, and the camp is full. People's lives are so much more exposed in a campground. We marvel at the variety of pop-ups, mobile homes, fifth-wheels, trailers, and tents of every size and shape. The air is full of the sounds of children, excitement that is contagious in their high-pitched little voices. Before us a huge mobile unit pulls in. It is the Cadillac of the line, the castle of the campground. Two elderly women climb down to guide the camper, driven by an elderly man, into its tiny slot in the woods. This scene develops for a good thirty minutes. Pull in. Back up. Over to the right. Now to the left. Watch the tree limb. They manage this tricky maneuver with patience and affection. We guess the three are in their seventies. Perhaps one of the women has lost her partner. How wonderful it is to see folks taking care of one another, living full lives. When they are finally properly positioned, the man pulls out a rug, three chairs, and a small plastic table. It is now dark, but he unrolls the overhead awning from the side of the trailer, covering the little outdoor living space. The ladies emerge from inside with drinks and snacks. The three make a toast. The weekend has begun.

The black night is lit here and there by bobbing flashlights, hanging lanterns, and campfires. Crickets compete in the darkness. Muffled conversations are interrupted by the sudden pop of a burning log. Laughter briefly rises and quickly quiets. The scent of burning pine wafts through the air. Our own coals glow bright red and fade.

Just before falling asleep, I ask Judy, "How's the mattress?"

"It feels like it's full of cookie dough," she answers, longing for her tent.

Total Walked	259 Miles
Walked Today	14 Miles
Walking to Do	39 Miles

Chapter 19
Burt Lake to Cheboygan

Friday, August 29

And the days are not full enough
And the nights are not full enough
And life slips by like a field mouse
Not shaking the grass.

> —Ezra Pound, "And the Days
> Are Not Full Enough"

It is hard to believe that we are nearing the end of our walk. Judy is already a bit blue. Miles and days, stretching endlessly before us not long ago, are abruptly running short. We have hit our stride, found our rhythm. Our patterns are established. In the right pocket of my shorts are my maps for each day. Judy teases that her memory of me will be pulling those faded scraps from my pocket, gingerly unfolding the worn paper, checking our location, calculating our remaining distance, then carefully refolding and pocketing the maps as if they are sacred documents. I do this every few hours. Each time, she asks me, "How much further?" I respond, and we proceed. She never questions my answer. It has taken me longer than it should to realize it's because she doesn't care. She's content to be on our journey, no matter what. So, for now we will try to savor our last two days, walking today beside the shore of Mullett Lake and tomorrow along the Straits of Mackinac.

Over breakfast at Wilson's we (no surprise here) pore over our map, engraving in our minds points of interest and calculating the miles to Cheboygan. To pass the time we drink too much coffee and watch the early shift of regulars come and go until 8:00 A.M., when the ranger station opens and we can store our sleeping gear again.

Leaving the park, we cross Old 27 and walk into the small resort town of Indian River. Pausing at midpoint in the bridge over the river of the same name, we admire the small watercraft that are docked snugly in front of manicured lawns leading invitingly to pretty cottages. It is an idyllic summer scene that might well appear on a brochure touting the vacation attractions of the area. Below us the river flows gently into Mullett Lake. Gazing deeply into the clear currents, it is easy to drift back in time and imagine Native Americans paddling birch bark canoes heavily loaded with beaver pelts through the same waters.

We pick up the trail on the other side of the bridge. Our path is bordered by an abundant variety of berry bushes. Every color that might be found in a kindergartner's crayon box is clustered among the bushes—black, blue, orange, yellow, white, and a multitude of reds—festively decorating the trail and previewing autumn's dazzling display of color. We marvel at this bounty of berries, noting ruefully that we have no idea which are edible. Luckily, we were fed at Wilson's. Left to our own devices, we could have bad tummy aches. Nearby are vines of sweetpeas, which delight Judy but prompt me to prattle on about Popeye and Olive Oyl.

The surface underfoot is a great improvement over yesterday's larger stones, when we found ourselves rocking and twisting back and forth over edges not yet worn by man or the elements. The constant pitch of our bodies required us to concentrate on keeping our balance. By the end of the day that vigilance had extracted a certain amount of extra energy. Our walk this morning is less demanding, and we bask in its ease as we glide along the path through thickets of maple, pine, and the now ever-present aspen and birch.

We enter a marshy area formed by excess runoff bleeding from the Indian River and from the southern reaches of Mullett Lake. The marsh appears to be covered by waterlilies. In the distance is a pair of swans. Their white plumage and long regal necks starkly grace the green-covered waters. A softly melodious series of muted notes rises over the marsh. The birds are preparing for flight.

With the beauty of the swans and the lilies and the watery marsh also comes the pesky mosquitoes. I am under attack. In Alaska we wore folding headnets, which looked a bit unusual but did the trick. It is the females that do the damage, latching onto me to acquire a blood meal for the development of their eggs. The males do not bite but obviously are not blameless. They do play a key role in producing the females that are tormenting me. There are over sixty mosquito species in Michigan. In my fifty-two years here I believe I've encountered them all. Out come our bandannas, and I swat away as Judy dips into her pack for the repellent spray. I shut my eyes and rotate my body on her command, feeling like a child blindfolded and playing pin the tail on the donkey. Instantly, the juice goes to work, and we are spared.

Ahead I spot what looks like the outline of a family. As we approach each other, we can see a helmeted ten-year-old boy tightly gripping the handlebars of his junior mountain bike. Indeed, his hands are so tightly holding on that the blood has drained from his chubby little fingers. Sensing his nervousness, we move to the side of the trail. We are rewarded with a "thank you" through clenched teeth. This is a very polite child. We wish he was having a little more fun. His parents follow with a dog in tow. The dog, too, is intimidated by us. This is a first! The poor thing cowers to the other side of the trail, putting his masters between himself and us.

A mile up the trail I almost fly into Judy's arms when our presence flushes out a squadron of doves tucked in the bushes. The sudden noise and the rush of air from the simultaneous flap of hundreds of not so peaceful wings almost takes my breath away. A variation of this phenomenon occurs again not thirty minutes later, when two pheasants repeat the surprise. One moment we are lulled by the surrounding tranquillity, and the next every nerve ending is quivering. While these beautiful creatures are harmless, it is still quite disconcerting to have your emotions swing so dramatically. Of course, it is the unexpected, both the beauty and the danger, that is part of the allure of the natural world.

The trail now reaches the southern shore of the lake. We are taken aback by how quiet and abandoned the area feels. It seems peculiar to us that this splendid place would be absolutely devoid of people on the last official weekend of the summer. It is as if the vacationers have offered the day to the gods in thanks for the blessings enjoyed here during the rest of the summer. The path follows the water's edge. We walk in silence. No motor spoils the quiet. No other human is in sight. Fish jump in the lake. They are safe. We are happy.

At the six and a half mile point of the day we enter the tiny village of Topinabee. Topinabee runs up a steep hill from the shore of

On the trail along Mullett Lake

Mullett Lake. It was founded in 1881 at the behest of a railroad official who was anxious to have a resort on Mullett Lake. The hotel operator who platted the village named it for the Potawatomi chief who concluded the treaty giving the white man the site of Fort Dearborn, now the city of Chicago. This village, unlike most others through which we have come, was never a lumbering center, so it never suffered the struggles of the aftermath of that era. It is easy to see why the railroad executives passing this lovely spot on the lake would plan their own little resort.

Ahead is the old railway station sitting not twenty yards from the lakeshore. It has been converted into a handsome public library similar to the one we saw in Wolverine. The conversion of these old stations into community buildings has been quite successful in Michigan and elsewhere. Port Huron, New Haven, and Mount Clemens, in my congressional district, celebrate the boyhood presence of Thomas Edison and have turned their old stations into museums.

Ann Arbor has converted its station into a popular restaurant called the Gandy Dancer, descriptive of the workers on the railroad. On a far larger scale, in Washington, DC, after several staggeringly unsuccessful tries, Union Station has been redeveloped into a stunning site for shops, restaurants, and movie theaters while still fulfilling its railroad functions.

Scattered on the steep hills rising quite dramatically from Mullett Lake are several small resorts, campsites, and cabins. We can almost hear the deep sonorous blasts of the horn on the public steamer earlier in the century as it stopped here on the inland water route to drop off picnickers in the morning and pick them up in the late afternoon. Next to the rail bed is a sign for Cafe Noka, which sits a few yards away across the road. Near the sign is a black cut-out silhouette of a bear—our one and only encounter! Judy, seizing the moment, wraps her arms around our wooden friend, and I snap a picture.

The cafe is charming. Several families with small children are finishing up their breakfasts among the six tables. We grab swivel stools at the counter and order pie and coffee. I choose rhubarb (Macomb County was once the rhubarb capital of Michigan), and Judy has coconut cream. Of course, we also exchange bites of each other's treat. Our waitress, in her mid-thirties, blonde, athletic and friendly, draws our attention to the back of the menus, where we read the legend of Noka and Topinabee.

"Within the culture of the Ojibway Indians there once existed the Society of the Good Hearted Ones. Its members strived for inner peace and good health by combining medicine and song into ritualistic ceremonies. Where these ceremonies took place, patron images could be found carved in totems. Noka, or bear, would be placed at the entrance and exit to guard the proceedings."

Michigan's proud Native American history tells us that the Ojibway, also known as the Chippewa, inhabited the northern part of the Lower Peninsula. They were descendants of Algonquin stock whose history can be traced back to at least a century before the coming of whites. Étienne Brûlé, the first white man to set foot on Michigan soil, landed at the site of Sault Ste. Marie in 1618. (Ed Bruley on my staff has been able to trace his family roots back to the same town in France where Étienne Brûlé lived. It's hard to believe that they aren't related.) The Algonquin originally were an agricultural people who depended more upon producing vegetables than

Our only bear sighting—in front of Cafe Noka in Topinabee

hunting. They grew corn, wild rice, squash, kidney beans, and tobacco. As the Chippewa moved north, good agricultural land became scarce. Out of necessity they turned to a nomadic hunting and trapping existence, fueled by European demand for furs.

"More coffee? Another slice of pie?" our waitress asks. Business has slowed. Now there is time to talk. The conversation turns to our walk. She too loves the out-of-doors and hiking, but her life has changed recently with the birth of her child. Pictures of the baby are eagerly pulled from her purse. She can hardly tear her own eyes away from the photos to show them to us. Joy and pride and wonder bathe her face in a radiant smile. I believe she is a "good-hearted one" who, as the legend tells us, has found inner peace.

Leaving Topinabee, we finally spy two fishermen in an old rowboat on the lake. One is casting, his line stretching out over the calm waters and falling with just the barest splash. The other rows slowly, hypnotically, oars creaking in their rusty locks. As the oars lift from the water, they appear to be strung with diamond necklaces.

We leave the trail at Veery Point to make a phone call at the Veery Point Motel, across the road. Judy and I have decided that it is fitting to celebrate our walk across the bridge on Labor Day by supporting the strikers and locked-out workers at the *Detroit News* and the *Detroit Free Press,* the two largest newspapers in Michigan. Our plan is to lace our "No News or Free Press Wanted Here" signs through our backpacks. My call now is to Emily Everett of the *Sunday Journal,* the union newspaper, which was founded after the strike began. We want to reiterate our support for their efforts against two giant conglomerates, Gannett (the *News*) and Knight-Ridder (the *Free Press*), that made the decision to bring in replacement workers, bust the unions, and in the process tear apart our community. The National Labor Relations Board (NLRB) ruling on June 19 that the company was at fault for unfair labor practices and must rehire the workers to their jobs was a huge victory but short-lived. The *News* and *Free Press* and their joint operating company, the News Corporation, immediately appealed in the federal district court, and the decision has now been overturned by Judge John Corbett O'Meara, a disappointing setback. The workers need support now as much as at any time in their struggle. They have been locked out of their jobs for two years.

Just last month, on July 11, I joined five union brothers and sisters to protest the actions of the newspapers toward their own workers. We walked into the lobby of the *Detroit News* and asked to see the editor or publisher. A courteous but nervous security crew scrambled about the lobby as our request was forwarded upstairs to the executives. Our group also included Father John Nowlan, pastor of St. Hilary's Catholic Church in Redford; Bob King, now vice president of the UAW for organizing; Gloria Cobbin, chair of the Fifteenth Congressional District and secretary-treasurer of the Metro-Detroit AFL-CIO; Vanessa Sylvester, organizing director for the United Food and Commercial Workers Union Local 951; and Brad Markel, from the Wayne State University School of Labor Studies. Our message was simple: the newspapers should obey the law and the NLRB ruling by calling back the workers who are now being locked out of their jobs. After a contentious confrontation with an assistant editor in the lobby, the editorial page editor, Thomas Bray, appeared and invited us up to his wood-paneled conference room.

Father Nowlan, Bob King, and I politely but strongly made our case on behalf of the workers and the need to heal the breach in the community. After thirty minutes of conversation, I asked to speak with the CEO of Gannett, John J. Curley. We were told that it would be impossible. Mr. Bray requested that we leave. Men and women who had labored to make these newspapers great and viable and who had labored so that this man could have a paneled conference room had been without paychecks or the dignity of their jobs for two years. We declined. Furious, Bray left the room to call the security and the Detroit police. We in turn started dialing our cell phones and calling the other media outlets in Detroit and CNN in Washington, DC. Mr. Bray soon returned and flew into a rage. He tried to wrestle my phone out of my hand but only succeeded in breaking the antenna. Soon Inspector Whitty of the Detroit police arrived in the room and told us we were on private property and must leave. When we refused, he asked how we wanted to be removed, with or without a struggle.

We agreed to walk out under arrest to a waiting paddywagon in the downstairs garage. In the elevator on the way down we were stuck between floors for ten minutes, much to the consternation of the *News* security person who was trapped with us and Inspector Whitty, whose brother happens to be a supporter in my campaign.

In the garage we were loaded into the paddywagon. A young police officer accompanied us in the back and volunteered that he had once worked in the United States Capitol as an intern and was fascinated by the experience. We continued to call CNN and the Associated Press, along with local radio stations WJR and WWJ. As the paddywagon pulled out, we could hear the cheers of hundreds of supporters, including Judy, who had been marching outside while we had been inside. Local radio and television stations were arriving for live coverage. We were successful in creating a news story that delivered our message: The conglomerates are breaking the law by not returning the workers to their jobs. And the federal judge of the NLRB had ruled that the newspapers were responsible for the impasse. When the story is about the media, it is enormously difficult to get coverage. Our tactics had worked.

A short ride later we arrived at the police station near Greektown, where we were booked and fingerprinted in the police gym. The officer who booked us was Joe Kaptur, who asked me if I knew his cousin Marcy, the congresswoman from Toledo and champion of working people. I assured him that I did and shared his admiration for her work.

The irony would be humorous if it weren't so harmful. Within one hour we had encountered three Detroit police officials with personal links to us and the very values we represent. The newspapers, in contrast, with all their wealth and power, are sadly out of touch with the community in which they are located. Subscriptions to the *Detroit News* and *Free Press* dropped dramatically as a result of the management-labor dispute.

On this Labor Day weekend we again want to show our solidarity with the workers. Normally, we would march with thousands in the Detroit Labor Day Parade. This year at the same hour we will walk five miles across the Mackinac Bridge with our signs, taking the struggle north to salute the courage of the workers and to demonstrate our respect for the union movement. Emily tells me that folks are really crushed by Judge O'Meara's ruling but that they vow to "last one day longer." Funny how that is exactly where we are on our journey—one day longer.

Back on the trail we come upon the aptly named lake settlement of Birchwood. An elderly man of the World War II generation works in his front yard.

"Howdy! Can you tell me how far to Cheboygan?" I call out.

"Oh, about eight miles," he says with certainty. He's happy to be interrupted and likes to talk. He's equally positive that he once walked ten miles an hour in full battle gear in the service. Boy, are we ever slackers. "Oh yes, you are eight miles from Cheboygan. Less than an hour away," he repeats, firmly. He is engaging, enthusiastic, and entirely wrong. Time and distance assume a different dimension when memories are of fifty and sixty years ago. On the verge of forgetfulness ourselves, we respect his version of his life. Who knows what the circumstances were in his war. We thank him and move on.

Next we encounter two vibrant, sociable retired teachers on bikes, the old-fashioned kind with fat tires and baskets over the handlebars. Stopped at an intersection of the trail and a road leading to the lake, we engage in conversation. They want to know where we have come from and where we are headed. They are from Cincinnati, Ohio. Judy tells them her mother grew up there. I ask, "Do you miss school this time of year?"

The one with the red bike and a sweater stuffed in her basket pinches her thumb and index finger together, holds them at eye level, and laughingly says, "I miss it about this much."

The other one chimes in. "I enjoy a second cup of coffee in the morning."

Are there any more important people in our society than teachers? They shape our children's lives in the most profound ways. Earlier in my life I struggled between choosing a life as a teacher and one in politics. On my bad days I sometimes think of the line from Robert Bolt's play, *A Man for All Seasons,* when the ambitious young man, Richard Rich, begs Sir Thomas More for a position of power in the government and More responds time and time again, "Be a teacher. Be a teacher."

The quaint village of Mullett Lake is ahead. Although the village was named for the original surveyor of Cheboygan County, whose name ended with a double *t,* in 1873 the post office adopted an inaccurate version spelled with only one *t.* For some seventy years, much to the annoyance of the inhabitants, the names of the town and the lake were spelled differently. Finally, on June 1, 1944, the error was corrected. It takes only minutes to walk through this town, which rather appears to be a movie set. It is perfect in every way, but there is not a person to be seen or heard. We marvel at the well-tended flower gardens, neat yards, white picket fences corralling shuttered cottages, gently lapping clear water, and fresh and invigorating lake air. It certainly is peaceful. We find ourselves skirting a golf course at the edge of town, and we also find all the cottage dwellers. So much for serenity. In the woods next to our trail a golfer in tam-o'-shanter searches longingly for his ball.

"Good luck," says Judy.

"I need it," he responds, pushing aside a bush with his pitching wedge.

We have run out of lake shore, but it has been a glorious ten miles along the edge of Michigan's second largest inland lake. Up ahead at a railroad crossing we find ourselves a patch of grass away from the mosquitoes and indulge in a sugar break—feasting on dried fruit and a Milky Way bar. On the other side of the tracks we find ourselves in farm country. Gone are the tree-lined borders of our trail. It is liberating to be in the open, where the land stretches far to a distant horizon. The woods are lovely and almost cozy but can be confining too. Suddenly, we feel free. But all freedom is at once invigorating and daunting. There is a renewed zest in our step as we stride forward to cover the territory ahead. At the same time, we are reminded of how small we are on this great earth.

For three miles we walk between farms and pastures. Vast purple-blue clover fields are a breathtaking sight. We are even more grateful for their sweet fragrance, which drowns the chemical smell of mosquito repellent. Giant circles of hay weighing as much as fifteen hundred pounds each dot other fields. They look to me like huge brown rolls of steel. Horses and cattle feed near the fences. A semicircle of cows gazes at us forlornly, reminding me of a picture that hangs in the Press Gallery just outside the chamber of the House of Representatives. There a similar formation of cows looks out from the photo with a glassy-eyed, steady stare. It is entitled *Press Conference*. Anyone who has faced a group of disinterested reporters just going through the motions of covering your "important news" knows the sick humor of this picture. Of course, I could be charitable and try to look at it from the reporters' point of view—it must be tiresome to be part of a herd listening to just another "dull" politician.

In the distance I spot what looks like a bull. Or is it a herd of bulls? That doesn't make sense. I take out the binoculars and alert Judy. "Oh my gosh," I exclaim, "a herd of bison." These large-hoofed animals actually are part of the cattle family. They are short horned, humped, and have shoulders that slope down to their hindquarters. While only five feet in height, males can grow to nine feet in length and weigh as much as twenty-five hundred pounds. At the beginning of the nineteenth century there were sixty million bison grazing on the prairies and open spaces of North America. Within fifty years they were extinct east of the Mississippi River. By 1900 there remained only two wild herds in North America, one in Yellowstone National Park and the other in Canada. Protective legislation was passed beginning with a 1908 law establishing a national bison range in Montana, and since then the population has risen to twenty thousand. Some are now domesticated like our herd. We just can't resist the temptation to break into song.

> Oh, give me a home, where the buffalo roam,
> Where the deer and the antelope play;
> Where seldom is heard a discouraging word,
> And the skies are not cloudy all day.
> Home, home on the range . . .

All the creatures are happy when we stop, no doubt. Curiously, this song by an unknown author, though first printed in 1911, is said to have been popularized when it was sung on the doorstep of Franklin Delano Roosevelt's home by a group of newspaper reporters the night he was first elected president.

The trail takes us into Cheboygan. Pausing on Lincoln Road to figure out how to get to our motel, Judy and I huddle over our map. Extended from my backpack is the billy club. I turn suddenly to check out our street location. The club catches Judy hard in the face. It is a solid whack. I fear that I have broken her jaw. We are both momentarily stunned, but, luckily, there does not appear to be real damage. We have traveled almost three hundred miles with pepper spray and club, unneeded, only to come to this. Considerably cha-grined and apologizing profusely, I guide my stricken wife the few blocks to our motel on the Cheboygan River.

Cheboygan, population five thousand, is located at the mouth of the Cheboygan River, where it empties into the South Channel of the easternmost end of the Straits of Mackinac. The river served as the traditional boundary line between the Ottawa and Chippewa Indian tribes. The name of the city may originate from one of those early camping grounds that was known as *Shabwegan,* meaning "Chippewa water." There is also the possibility it may be an Ottawa Indian name. In that language *chc bois-gan* meant "harbor" or "portage" and *ja-bo-ga-ning* meant "passage through."

In 1844 Alexander McLeod traveled from Mackinac Island and constructed a small log cabin on the riverbank, a dam in the river, and a sawmill. Lumbering flourished here, reaching its peak in 1895. Lumberjacks and mill workers also kept forty-two saloons bustling during this period. Remaining at Watermill Field after the demise of the lumber industry is the world's largest sawdust pile, standing an astonishing 1,000 feet long, 600 feet wide, and 100 feet high. People today still take sawdust from the site to use as mulch on trees and flowerbeds. Now the economy of the city is based upon agriculture, light industry, and, of course, tourism.

A peppy clerk greets us at the Best Western River Terrace Motel. Waiting for us is a letter from Judy's mother, a fax from Chris Koch, and phone messages from my father and my colleague Bart Stupak. Our room overlooks the river. We are anxious to get out of our grubby clothes, shower, and head for the indoor swimming pool. Once again we are lucky to have the pool and whirlpool to ourselves. It is heavenly first to suspend our tired bodies in the heated waters of the whirlpool. Our well-used muscles and joints revel in this unaccustomed weightlessness. Floating is divine relaxation. Then we take to the pool and slowly swim a few laps, luxuriating in stretching and a different form of movement than we're used to. Slowly, the waters work their invigorating ministrations, and we take turns plunging in and out of the cool pool and hot whirlpool.

We "dress" for dinner in clean shorts, T-shirts, and socks with our flip-flops. No one else at the River Boat Restaurant looks quite as casual as us, but no one seems to care either. We call for a ride to the restaurant, but we walk back. This is our last night before our last day.

Total Walked	280 Miles
Walked Today	21 Miles
Walking to Do	18 Miles

Chapter 20
Cheboygan to Mackinaw City

Saturday, August 30

> *Friendship is a relationship that has no formal shape, there are no rules or obligations or bonds as in marriage or the family. It is held together by neither law nor property nor blood, there is no glue in it but mutual liking. It is therefore rare.*

— Wallace Stegner, *Crossing to Safety*

My wife is my best friend. It is that piece of our marriage, the "mutual liking," that is the significant subtext of our journey. Judy describes our walk in her journal as "a nomadic life anchored by being with her best buddy." She repeatedly says that she does not want to stop, that she would like to just keep walking. I delight in the joy our adventure brings to her and revel in her commentary on all the wonders of nature that unfold along our path. Now her feelings of nostalgia about the end of our walk leap ahead of the actual event. I tempt her to enjoy today by altering our route.

This morning I suggest we get off the main street and walk through an adjoining neighborhood. My father, a former mayor of East Detroit (now Eastpointe), had once come to Cheboygan for a mayor exchange week in the 1960s. I recall him speaking approvingly of the fine old neighborhoods. We cross the road from the motel and walk down wide tree-lined streets, past large frame houses, some with sprawling verandas and antique wicker chairs and swings tucked under their overhanging roofs. The historic white colonial Cheboygan county courthouse is draped in festive patriotic bunting for the holiday weekend. The flag of Michigan and Old Glory hang on either side of the screened front door. The grandam of structures is the Victorian Opera House, built in 1877. It was razed by fire and then rebuilt, the latest restoration in 1984.

Today it serves as the city hall, but it also hosts an acoustically superb theater that is filled throughout the year with music, dance, and drama.

A sparse farmers' market sits forlornly in a church parking lot. It offers little. The only tempting item is a small basket of sour cherries. We ask two fellas who are guarding the cherries where we can pick up the trail to Mackinaw City. "Half a mile up the road on your left," is the response. One of the farmers points the way, his long, sinewy arm protruding from bib overalls. His friend, chewing a wad of tobacco and wearing a John Deere cap, nods in agreement. In reality the trail is less than a block away.

We ponder our choices. The trail—safe, quiet, but screened from the straits and mosquito infested. The road, US-23—great views, wide shoulder, but noisy with heavy Labor Day weekend traffic. We pick the trail. Since we are only fifty yards off the road, we decide that we can dip in and out and vary our walk. The views of the straits are gorgeous, with Bois Blanc Island and the Les Cheneaux Islands to our north. Closer to Mackinaw City, Round Island and historic Mackinac Island come into view.

Sure enough, we are greeted at the entrance of the trail by a swarm of mosquitoes. But we're prepared. Out come the bandannas and spray, probably for the last time. Walking is easy; the trail is smooth and level. A remarkable abundance of flowering goldenrod borders our path. A large blue heron is flushed out in front of us. I try to catch a photo of the bird in flight, but neither my camera nor my skill is up to the challenge. On our left are cottages hidden in the woods connected to US-23, the shoreline road, by driveways that cross the trail. These openings in the trees allow us to glimpse the straits on our right. Though there is a miniature warning sign for each driveway, we see no one—until, that is, we come across a crew putting down fresh asphalt. I lead us out to the road in order to avoid imprinting our boots on the hot mineral pitch. The owner of the property is watching the process and is startled to see us. "Aren't you the congressman?" he asks curiously. We stop. I'm surprised to be recognized here. He confesses to being a C-Span junkie and concludes with a familiar "Good to see you, Dave," as if we were old friends. The power of television.

Across the road the Straits of Mackinac drain the waters of Lake Michigan into Lake Huron. The straits have long been the passageway of commerce for Michigan. During the waves of European immigration throughout the nineteenth century demand grew for coal, foodstuffs, and merchandise from eastern ports. The ships then returned with iron ore from the Upper Peninsula and produce from the rich farmland on the western shore of the state. It was often risky travel, however. Violent storms, narrow channels, and numerous reefs and shoals have caused an estimated five thousand wrecks on the Great Lakes since navigation began. These waters are among the most treacherous in the world. Natural harbors are scarce, fog is common, and the channels that connect the lakes, such as the Straits of Mackinac, are notorious graveyards for ships.

Since the early 1800s countless shipwrecks have occurred in the straits between Beaver Island in the west and the Les Cheneaux Islands in the northeast. On October 16, 1880, one of the worst storms of the century caused over 90 ships to be wrecked and 118 lives lost. The "Big Blow" of November 1913 stranded 19 ships, 6 others were driven to the shore as total losses, and 12 others completely vanished. Between 250 and 300 people died in that storm. It is hard to imagine all that fury as we walk on this perfect sunny late-summer day. The sparkling blue water of the straits benignly laps on the thirteen-mile southern shoreline of Bois Blanc Island. Beyond the elongated western tip lies the much smaller and uninhabited Round Island and then the more famous Mackinac Island.

We loop around the work crew and continue up our narrow corridor, mindful of the fabulous views of the straits, which are screened by the thin band of woods. "Let's take a rest at Point Nipigon on the water," I suggest. We cross US-23 to the entrance of a settlement of lovely homes with spectacular views of the nearby islands and the Mackinac Bridge in the distance.

"Big Mac" spans five miles over open water, the longest suspension bridge from anchorage to anchorage in the world. In the United States only the Verrazano Narrows linking Staten Island and Brooklyn and the Golden Gate linking San Francisco and Marin have longer main spans. Big Mac appears to stretch farther, however, because it seems closer to the water. The dream of a bridge connecting our peninsulas reaches back to 1854, when it was first suggested and dismissed as "impossible." In the 1930s the Michigan CCC constructed 504 bridges. In 1935 an application to the Works Progress Administration to link our state across the straits with the world's longest bridge was turned down. The idea and dream persisted, and a generation later, in the more prosperous times following the Depression and World War II, it became a reality. The Mackinac Bridge was completed in November 1957.

The sun is now bright in the sky. We make ourselves comfortable on a grassy knoll that leads to the gates of Point Nipigon. Sapping what little remaining energy I possess, the sun quickly lulls me into a trance. Above us on poles the flags of Michigan and the United States flutter in the breeze off the straits. Closing my eyes, I am transported by the sound of the whipping cloth to the deck of a sailboat on waters where we've boated with friends at the southern end of Lake Huron. Within moments I've drifted from my reverie into sleep. Thirty minutes later I'm roused by Judy gently rubbing my shoulder. I've napped long enough. It is time to finish. We gather ourselves and stumble back to the trail, still not fully alert.

The secluded trail quickly grows monotonous again. Furthermore, it not only obscures the straits but hides the sun as well. We are soon ready for another peek at the world beyond our borders. Exiting at a designation called Grand View, we are greeted by just that. I do not have the capacity to describe the colors of blue.

Totally absorbed in the sight before us, we are startled by a penetrating "Yo" ringing in the air. A woman our age on a cycle is heading north and wants our attention. We cross the road to meet her, and I ask, "Can I help you?"

"Saw you walking through Gaylord a few days ago," she answers. "Did you take the trail?"

The three of us huddle on the wide shoulder and share our stories. Bonnie Vance and her husband, Ron, operate the Vance Rehabilitation Center in Gaylord. They have just spent the past few days vacationing with their family in Mackinaw City. She and her husband decided to ride their bikes the eighty miles to Gaylord, but the wind is proving too much, and Bonnie has turned back. The kids will still be in Mackinaw City when she returns. Fully empathizing with such challenges, she is thrilled with our adventure. Bonnie is a big supporter of the rails-to-trails efforts. She also informs us of the annual four-day bike ride from Lansing for the bridge walk.

While we are chatting, someone down the road near a roadside park yells, "Congressman Bonior." What is going on here? It's David Lossing and his wife, Suzanne. David works for Senator Carl Levin, and they are taking advantage of the senator's vacation to get a few days of rest and relaxation at a favorite beach off Route 2 near St. Ignace. Now five of us cluster, and I introduce people to one another.

We are losing the day, so before we become engaged with other acquaintances, new or old, we head back to the trail for a final burst of serious walking. An official sign with the single word *Freedom* draws our attention. Our map confirms our discovery of such a place. But, curiously, there is no concrete evidence of Freedom. Maybe it's just an idea.

> Oh Freedom, Oh Freedom
> Oh Freedom over me,
> And before I'll be a slave
> I'll be buried in my grave
> And go home to my Lord
> And be Free.

Judy teaches me this hymn of the civil rights movement. This is a powerful song. Unfortunately, Judy cannot really even carry a basic tune, but she surely does care. Our burdens feel lightened as we lift up our voices and stride together to the cadence of this great song of social justice. Yet, when we stop singing, there is a terrible silence. Out of respect for the past. Out of sorrow for the present. Still too often, our family, our friends, our nation, feel the painful sting of racism.

Freedom fighters introduced a nation to these songs. In the basement of a church near the campus the young national chairman of the Student Nonviolent Coordinating Committee (SNCC), John Lewis, retold his true stories of the civil rights movement—the sit-ins, the marches, the freedom rides, the bombings, the beatings, the fires, the lynchings, the jails. The soft-spoken, modest man was no more than twenty-four years old, but he was already a hero. Judy had been active in the University of Iowa SNCC, trying to raise awareness, support, and money for the actions across the South. Then, in the early spring of 1964, she experienced a night that she would never forget.

Years later, as a colleague in the House of Representatives, John Lewis has had the same impact on me. Of course, long ago I was somewhere on that same campus, that special night. Still, the fact that Judy and I now share John Lewis as a touchstone in our lives strengthens our commitment to each other. I may have come later to the songs, but the themes define our American history and our core values. For justice and freedom to prevail people must stand up, speak out, organize, fight back, and sometimes die, even in the United States.

Ahead is Mill Creek State Park. This historic place, Michigan's oldest industrial site, was discovered by a local history teacher and archaeology buff in 1972. In the late 1700s a mill was established at this location and powered by water. The wood planks made here were used in the construction of Fort Mackinac on the island. We ford the little creek and walk up wooden stairs into the reconstructed park. A number of rough-hewn buildings house artisans demonstrating their old-fashioned skills. The mill house straddles the creek, and sawyers operate the water-powered machine for timber cutting.

The bustle of vacationers is quite a contrast to our quiet trail. The park itself is 625 acres overlooking the straits and Lake Huron. A small concession stand sells food and drinks near a shelter with picnic tables. Little children rush about trying to feed their crumbs to a chipmunk that wants to eat but is terrorized by the noise and confusion. There is a mounting level of frustration on both sides. The children are becoming hysterical. The chipmunk is too.

We make our escape and head back to the road for our final push into Mackinac country. Jean Nicolet was the first white man to explore the straits, when he canoed through them in 1634 while seeking a waterway to the Orient. The French and Indian cultures clashed in the upper lakes region, which was designated the long and confusing name of the Province of Michilimackinac. The use of the *c* at the end signified the French inclination to maintain the integrity of this essentially Indian word. The name itself is Chippewa, meaning "at the place of the big turtle," and refers to the island. When viewed from the lake, the island resembles a turtle, an animal with religious significance to many of the tribes that lived here. Eventually, the French shortened the name to Mackinac and applied it to the island and the straits. The spelling of the name of the bridge also followed this example.

When the British arrived in 1761, during the last phase of the French and Indian Wars, they began to spell the word as it was pronounced, *Mackinaw*. This spelling was applied to the heavy rain gear that originated among traders and fur trappers. And, finally, this British spelling was adopted by Mackinaw City. No one seems inclined to reconcile the difference. After 240 years the disparity lingers, to everybody's confusion.

We take turns peering through our binoculars over the straits to their most famous island. Rising out of the channel between Lakes Michigan and Huron, the green hills thrust up from the blue water.

Mackinac Island ascends from the water on six terraces. Geological evidence in the rock formations suggests that in ancient times the island was entirely covered by an inland sea. As the water receded, the rocky limestone pinnacles gradually emerged until the lakes reached their present level. This reaction of the sea wore away the less resilient aspects of the rock, resulting in such natural wonders as Arch Rock and Sugar Loaf Rock, popular tourist sites. Pine and cedar grow on the cliffs. A host of natural springs gushing from the limestone compensate for the absence of lakes or rivers on the island.

Magnificent summer houses built in the 1880s line a terrace on a bluff not far from the renowned Grand Hotel, a five-story structure erected in 1887. The Grand Hotel, one of the treasures on the island, is a modified colonial design and is one of the few large wooden resort hotels of that period still standing today. Its classical columned veranda is one of the enduring images of Mackinac Island. This porch is billed as the longest in the world, running the hotel's eight hundred–foot length and rising three stories high. From the shore it is also possible to see the fort the British built after abandoning the captured Fort Michilimackinac in Mackinaw City. Next to the fort, high above the village, is the lovely summer residence of the governor of Michigan.

In the village is where John Jacob Aster made his fortune in fur trading. Taking advantage of the federal government's prohibition of pelt trading by foreign countries on U.S. soil, Aster set up his American Fur Company in 1817 after the Treaty of Ghent ended the War of 1812 and the British withdrew from the island, which they had only recently recaptured. The peak of the Mackinac fur trading industry came in 1822, when pelts valued at three million dollars were cleared through Astor's company, which seasonally employed two thousand voyageurs and four hundred clerks. Voyageurs were trappers and procurers of pelts, often trading with the Native Americans. A hundred skilled men were employed in July and August to grade the pelts according to size, quality of fur, and shade of color.

The fur-trading crowd on Mackinac Island represented a racial cross-section of upper North Americans. As many as three thousand Indians camped along the beach, their wigwams often two or three rows deep. American soldiers of varied stock and lineage occupied the fort the British had built with wood from the Mill Creek sawmill. Missionaries came to discover new lands and save souls. Thrown in also were thousands of voyageurs and, for good measure, add the *coureurs de bois,* unattached woodsmen who worked when necessary and otherwise lived an undisciplined life. For a time it was a wild, unruly place.

By 1830 the fur trade was already in decline. There was little wildlife left to trap. Astor closed his company, and the island population shrank precipitously. The island turned to promoting itself as a resort center. A number of wealthy southern planters built homes there, but the Civil War disposed them of their fortunes. After the Civil War the island attracted rich Chicagoans and once again became prosperous.

Today the island remains a throwback to the past. Its most distinguishing characteristic is the reliance on horse and buggy for transportation. M-185 circles the island, but no automobiles are permitted. Bikes are also widely used, and hundreds are available for rent to the tourists who come by ferry from Mackinaw City and St. Ignace. Both the Grand Hotel and Mackinac Island are designated as National Historic Landmarks, evidence of their distinctive significance.

The road into the city offers exhilarating views. I'm glad to be off our suffocating trail. At the state highway sign announcing Mackinaw City, we take each other's picture, posed in reversals of fact. Judy's smile while hugging the sign pole belies the deep sadness she feels about the end of our journey. I suck in my stomach and flex my biceps, Charles Atlas style, to mask my arrival in such a bedraggled state. I console myself with the reality that I have just walked three hundred miles. Judy could continue up to the Hudson Bay. She is the real muscle on this trip.

A wave of nostalgia grips me as we approach the city. Forty-three years ago my parents and my Aunt Nell piled my sister Nancy, cousin Jerry, and me into our 1953 lime-green Plymouth for a grand tour up north. Mackinac and the Upper Peninsula were our destinations. A week's vacation was a rare opportunity for us. There was no interstate highway. It felt like forever slowly following the asphalt ribbon running to the top, all squished in the back seat. Waiting for us was the bridgeless strait. As evening approached, our job was to spy vacancy signs on the motels. It seemed the closer we came to Mackinaw City the more red neon "No Vacancy" signs we saw. Then we unexpectedly pulled up to a string of simple log cabins overlooking the fog-shrouded straits. Our cabin was knotty pine,

The end is bittersweet

all twelve-by-twelve feet of it. I recall sitting outside our cabin in the cool night air, watching the fog drifting and imagining the wonders of the island and the wilds of the UP. The anticipation I felt was palpable. Could I have bottled it, I would have had enough adrenaline to have hiked Nester Township.

In the morning I turned over in my bed and pulled back the drapes to reveal the treasures of Mackinac country. And there it was, the island. Then we were into the car and off to the queue to wait our turn on the car ferry that would take us to St. Ignace, where we would catch another ferry to the island. The line for the car ferry was long. During the peak summer weeks it sometimes stretched ten miles from the dock along the shoulder of the road. The ride across took fifty minutes but seemed like forever to us, as we sat up on deck watching Mackinac go by, knowing we had to cross all the way over before we could return again and actually reach the island.

At the end of the day we drove to Sault Ste. Marie, where my

Bedraggled but victorious

mother's father came to the United States from Canada. Here also are the famous Soo Locks that facilitate Great Lakes vessels carrying copper, iron ore, coal, and winter wheat. We took a memorable cruise up the Tahquamenon River, winding through a mysterious wilderness for hours. The river plays a prominent part in Longfellow's epic poem *Hiawatha*. The boat passed thickly forested ridges, stretches of aromatic cedar, and stone cliffs rising to a hundred feet. My father was shooting his new 8 mm camera and captured a deer swimming across the river. As we approached the Upper Falls, the low thunder of the water grew to a roar. We docked and walked the foot trail to the brink of the falls, which extends two hundred feet in a sweeping arc between high sandstone walls. The pounding waters crash forty feet over the face of the cliff. My nine-year-old self was mesmerized.

Four decades later the place is unrecognizable to me. Inside the city limits along the shore road are a string of modern new hotels, conference centers, restaurants, and curio shops. The conference centers overlook the straits through vast stretches of glass. The motels offer indoor pools with similar views. It all looks brand-new. The 1980s and 1990s have been very good to the economy of Mackinaw City. Nothing seems familiar to me. This is another world from the one I experienced as a boy.

I feel old. Very old. It's like looking at yourself in a dusty family photo album. A gentle breeze of self-pity wafts over me. I linger in this mood, privately indulging in melancholy as we walk the bright, white concrete sidewalk into the center of town.

Above all, Mackinac is a crossroads. A conjunction. A place where people connect and disconnect. The two peninsulas, the island, the lakes—all meet here. So frequently the focal point of our rich history, this place of enormous beauty has also seen horrific exploitation. The Native population was the first victim, cheated out of land and water rights. Astor and his ilk depleted the beaver and contributed to the eradication of the gray wolf, fisher, and pine marten. The lumber barons denuded the state of virtually all its virgin stands, taking with them forever the woodland caribou and the grayling trout. The mineral magnates were right behind to claim the rich veins of copper and iron revealed by Burt and Houghton.

As a nation, we have traditionally operated under the illusion that these resources are inexhaustible—but they are not. To our right beyond the old car ferry docks is, next to our people, our greatest natural resource: fresh water. Ninety-five percent of the country's fresh water and 20 percent of the world's fresh water is here in the Great Lakes. It has helped to make this region the wealthiest of any place on the planet. Its power and bounty are often overlooked and underestimated. It, too, is presumed to be inexhaustible. But, just as Astor craved furs and Clements sought trees and Boston investors targeted minerals, so too do others desire our fresh water. With a world population approaching six billion and the demand for fresh water increasing exponentially, we need to be vigilant. Perhaps technology will save us from ourselves. Desalinization may rescue us from our long history of "Help yourself." But perhaps not. We struggle with the false notion of inexhaustibility, which is built upon the destructive idea of the rights of "rugged individuals" to act in an "unfettered free market." We need to be vigilant because already corporations and governments have proposed selling our fresh water. The rush may already be on.

The process of economic exploitation, which has been steady from our earliest days, has naturally enough been applied to human beings as well as to resources. The Indians were the first but not the last victims. It would take establishing a community and the rule of law to bring justice and equality to the greatest resource of the state, its workers and their families. The labor union was critical in achieving the balance referred to by Alexis de Tocqueville when he visited and wrote about the United States, including Michigan, some 160 years ago: "Among the laws which rule human societies, there is one which seems to be more precise and clear than all the others. If men are to remain civilized, or to become so, the art of associating together must grow and improve in the same ratio in which the equality of conditions is increased."

When my grandfathers came to the United States at the beginning of the twentieth century there were no rights or protections for the workers who created fortunes for others and pennies for themselves. We are here this Labor Day Weekend to honor all those who struggled to achieve "the equality of conditions" that has made the United States the envy of the world.

Ahead Fort Michilimackinac sits beneath the bridge, like Mill Creek State Park, a reconstructed memory of itself. We turn away from the water and walk up Center Avenue. The aroma of sweet fudge collides with the invigorating lake air. It smells like vacation. The sea of tourists dipping in and out of gift shops is a blur of moving color and chatter. Our backpacks are too bulky for the crowded sidewalks.

A middle-aged couple stops to tell us that they saw us walking near Houghton Lake. They act as if they know us—seeing us now for the second time means we are old friends. It is a feeling of connection. We shared that sense of communion with a green heron near the Grampian Hills almost three weeks ago. I wonder if Bonnie Vance has been reunited with her family, happy to be out of the wind. Or if the Ukrainian exchange student we met along the Saginaw Bay is here joining her fellow visitors to our country. Or whether our snowmobiling rotarian who told us of the trail outside Gaylord made it to the other side of the straits. Or if Jenny Anderson, who drove our car up here, has found her brothers and sisters of the Seafarers International Union. We have all come together here to celebrate our sense of community.

A low heavy pewter sky hides the sun. Looking ahead, we see our car in a motel parking lot. I reach for Judy's hand and squeeze it gently. A soft rain is falling.

Miles Walked	298 Miles
Walked Today	18 Miles
Walking to Do	The Bridge

Epilogue

To travel hopefully is a better thing than to arrive.

—Robert Louis Stevenson

It is Labor Day. The air is cool, and the sky is overcast. The Straits of Mackinac are foggy and Mackinac Island invisible.

Yesterday we spent a warmer and sunny day on the island. After arriving by ferry from Mackinaw City, we rented bikes for the eight-mile ride around the perimeter road. Even at a leisurely pace, the scenery seemed to whiz by compared to three weeks of walking. In the early evening we returned to the harbor to meet Bart and Laurie Stupak. Bart is my colleague in Congress. He represents the Upper Peninsula and northern Michigan, including the Island. The four of us walked up to Huron Street, where carriages pulled by Clydes-dales, Percherons, and Morgans line up along the curb waiting to be rented. The horses strained to pull our carriage up a steep hill near the Grand Hotel. The slow, rhythmic clop, clop of the hooves carried us to the Woods restaurant in the Island's forested interior. Inside the opulent Tudor mansion is a comfortable atmosphere of old-world Bavarian charm. Over dinner, like students returning to campus in the fall, we exchanged summer stories. We caught the last ferry back to St. Ignace. One last night. The bridge awaits us.

Closing a bridge to vehicles and opening it to people has great popular and symbolic appeal. On that occasion we actually pay attention to the connection between the two ends. We are part of something larger than ourselves, part of a joyous throng that for a brief, magical time erases barriers, bonds strangers, proclaims a community. I experienced that exhilaration in 1986 when I joined 25,000 others running across the Verrazano Bridge at the start of our twenty-six-plus miles in the New York City Marathon. And again when Judy and I were part of 200,000 Americans and Canadians walking across the new second span of the Blue Water Bridge connecting our two countries at Port Huron, Michigan, and Point Edward, Ontario.

The excitement today is no less palpable as we join ranks and

Laurie and Bart Stupak with Judy on the Mackinac Bridge

assemble for our march to the other side. Some 50,000 of us are drawn to this annual event. Beckoning us is a wondrous structure, which for centuries experts thought was impossible to erect.

Dr. Kenneth Landes, chairman of the University of Michigan Geology Department, and his colleagues studied the rock formation underlying the Straits in 1944 and concluded that "a suspension bridge over the Straits of Mackinac could lead to a possible disaster of shocking proportions." They were convinced that the rock formation could not support the terrific weight of the span. Engineering geologists would later dispute Landes's claims, and, together with the political leadership of Governor G. Mennen Williams and United States Senator Prentiss Brown, the authority for the bridge was established in 1950. Groundbreaking occurred on May 5, 1954, and three and a half years later, on November 1, 1957 the bridge was opened to the public.

Our salute to Labor Day

We are here today on Labor Day to honor the workers who forty years ago toiled with strength, skill, and courage over these cold, wind-swept waters. Men worked 552 feet above the water on the two main towers, which also extend 210 feet below the water's surface into the bedrock. In all an estimated eleven thousand workers had a hand in building the five-mile span: three hundred engineers, thirty-five hundred workers on site, and an additional seventy-five hundred who worked in the quarries, shops, and mills. "One thing about the Mackinac Bridge," said Mike Gleason, who bolted iron on the north and south approaches from 1954–55, "there were nothing but top-notch men on the job. I made some lifelong friends on that job." Mike Gleason has also been a friend to me. He was one of my early supporters. Today his son Patrick (Shorty) Gleason, following in his dad's footsteps, is president and business agent for Iron Workers Local 25. Shorty, too, is a top-notch man and a great friend and ally.

Ending our walk on the Mackinac Bridge

Five workers gave their lives to this monumental enterprise. Clifford Mumby, a retired union iron worker who labored on the bridge in 1956–57, recalls: "There is a certain camaraderie among bridgemen. You know your life depends upon the other people who are up there with you everyday. They truly are your brothers. It was dangerous work, and some days you just had the feeling that it wasn't your day. You could walk off, and no one would say anything."

Just as it took courage to build the bridge over a seemingly impossible expanse, so also did it require extraordinary fortitude to explore these unknown waters. In 1671 Louis Joliet canoed from Sault Ste. Marie down to Lake Erie, becoming in all likelihood the first European to make that trip by way of what we now call Lake Huron, the St. Clair River, Lake St. Clair, and the Detroit River. Thirty years later Commandant Cadillac, who had earlier led his troops at Michilimackinac, crossed these same waters to found a fort "at the narrows" (*d'étroit*).

Three centuries ago these intrepid men explored the eastern boundary waters of Michigan. Today the drive from Detroit to Mackinaw City is four and a half hours on Interstate 75 through the heart of Michigan. But what do we really know of a place when we hurtle through it along efficient but soulless connectors and see only an undulating median strip and interchangeable interchanges?

Judy and I wanted to feel the pulse of where we live, to meet Michigan face to face. We looked to these historical figures as our inspirational guides. Our challenge was to explore Michigan for ourselves and perhaps in the process to discover more about ourselves and our relationship to each other. Undeniably, it was the exploration of self, the redefinition of our marriage, that required the most courage in our journey.

I have through training and temperament always been drawn to a challenge. The more difficult, the greater the appeal. In *Letters to a Young Poet* Rainer Maria Rilke writes, "If only we arrange our life according to that principle which counsels us that we must always hold to the difficult, then that which now still seems to us the most alien will become what we most trust and find most faithful."

I have been blessed in my life by parents, teachers, priests, coaches, military officers, coworkers, and mentors who have demanded discipline, the ingredient of both personality and character most necessary to "hold to the difficult." People who would push me beyond what I might never have imagined possible forged my essential self. Over time the rigors of these experiences deliver their own intangible satisfactions. Each effort builds toward the next until finding trust and faith in difficult places becomes its own reward.

Armed with this self-confidence, I convinced Judy that we could undertake the challenge of this walk together. It seemed the right time. For ten years we had worked side-by-side in the U.S. Capitol, and, when Judy retired from her job at the end of 1996, after twenty-one years as a staff person in the House of Representatives, the separation was difficult. The last two years had been particularly stressful. The legislative and political battles were hard and often bitter. I missed her very much during the day, her counsel and encouragement. But I was confident we could construct our lives together in other ways. Our walk was to be the path to building upon our relationship through a new adventure, a different dimension. I wanted to create a shared experience so memorable that it would be engraved in our hearts and minds forever. A journey that was not a race or a single event but something more permanent, something that required planning, patience, understanding, and partnership. Something that would inspire a pioneer.

What I found on our journey was how much I drew from Judy's strengths. Her stamina, persistence, good humor, and advice seemed to always be there in the right proportions at the right times. But, more than any one of these virtues, I learned from her ability to enjoy each step—to experience the present without dwelling in the past or, even more difficult for me, without skipping ahead to the future. Oliver Wendell Holmes observed, "What lies behind us and what lies before us are tiny matters compared to what lies within us." For three weeks in August 1997 I was able to snatch moments of the present and begin a journey of awareness—a gift from my wife and Michigan.

It is nearly time to walk our last five miles. We mingle with the building crowd. Festivity is in the air. Many of Bart's constituents come by to greet him and Laurie. Judy and I take turns threading our newspaper protest signs through our backpacks. Somewhere ahead of us the crossing has begun. People surge forward.

Together Judy and I take our first steps onto the bridge.

Selected Bibliography

Badger, Curtis J. *Salt Tide.* Harrisburg, PA: Stackpole Books, 1993.

Bailey, Anthony. *A Walk through Wales.* New York: HarperCollins, 1993.

Brockman, C. Frank. *Trees of North America,* rev. ed. New York: Golden Press, 1986.

Bryson, Bill. *A Walk in the Woods.* New York: Broadway Books, 1998.

Carson, Rachel L. *The Sea around Us,* rev. and illus. ed. 1950. Reprint. New York: New American Library, 1961.

Catton, Bruce. *Michigan, A Bicentennial History.* New York: W. W. Norton, 1976.

Doebler, Wally. *Summers along the Clinton.* Ann Arbor, MI: Members First Publications, 1996.

Encyclopedia of Michigan, 2d ed. New York: Somerset Publishers, 1989.

Foehl, Harold M., and Irene M. Hargreaves. *The Story of Logging the White Pine in the Saginaw Valley.* Bay City, MI: Red Keg Press, 1995.

Green, Libereta Lerrich. *The Beacon Tree, A Tail of the Underground Railroad.* Bulletin of the Detroit Historical Society. Ed. Patricia S. Sawyer. 1923. Reprint, Mount Clemens, MI: Macomb County Historical Society, 1976.

Hansen, Dennis R. *Trail Atlas of Michigan—Nature, Mountain Biking, Hiking, Cross Country Skiing.* Okemos, MI: Hansen Publishing Co., 1996.

Headlight 3, no. 1. *"Bath City" Mt. Clemens, Michigan.* 1897. Reprint. Mount Clemens, MI: Macomb Historical Society and Mount Clemens Public Library, 1987.

IWW Songs. 19th ed. 1923. Reprint. Chicago: Charles H. Kerr Publishing Co., 1989.

Jenkins, Peter. *A Walk Across America.* New York: Ballantine Books, 1983.

Jenkins, Peter, and Barbara Jenkins. *The Walk West: A Walk Across America 2.* New York: Ballantine Books, 1984.

Kurta, Allen. *Mammals of the Great Lakes Region,* rev. ed. Ann Arbor: University of Michigan Press, 1995.

Letters of Father Pierre DeJean, 1825–1826. *Along the Huron River.* Ed. Patricia Schott Sawyer. Trans. Donald E. Worrell Jr. Mount Clemens, MI: Macomb County Historical Society, 1986.

Little, Elbert L. *The Audubon Society Field Guide to North American Trees (Eastern Region).* New York: Alfred A. Knopf, 1980.

Logue, Victoria. *Backpacking in the '90s: Tips, Techniques and Secrets,* 3d ed. Birmingham, AL: Menasha Ridge Press, 1995.

Lund, Harry C. *Michigan Wildflowers, in Color.* Holt, MI: Thunder Bay Press, 1985.

Magee, Dorothy M., ed. *Centennial History of Mount Clemens, Michigan, 1879–1979.* Mount Clemens, MI: Mount Clemens Public Library, 1980.

Michigan Atlas and Gazetteer, 5th ed. Freeport, ME: DeLorme, 1995.

Morland, Miles. *A Walk across France.* New York: Ballantine Books, 1994.

National Audubon Society Pocket Guide. *Familiar Butterflies of North America.* New York: Alfred A. Knopf, 1990.

Newhof, Susan J. *Michigan's Town and Country Inns,* 4th ed. Ann Arbor: University of Michigan Press, 1998.

Peattie, Donald Culross. *A Natural History of Trees of Eastern and Central North America.* 1948. Reprint. Boston: Houghton Mifflin, 1991.

Peterson, Roger Tory. *A Field Guide to the Birds.* 1934. Reprint. Cambridge, MA: Riverside Press, 1996.

———. *A Field Guide to the Birds East of the Rockies.* Boston: Houghton Mifflin, 1980.

Powers, Tom. *Michigan State and National Parks: A Complete Guide,* 3d ed. Davison, MI: Friede Publications, 1997.

Public Sector Consultants, Inc. *Michigan in Brief, 1998–99.* 6th ed. Grand Ledge, MI: Millbrook Printing Company, 1998.

Roth, David Luther. *Johann Roth: Missionary.* Greenville, PA: Beaver Printing Co., 1922.

Smith, Greg, and Karen-Lee Ryan. *700 Great Rail Trails: A National Directory.* Washington, DC: Rails-to-Trails Conservancy, 1995.

Smith, Richard P. *Understanding Michigan Black Bear.* Marquette, MI: Smith Publications, 1995.

Tekiela, Stan. *Birds of Michigan Field Guide.* Cambridge, MN: Adventure Publications, 1999.

Terres, John K. *The Audubon Society Encyclopedia of North American Birds.* New York: Alfred A. Knopf, 1980.

Thurston, Herbert J., and Donald Attwater. *Butler's Lives of the Saints,* 2d ed. 1956. Reprint. Allen, TX: Christian Classics, 1996.

Tocqueville, Alexis de. *Democracy in America.* Vol. II. Trans. Henry Reeve, revised by Francis Bowen, with introduction by Phillips Bradley. New York: Alfred A. Knopf, Inc., 1945. Reprint, New York: Vintage Books, 1990.

Writers' Program. *Michigan, A Guide to the Wolverine State.* 1941. Reprint. St. Clair Shores, MI: Somerset Publishers, 1973.

Zim, Herbert S., and Alexander C. Martin. *Flowers, A Guide to Familiar American Wildflowers,* rev. ed. New York: Golden Press, 1987.